# from BOARDROOM to WHITEBOARD

# PHILLIP V. LEWIS
### with
## MARILYN HERMANN LEWIS

# from BOARDROOM to WHITEBOARD

*A New Generation of Leadership*

TATE PUBLISHING & *Enterprises*

Published by Tate Publishing & Enterprises, LLC
127 E. Trade Center Terrace | Mustang, Oklahoma 73064 USA
1.888.361.9473 | www.tatepublishing.com

Tate Publishing is committed to excellence in the publishing industry. The company reflects the philosophy established by the founders, based on Psalm 68:11,
*"The Lord gave the word and great was the company of those who published it."*

Book design copyright © 2011 by Tate Publishing, LLC. All rights reserved.
*Cover design by Christina Hicks*
*Interior design by Kellie Vincent*

Published in the United States of America

ISBN: 978-1-61777-793-6
1. Business & Economics, Leadership    2. Business & Economics, Education
11.06.28

In memory of our parents
Walter Vernon and Doris Mintie Lewis
Charles Paul and Erma Pauline Hermann
For their example of faithful Christian leadership

# TABLE OF CONTENTS

## II. LEADERSHIP CHALLENGES

## III. LEADERSHIP STRATEGY

# INTRODUCTION

A leader's role is to raise people's aspirations for what they can become and to release their energies so they will try to get there.

—David R. Gergen,
American journalist and US White House advisor

# INTRODUCTION

Modeling provides the basis of all true leadership. Leaders must set the example for their followers. The number one management principle in the world is this: People do what people see.

—John C. Maxwell

As iron sharpens iron, so a friend sharpens a friend.

Proverbs 27:17

If you are a recent leader, a current-day leader, or an aspiring leader, I have a question for you. Where are you headed as a leader?

The reason I ask is: You and I can't lead people somewhere we're not willing to go ourselves. I don't have to be perfect to get there, but I do need to be on the right path. My experience with leaders, past and present, is this: The majority of them give up too soon. They hit a wall, get discouraged, and don't keep moving. They don't do the difficult, sometimes agonizing work it takes to overcome mistakes, failures, or failed attempts. They fail to look deep inside themselves or to seek outside for the courage and strength to overcome. They bog themselves down with tactical decisions and never get to strategic thinking. Thus, my experience has been that too few leaders have the tenacity to do the long, hard work that success requires. They are content with being ordinary, to be one of "the guys." They are unwilling to accept the challenge to be extraordinary.

If you are an aspiring leader or someone who wants to be an improving leader, here's your personal question. Are you ready to learn how to lead effectively? If you are, your answer will raise more questions for us to consider. Are you ready to do the long, hard, gut-wrenching work that success requires? Are you ready to transition from employee to manager or from manager to leader? Are you willing to abandon being an ordinary leader to become an extraordinary leader? Each transition creates new possibilities for failure, new issues and crises calling for you to accept responsibility, new power choices to take control of the situation, and new opportunities for success.

This book is based on the optimism that something desirable will happen as you and I walk down our leadership road together. There will be a positive outcome related to our experiences. The path we will be traveling is paved with three layers of my confidence in you.

First, I am confident that you will find my knowledge and experiences understandable and adaptable, and at the same time warm and engaging. These experiences and knowledge were acquired as a businessperson, educator, business mentor, and spiritual mentor. In addition to business experience and consulting, I have served as the dean of a College of Business Administration at three different universities in three different states for over twenty years. You will find what is imparted to you to be worthy material. It will motivate you to become a great leader.

Second, I am confident that you will allow me to connect with your heart, head, and hands. Our heads, hearts, and hands address the three motivational systems that affect us—cognitive, affective, and practical. The *cognitive* is concerned with the acquisition of knowledge by reasoning, intuition, or perception. The *affective* relates to an external expression of emotion associated with ideas, words, or actions. The *practical* is concerned with matters of fact, real life, and experience.

To illustrate: The *hands* are about the practical—sensible, realistic, no-nonsense, matter-of-fact action and physical effort. The *heart* is about the affective—emotions, sentiments, touching moments, and feelings. The *head* is about the cognitive—knowledge acquisition, logic, and understanding. When we are doing something new or different, we often have to have full commitment involving our heart, head, and hands to make it work effectively.

Third, I am confident that you will allow me to build a mentoring relationship with you as a member of the current or next generation of leaders. Your generation may be called the Net or Millennial Generation, the X or Y Generations, or the Boomer Generation. No matter the label, all of us need mentoring of one sort or another to be all that we can be as a leader. In fact, one of the most valuable assets your career can have is to have a great mentor or even several mentors along the way, even in different areas of expertise. Some people mentor by teaching, small group studies, club sponsor, adopting a college student for a year, Big Brother/Big Sister, tutoring, or coaching. Others mentor by writing letters, sending e-mails, starting a blog, or being active on Facebook or Twitter. Some meet individually or in a small group to pass on their experiences and learnings. I have chosen to put my leadership thoughts in a book. Read it and think of me sharing the wisdom of the business world with you as a mentor.

Each chapter will involve a harmony of beliefs, values, actions, and experiences. As you observe each component, I trust you will begin to fully appreciate the strength of your character, honesty, and hard work. Your consistency in life, as you work with your hands, head, and heart, will pay dividends beyond measure. You will be called upon to make new decisions and choices for your life and career, and you will also uncover new directions for recovering from poor choices and decisions.

## UNDERSTANDABLE AND ADAPTABLE

King Solomon wrote in the Old Testament: "Be careful, for writing books is endless, and much study wears you out" (Ecclesiastes 12:12). This statement could easily be said about writing and publishing leadership books. Or an author might glibly say about his or her leadership book (as Solomon wrote in Ecclesiastes 12:13), "That's the whole story. Here now is my final conclusion." Yet she or he knows that there will certainly be more books to come. In our knowledgeable society with emphasis on living organizations and lifelong learning, mentors and protégés must always be growing in knowledge and gaining in understanding. The "final conclusion" results in affirmations for *your* leadership goals.

## HEAD, HANDS, AND HEART

The *head* involves intellect and persuasion through logical and rational arguments. As consultant James R. Lucas has written, "Leading with the head means that we never leave reason out of the equation, even as we avoid making it the whole equation. We should lead with the head—by using it as a thinking tool, not a battering ram."

The *heart* involves excitement, passion, and fun. Perhaps that is why Friedrich Nietzsche, a nineteenth-century German philosopher and classical philologist, wrote, "Nothing ever succeeds which exuberant spirits have not helped to produce." Both the head and the heart are involved in getting messages across. As Israel's King Solomon wrote in Ecclesiastes 5:20, "They seldom reflect on the days of their lives; because God keeps them with the gladness of heart" (TNIV).

The *hands* involve creation, demonstration, and involvement. Arnold Bennett, English novelist, wrote, "There can be no knowledge without emotion. We may be aware of a truth, yet until we have felt its force, it is not ours. To the cognition of the brain must be added the experience of the soul." So whether you are an idea person, an emotional and passionate person, or an action-oriented person, I know you will find something in the pages to come that will stimulate you to increase your effectiveness as a leader.

## MENTORING RELATIONSHIP

Benjamin Disraeli, a former prime minister of England, said, "The greatest good you can do for another is not just to share your riches but to reveal to him his own." Therefore, good leaders deliberately seek out and find other possible leaders. Great leaders not only find these potential leaders but also mentor them to be great leaders. A mentor teaches, demonstrates, allows the protégé to try, and evaluates the attempt. The mentor typically is perceived to have great relevant knowledge, wisdom, or experience. The protégé is perceived to have less knowledge, wisdom, or experience. Therefore, I have a request for you.

Think of my mentoring you as a personal relationship where you are seeking coaching from someone more skillful and knowledgeable. If you are asking yourself, "Why should I listen to you as a mentor?," consider the following. The people I have mentored in business have gone on to become supervisors, managers, a vice president of an international airline, business owners, founders and cofounders, and top salespeople. Those I have mentored in academia have gone on to become professors, department heads, editors, deans, assistant deans, MBA directors, vice presidents, and presidents. The people I have mentored in public life have gone on to become state representatives, state treasurers, and civic club leaders. Those I have mentored in the spiritual arenas have gone on to become Bible class teachers, ministers, deacons, elders, and ministry directors.

It is especially important that professional women find mentors, someone with whom they can build a mentor-protégé relationship. Beth Hughes Swanson, manager of editorial communications for Wendy's International Inc., has written, "The bottom line for professional women is that they shouldn't feel desperate if they don't have a traditional business mentor. But in some form or fashion, they should seek out wise and supportive counsel." Angela Ahrendts, CEO of Burberry, would agree. Although she is recognized as the woman behind Burberry's success because of her business acumen, down-to-earth product selling, and being technically savvy, Ahrendts says she learned her analytical skills from Linda Wachner, former CEO of Warnaco, and her right-brain skills from Donna Karan, creator of the Donna Karan DKNY and New York clothing lines. Mentors can be very important to a leader's success.

A reason why mentoring is especially important for professional women is that in many ways pay, succession, and future planning it is still a man's world. There are many more men in senior leadership roles than women. Unfortunately, men do not always relate well to women, and women sometimes do not trust women. If a woman wishes to move upward, however, she will often have to seek out a male leader to guide her through a traditional mentor/protégé relationship. That's why organizations like the Christian Business and Professional Women's Ministries designed their mentoring program for those wanting to relate professionally, personally, and spiritually.

Barry Bozeman, Regents professor at the Georgia Institute of Technology, and Mary Feeney, professor at the University of Illinois, mined the following meaning from their research for our understanding of our mentoring relationship: "Mentoring is a process for the informal transmission of knowledge, social capital, and the psychosocial support perceived … as relevant to work, career or professional development." In addition, they emphasize that mentoring entails informal face-to-face communication over a sustained period of time.

Taken in this manner, our mentoring relationship (yep, you and me) will be an important influence in your professional development. The war for talent in the business world is always active. It is to your advantage, therefore, to read and study the chapters that follow in order to enhance your performance, commitment, skill set, and knowledge.

## CONCLUSION

As your mentor, I will serve as a trigger, guide, or release mechanism for the motivation that lies within you to be the best leader possible. Are you ready? If so, think of this book as an action plan that will help you move toward both growth and reward. Think of our relationship as an investment in your future. At times, we all need help.

For forty years I've spent an inordinate amount of time in corporate and educational boardrooms, holding seminars, consulting, teaching, and leading. For the last twenty years I've been leading from my own boardroom. In the beginning, we had flip charts, and then we moved to transparencies and finally to PowerPoint presentations. Then one day chalkboards were replaced by whiteboards, and almost every conference room put one up. You could write on it *and* show slides. A whiteboard is what I am asking you to imagine as you continue to read and study this book. Think of it as a whiteboard that I am using as your personal consultant.

When we lived in California, there was a Presbyterian church within walking distance of our home. A small sign at the entrance to the parking lot said, "Enter to Worship"; at the parking lot's exit, another small sign said, "Leave to Serve." Great advice for that church's worshippers. For our purposes, I'd like to change that sign to read, "Enter to Learn"; when you exit at the end of this book, the sign will say, "Leave to Lead."

Albert Schweitzer, Franco-German theologian and physician, said, "In everyone's life at some time, our inner fire goes out. It is then burst into flame by an encounter with another human being. We should all be thankful for those people who rekindle the human spirit." Let me help you start or rekindle that fire via our whiteboard chats.

Or, if you prefer the words of Stephen Curtis Chapman, Christian singer and songwriter, "Saddle up your horses; we've got a trail to blaze." Are *you* ready to be a trailblazer?

# LEADERSHIP

Leadership is much more an art, a belief, a condition of the heart, than a set of things to do. The visible signs of artful leadership are expressed, ultimately, in its practice.

—Max DePree,
founder of Herman Miller Furniture Company

1. Are You Going to Lead, Follow, or Get Out of the Way? The Nature of Organizational Leadership

2. Is the Color of Your World Changing? An Organizational Revolution

# ARE YOU GOING TO LEAD, FOLLOW, OR GET OUT OF THE WAY?

## THE NATURE OF ORGANIZATIONAL LEADERSHIP

One does not "manage" people. The task is to lead people. And the goal is to make productive the specific strengths and knowledge of each individual.

—Peter Drucker,
writer, management consultant, social ecologist

In his grace, God has given us different gifts for doing certain things well. So…if God has given you leadership ability, take the responsibility seriously…

Romans 12:6–8

Have you had the experience of walking a famous battlefield like Gettysburg? If so, you may have experienced the emotion of war firsthand or lived through the war yourself. The battle between the North and South may have come to life for you. Reenactments and movies have helped us further visualize soldiers performing under fire, communicating, following orders, and inspiring their compatriots. You perhaps envisioned leaders being guided by a new mission. You imagined how it was possible to manage through confrontation, chaos, uncertainty, and change. The outcome was a new path for the uniting of divided states.

One hundred and fifty years have passed since the War Between the States. New winds of change were blowing then, and these winds are continuing to move across our nation, lives, and jobs. Are you aware of the direction and force of that wind? Can you recognize the dangers, attempt balance among groups, and discover how to convert losses into successes?

---

Let's get personal.

In the business world, those organizations that were designed during placid times will not withstand the pressure of chaotic times. In the past, inflexible, rule-driven mass producers were staffed by persons who "knew their place." Today, organizations must be flexible, porous, adaptive, and fleet-of-foot. Warren Bennis, organizational consultant and author, described it this way:

> Today's organizations are evolving into federations of networks, clusters, cross-functional teams, temporary systems, ad hoc task forces, lattices, modules, matrices—almost anything but pyramids with their obsolete top-down leadership. The new leader will encourage healthy dissent and value those followers courageous enough to say "no."

How is it possible then that a study from the Leadership Trust Foundation of Herefordshire, England, found that 73 percent of CEOs removed from their posts were fired as a result of "ineffective leadership"? That percentage is higher than the number of executives fired for unethical behavior. In this day and age, how is it feasible that a lack of adequate leadership skills is becoming epidemic? That business incompetence can bloom at the most prestigious corporations?

Groundbreaking changes are occurring in a world increasingly becoming flat. These changes will forever alter the way leaders meet the needs of followers and rally to their needs. These changes are so profound that they sometimes seem overwhelming. Leaders must chart new courses, hustle, and be engaged fully while constantly improving everything. They must be allies with their followers—locally, nationally, and internationally.

## EFFECTIVE LEADERSHIP

As a leader, you must be in touch with these changes. If you don't, you will quickly become obsolete. You must challenge the *status quo*. You have to answer the challenges to avoid catastrophic, misguided action. In short, you must be an effective leader, one who knows the right things to do. This can be difficult because of what is called the duality of leadership. As consultant James R. Lucas has observed:

> Every situation for a leader is a composite of conflicting and opposing considerations, each of which is valid from a certain point of view. Each has its pros and cons, which have to be evaluated. The leader must be able to hold opposing ideas in mind and balance them judiciously. Otherwise, decisions become extremist answers with disastrous results.

New ways of thinking and new models are therefore needed in business, education, and government—all of organizational life. There are interpersonal relationships, communication, change, conflict, motivation, and influence issues that must be dealt with. Our organizations today need visionary, passionate, creative, inspiring, trusting, warm, and results-oriented leaders. John Kotter, professor at the University of Michigan and author, established the following key distinctions about leaders:

1. Leaders produce change and adaptability to new products, new markets, new competitors, new customers, and new work processes.

2. Leaders have a vision of what the organization can become and mobilize people to accomplish it.

3. Leaders elicit cooperation and teamwork from a large network of people and keep the key people in the network motivated by using every manner of persuasion.

4. Leaders produce change, often to a dramatic degree, such as by spearheading the launch of a new product or opening a new market for an old product.

5. Top-level leaders are likely to transform their organizations.

6. Leaders create a vision (lofty goal) to direct the organization.

The effective leader will need to be inspirational to capture the attention of followers and get them to move forward in a positive manner and attain desirable outcomes. Fortunately, there are leaders in our business world who are able to demonstrate honesty and integrity, purpose, kindness and compassion, humility, courage, justice, and fairness. Some of those examples include: Warren Buffett, CEO, Berkshire Hathaway; Steve Jobs, CEO, Apple; Anita Roddick, CEO, The Body Shoppe; Aaron Feuerstein, CEO, Malden Mills; Charles Pollard, CEO, Service Master; Peter Brabeck-Letmathe, CEO, Nestle's; Ray Gilmartin, CEO, Merck; Alan Mulally, CEO, Ford Motor Co.; John Tyson, president and CEO, Tyson Foods Inc.; and many others. How many effective leaders could you name? Do you work with one or several?

In chapters ahead, we will look at the traits of an effective leader. In later chapters, you will discover how to acquire those traits. You will come in contact with what has made the leaders such as those mentioned above so successful in their chosen paths.

## LEADERSHIP MUST-DO AND MUST-NOT-DO LISTS

Leaders, even the good ones, make mistakes. You have. I have. We all have. Sometimes we recognize them and overcome them. Sometimes we are oblivious to what we've done. Fortunately, we at least recognize those items in which we ought to be involved. My experience in working with leaders has resulted in the following things I hear most frequently mentioned that a leader must do (in no certain order of importance or frequency). A leader must:

1.  Place a high value on people; take care of people.

2.  Lead by being visible; manage by walking around (MBWA).

3.  Have a clear, encompassing, far-reaching, and engaging vision.

4.  Communicate the vision; deliver the message.

5.  Maintain integrity and credibility; live the code.

6.  Be trustworthy; trust others.

As you might suspect, leadership can be a risky way to spend your life. Your thoughts, behaviors, and actions are vulnerable. What item(s) on this list, therefore, would you consider to be the most important when working with and leading others? Which one of these items would you least put up with in a leader you admire? Which one is a deal breaker for you?

When it comes to leader mistakes, the list is almost twice as long. The following is the list I hear most frequently mentioned about what a leader must not do (in no particular order of importance or frequency). A leader must not:

1.  Communicate poorly or not at all.

2.  Have a top-down authority attitude and be a dictator in decisions.

3.  Engage in paperwork before engaging people.

4.  Demonstrate a lack of servant leader attitude.

5.  Experience success without mentoring successors.

6.  Fail to surround self with diverse thinkers.

7.  Fail to delegate responsibility.

8.  Demonstrate a lack of listening skills or stop listening.

9. Hire too fast and fire too slowly.

10. Blame others and not accept responsibility for own actions.

11. Fail to motivate people to do the best they can do.

12. Show favoritism or give preferential treatment to certain people.

13. Provide professional development or training.

As you think about the above mistakes, are there any items on the list (honestly) you already have a tendency toward? As your mentor, I will help you see where you can improve and strengthen in the above areas. I will help you improve your business serve or swing. I will assist you in keeping an open mind and being patient with learning or relearning a better way. However, you must be willing to make the changes required in thinking and actions taken.

If we want to achieve business success, we have to look clearly at the mistakes we make and stop repeating them. I've heard business owners say things like, "It was just a small mistake." In reality, however, there are no small mistakes. Why? A small mistake can have big consequences. Repeating "small mistakes" can lose customers, kill a business, or cost an employee his job. Such "mistakes" can break a leader; avoiding them can make a leader.

## LEADERSHIP LESSONS AND EXPERIENCES

A good mentor can be trusted to let you know when you're ready to go for your first leadership position or a promotion. This ability to see into the future is much like some airports that are difficult to land at because of the terrain, short runways, or air currents. Some pilots are not allowed to land until an experienced captain verifies that they know how to handle the plane and the situation—like the high Himalayas or Tegucigalpa. Weaknesses in knowledge and skills can result in fatal consequences. A mentor might begin your time with him/her by asking the following five questions:

1. When was your first leadership experience? (Define your point of time after age six, after age twelve, after age twenty-one, after getting into high school or college, or upon entering the workforce.) Was this leadership experience initiated by you, or did others nudge you into the role of a leader?

2. What are the important leadership lessons you learned as a child or early in life? How have those lessons changed over time?

3. What are some experiences early on that prepared you for leadership? Be specific.

4. How have success and adversity affected your role as a leader? Illustrate.

5. How has your leadership style evolved over time? Is it different in certain areas of your life or with different kinds of groups or group purposes?

As you think about answers for these questions, attempt to stay youthful in your thinking. Use reason instead of emotion, accept and entertain new truths, and have an adventurous mind. Look with new eyes and consider how your answers have impacted your leadership journey.

## First Leadership Experiences

One of my early leadership experiences was running for a high school office. You may have played some role like this. No matter how minimal that leadership role turns out to be, you are still remembered at a reunion as serving in that role. For example, I was class president. Every time I go to my high school class reunion, as soon as I walk in the door, our class coordinator announces to the group present something like this: "Hey, everyone, our president is here. Come over and say hello." Some people never forget—even at the fiftieth anniversary.

Other leadership experiences were in football, basketball, baseball, and track. Each sport taught me how to cope with winning, losing, following, and leading. Sometimes losing taught me more about leading than winning did. Two reasons: One is the fact that in many of the games I played, whether we were winning or losing, we spent a lot of time losing. Another reason is immediate feedback. You know instantaneously what is working or not working, what will work or won't work.

Lessons were also learned from observing and responding to coaches. How well I remember one autumn Friday evening as the school bus carrying the football team pulled up to and parked at the stadium. Before exiting the bus, our coach's pep talk for the game was short and penetrating. "Boys, tonight you get the hell beat out of you. Now get out on the field and warm up." Can you imagine how high or low our motivation was going to be in that game? How high or low would your motivation be if a coach said that to you and your teammates? What if a boss said something like, "You are being assigned to a new territory. You won't be able to meet your quota in this territory, but it's yours now!"?

If the truth were known, we may not have been as serious as the coach thought we should have been on that fifteen-minute bus ride to the stadium. But why such a prediction? As a leader, would you make such a statement to your followers? Especially if it involved a possible loss? Wouldn't you try to prepare your team just a smidge more positively?

Unfortunately, the coach was a soothsayer—a real gem! We lost 38–0. On the bus ride back to the gym, he didn't say a word, not even an "I told you so." None of us had anything to say either. It was a perfect example of no communication. During the next week, he never reviewed the game with us. There were no extra intensive practices, no added killer wind sprints. It was just business as usual. We practiced and planned for the next game as though last Friday night had never happened. We won that next game and had a winning season. Yet, to this day, I don't know what set off his hot prediction. He moved on to another job the next year, and (apparently) none of us had the guts to ask about that night. That event was untouchable.

On a lighter note, Jen-Hsun Huang, president and CEO of Nvidia, a maker of graphics chips in Santa Clara, California, says he learned to work with others by waiting tables at Denny's. If you've ever worked in a restaurant, you know what that's like. "Customers are always supposed to be right, but customers can't always be right. One must learn to make the most of all situations." After all, when one waits tables, tips are important. And to my knowledge, there are no threats of getting hell beat out of you like in football. Huang learned to make the best out of his situations, and you will have to make the best of a lot of strange, questionable circumstances and roll on.

## *Early Leadership Lessons*

I was one of those guys to whom people looked and expected to take a leadership role. Apparently, others thought I had the personality and character to lead. Yet I seldom sought these roles. Maybe they thought I could lead because I was taller than my classmates. Maybe it was because I was easygoing, likeable, got along with everyone, or had a sense of humor. Or maybe I was just gullible and easily influenced to take the reins.

Early in my freshman year in high school, the time arrived to elect class officers. The procedure was somewhat different than we read about or see in movies today. I went to a small high school (there were fifty-two students in my freshman class but only thirty-one students in my senior class). Homerooms and study halls were in vogue. Nominations for president were solicited in homeroom, and I was one of three candidates nominated for president. The three of us were asked to leave the room while our classmates voted. When we were told to come back in, it was announced that I had been elected president. The same thing happened my sophomore, junior, and senior years! Four straight years in the top class leadership role—can you imagine such a thing happening in high schools now?

To say I was surprised would be an understatement. Although in the beginning I was nervous, it gave me a new self-confidence in my own leadership that I had never analyzed before. If other people see this in me, why have I been ignoring it most of my life? Four years as president provided me the experiences of leading meetings, working behind the scenes with colleagues of influence, and interacting with superiors (teachers and administrators). Those early experiences provided me with skills I still use today.

My behavior and tendencies to seldom seek leadership experiences are reminiscent of the age-old debate as to whether leaders are born or made. My personal belief is that few, if any, are born to lead. However, at the same time, I also believe that some people may have a natural predisposition toward leading. Usually it is because they made choices in life to lead and acquired the necessary skills to do so. As Malcolm Gladwell, author and writer with *The New Yorker*, writes in the book *Outliers*, some people take their gifts, practice and study for thousands of hours, and turn their gifts into world-class talents.

## *Early Leadership Experiences*

How do you learn? I was an average-to-good student with the ability to learn both aurally and visually. My drawback was the lack of willingness to spend adequate time to make all As instead of settling for As and Bs. There were sports, friends, and girls in the way, I suppose. Yet, in retrospect, what needed a makeover was not my study skills. I had no motivation to be perfect. (I once told my wife about this tendency, and she just gave me a crooked grin and said, "You were just a lazy butt!") Good enough was good enough.

In addition, I had to learn how to deal with being an introvert. I was shy. Yet, remarkably, I was never horrified of talking to people, teaching, presenting, or being in front of people. Mostly, I was just quiet, never really seeing a need to insert myself in conversations others were having in my presence. Why spend time talking when there were always plenty of other people willing to do that for me? In my family, I was the oldest child of four. Everyone at school knew that, and perhaps that knowledge gave me some sort of power as being the oldest brother—the big brother.

I think the real reason for my hesitancy in talking might have been because I wasn't in control of those venues. For example, when I played quarterback in middle school and high school, calling the plays and giving directions didn't require much prose. As a leader in sports, few words were ever really required. Call the play, line up, and hit the opponent.

There did come a day, however, when sports and I had gone as far as we were going to go. About midterm one year, a college professor pulled me aside to let me know I needed to talk more in class. His reasoning? "You're a leader. Everyone looks up to you and pays attention to what you say. You have more experiences than most. You're adept at making the best of a state of chaos. And you're highly trusted. I need you to speak up more frequently. You need that experience, and your classmates need to hear your views.

So, from this point forward, a portion of your grade will depend upon your participation in class."

No one ever explained it more clearly. I suppose I could have challenged him. "Foul. That's not in the syllabus." But from that point forward, I set a goal to speak at least twice in every class meeting. My A was secured, and it was a great learning experience. (Although today, a soft elbow from my wife reminds me I'm lagging behind in my speaking up in Sunday school.) As a leader, you and I must be *heard* as well as seen.

Consider President Abraham Lincoln. His image is on the penny and on Mount Rushmore. In his own day, however, he was reviled in cartoons and the print media. He was a controversial figure right up to his assassination. Like President George W. Bush, he was ridiculed for his manner of speaking and homespun image. Yet Lincoln emerged as a leader dependent upon his public image, and he was an active participant in the development of his beloved, benevolent, and thoughtful public image. In the end, he had a profound impact on the public and in history as a commander-in-chief and the Great Emancipator. He was not only *seen* but also *heard.* More importantly, though, he was believed and trusted.

## *Success and Adversity Experiences*

Have you considered that adversity has the ability to introduce you to yourself? It clarifies what you value the most and helps you see the big picture. It forces you to embrace the challenge, fully commit to what is important, engage others, and take charge. You don't always have full control of all that is happening, but you are in charge of your own life. You may not have power over all the decisions, but you do control some. Often you can even positively influence the outcome. It *is* possible to stay focused on the decisions you control.

Rick Boxx, President and Founder of Integrity Resource Center, describes a situation a CEO he knows had with a disruptive, divisive employee:

> A longtime employee of his had been an adequate performer in the organization for many years. As the business grew, and more interaction between him and others became necessary, however, this employee's shortcomings became obvious. He would deride other employees, stir up dissension, and even make inappropriate remarks to—and about the business owner.

Naturally, no one wants to work with such a difficult person. Frustrations rise, morale goes down, and colleagues, customers, and vendors get upset. So what do you do with such a problem person—especially since he is a longtime employee?

You can't ignore him. You're going to have to intervene as quickly as possible and help get this person on the right track. If that is impossible, termination may be the only choice. To not take action is unfair to this employee, the employees with whom he works, and to the organization itself.

In my three ventures as the dean of a B-school, I have had to deal with any number of adverse circumstances. Here's one: the president of the university where I was first a department chairman fired someone who was a very popular dean at that time. As you might imagine, the business faculty were up in arms about that decision and ready to jump ship. The other department chair and I knew there was a tenuous relationship between the dean and president—the dean was raising more money than the president. We repeatedly recommended caution. Our wagons were hitched to a star, and if he crashed and burned, we would all crash and burn. Unfortunately, we couldn't stop the potential for retribution.

I was asked to fill the gap as dean for a couple of years until a replacement hand-selected by the president could be found. One of my first acts as dean was to call a faculty meeting. I invited the president to attend to share his vision about the future. It was obvious his vision was not our vision. Things started well and were proceeding nicely, but toward the end of his presentation, the faculty began to ask some challenging questions. Finally, the concluding moment arrived, and the president spoke his mind and heart. He had had all the questions he wanted.

His parting words were, "I know you don't all agree with what has recently transpired, and that's all right. We were looking for people when we found you, and we can do so again with other people. If you are unhappy with the way I'm doing things, don't let the door hit you in the butt on the way out." With that statement hanging in the air, he departed. We watched in amazement as the door slammed. There was no way I was going to be able to smooth the churning waters. I couldn't stick a finger in the dike, even though I tried with love and encouragement. During the next three years, a little more than one-half of the younger and more mobile business faculty reluctantly resigned—many of whom I had hired when I was the department chair—and took jobs at other universities. Then I also left. There was no way to keep hope alive in the minds of those leaving for new pastures. (However, I was fortunate to be able to continue the friendships and mentoring relationships with the majority of them and continue to encourage their growth and professional development from a distance.) Adversity is seldom pleasant.

So, if we learn more from losing than winning, we also might learn more from adversity than success. For example, on September 11, 2001, Bob Mulholland, senior VP and head of client relations at Merrill Lynch, had to respond to the terrorist attacks on the World Trade Center. He and his staff felt their building rock and watched as smoke poured out of a gaping hole in the twin tower across from them. Panic set in, and Mulholland knew he had to act.

He later said, "When there's a crisis, you've got to show people the way, step by step, and make sure you're taking care of their concerns." He calmed the staff and clients in the office by convincing them they needed to unfreeze their panic. He assured them they had enough time to escape via the stairs. Thanks to his calm and decisive leadership, he was able to minimize people's emotional responses and help everyone escape before the towers collapsed.

If you were a fan of the TV show *Lost*, the above illustration is not unlike one of the main characters—Jack Shepherd (Matthew Fox). One of the reasons Jack emerged as the leader was not only because he had a medical degree but also because normally he stayed calm and level. Or at least he appeared to when James Sawyer (Josh Holloway) or John Locke (Terry O'Quinn) weren't bugging him about something.

In the majority of instances, thankfully, we can keep hope alive in the minds of those who follow us. Hope can transcend the difficulties of the moment and focus on the potentials of tomorrow. It can help people bounce back, to find the will to move forward, and to once again aspire to greatness. Those following us need our insight, motivation, and willingness to lead them to higher or safer ground.

## Leadership Style Evolution

Over the last twenty-five years, my leadership style has evolved in various directions. I've learned to ask more questions than I did at one time. I've practiced looking around corners more frequently to see what's coming toward me. I've worked at allowing better intuition to develop. I've learned to see the forest and not just the trees. I've developed the patience to deal with ambiguity and/or complexity. I've attempted to become proficient at bringing unique perspectives to problem solutions. I've learned to set daily goals to become better at adding value to everything while staying prepared for anything and everything.

What about you? How have you changed in the last five to ten years? (You may have to ask others what changes they've noticed in you.)

Leadership style is not about fashion. It is about meeting the needs of followers and organizations. The demand of the situation, requirements of people, and particular challenges being faced result in a multitude of leadership style possibilities. Some of those leadership styles often discussed and researched include laissez-faire, autocratic, participative, visionary, situational, strategic, cross-cultural, charismatic, organizational, spiritual, and level five.

Plato, Greek philosopher and founder of Athens Academy, reminds all us that the unexamined life is not worth living. If you or I spent twenty-seven years locked away in deprivation, we would have plenty of time to examine our lives. Nelson Mandela, president of South Africa, 1994–99, was such a man. He, in fact, faced enough trouble for several lifetimes of examination. Yet he was able to liberate a country from violent prejudice. He united whites and blacks, oppressors and oppressed. He believed that overthrowing apartheid and creating a nonracial democratic South Africa "was not a question of principle; it was a question of tactics." Leaders come in all shapes and forms and intellectual directions. Like Mandela, leaders have the power to change people.

How we interact with, lead, and change people can happen through a variety of techniques. For example, if you haven't yet done so, you will need to develop skills developing a positive working environment, setting direction, delegating, being enthusiastic, building confidence in others, developing a team spirit, and providing feedback. We'll look at all of these ideas in the chapters ahead to guide you to leadership essentials that require your focus.

## EFFECTIVE FOLLOWERSHIP

An effective leader has followers. Can't be a leader without them. Before we conclude, we will take a look at the types and characteristics of those following you. Barbara Kellerman, lecturer at Harvard University, offers a typology that helps explain how followers differ from one another:

1. *Isolates.* Those completely detached. They do not care for their leaders. They just do their job without interest.

2. *Bystanders.* Free riders who are detached when it fits their self-interests. They have low internal motivation.

3. *Participants.* They engage enough to invest their own time and money to make a difference. They are sometimes for and sometimes against the leader and organization.

4. *Activists.* They are considerably engaged. They are heavily invested in people and process. They are eager to demonstrate their support or opposition. They feel strongly about their leader and organization.

5. *Diehards.* They are super-engaged to the point that they are willing to go down for their own cause. They can be an asset or a liability to the leader. They have a strong tendency to be whistleblowers.

Fortunately, not everyone you do or will work with is detached from the job or doesn't work at the job. Unfortunately, not everyone you do or will work with is passionately committed to and deeply involved with the job. All leaders and followers must find a way to work together to be effective so an unproductive disparity does not separate leaders from their followers.

## CONCLUSION

Some answers and illustrations for five important questions have been offered. As you ponder your own unique perspectives, consider the following example.

Ed Macauley is a former Boston Celtics basketball player who scored 11,234 points in ten NBA seasons and was inducted into the Basketball Hall of Fame in 1960. His uniform number, twenty-two, was retired by the Celtics. Three of his statements stand out: (a) "When you are not practicing, remember, someone somewhere is practicing, and when you meet him he will win." (b) "You always have to give 100 percent, because if you don't, someone, someplace, will give 100 percent and will beat you when you meet." (c) "Just remember that if you're not working at your game to the utmost of your ability, there will be someone out there somewhere with equal ability who is. And one day you'll play each other, and he'll have the advantage."

The message?

We must be prepared at all times. We must be prepared to give the game of life and business all we have. As Robert Thornton Henderson, American author, has said, "Most of the significant things done in the world were done by persons who were either too busy or too sick! There are few ideal and leisurely settings for the disciplines of growth."

Additionally, one remaining point touches our five questions. Somerset Maugham, English playwright and novelist, wrote in *The Razor's Edge,* "Nothing in the world is permanent, and we're foolish when we ask anything to last, but surely we're still more foolish not to take delight in it while we have it. If change is of the essence of existence, one would have thought it only sensible to make it the premise of our philosophy."

I have been leading others directly or indirectly for some time. I know how important the above discussion about leadership is in general and about leadership style specifically. I believe what humorist Arnold Glasow said: "The trouble with the future is that it usually arrives before we're ready for it." However, change is a critical component of our personal and professional life. It is so much a part of our world that we need to spend some time thinking about it. Why? Because change affects our leadership in so many crucial ways. It is the essence of our existence. And you, your followers, and your organization must be prepared for a revolutionary approach to understanding organizational leadership. Sometimes the only way to effect change is be in a leadership position. So are you going to lead, follow, or get out of the way?

# IS THE COLOR OF YOUR WORLD CHANGING?

## AN ORGANIZATIONAL REVOLUTION

Something is happening and it affects us all...With unsettling speed, two forces are converging: a new generation of business leaders is rewriting the rules of business, and a new breed of fast companies is challenging the corporate status quo....That convergence overturns 50 years of received wisdom on the fundamentals of work and competition. The result is a revolution as far-reaching as the Industrial Revolution.

*Fast Company* founding editors

Josiah was eight years old when he became king, and he reigned in Jerusalem thirty-one years ... During the eighth year of his reign, while he was still young, Josiah began to seek the God of his ancestor David. Then in the twelfth year, he began to purify Judah and Jerusalem, destroying all the pagan shrines, the Asherah poles, and the carved idols and cast images ... In the eighteenth year of his reign, after he had purified the land and the Temple, Josiah appointed Shaphan son of Azaliah, Maaseiah the governor of Jerusalem, and Joab son of Joahaz, the royal historian, to repair the Temple of the Lord his God.

2 Chronicles 34:1, 3, 8

In the children's book *The Cat in the Hat,* by Dr. Seuss, there is this peculiar cat that is perhaps the most famous of cats in these children's books. It appears in six books. If you remember, you know that this mischievous cat wears a tall, red and white-striped hat and a red bow tie and carries a pale blue umbrella. There's even a movie about him.

The cat brings an exuberant form of chaos to a brother and sister one rainy day while their mother leaves them at home unattended. He performs all kinds of wacky tricks. At one point, he balances a teacup, some milk, a cake, three books, a fish, a rake, a toy boat, a toy man, a red fan, and his umbrella while he's on a ball. (Do you think I've spent too much time with the cat?) Of course, the children love it.

Then the cat brings in a box with two creatures named Thing One and Thing Two, who begin to fly kites in the house. The cat's antics are vainly opposed by the family pet, an articulate fish. The children ultimately capture Things One and Two with a net and bring the cat under control. To make up for the chaos he has caused, the cat cleans up the house and disappears just as the mother arrives back home.

In how many directions is it possible for you be pulled? How many hats can *you* wear on any given day without losing your head? Is the chaos in your workplace anything like that described above? Is it possible for you to live up to what everyone expects of you and keep both them and you happy? How many balls can you juggle in the air at one time? Can you be successful and profitable while trying to move onward and upward?

Or do you just want to run away?

---

I hope you have the foresight and fortitude to stay and fix whatever is preventing you from staying on course. Not everyone can. Recall my experience in dealing with the unpleasantness of a president telling the faculty they would not be missed if they left the university, that they were easily replaceable. Little did he understand how untrue his assumption was. All those who left went on to other institutions and became their top leaders, researchers, and writers.

In such a situation as this, there did not seem to be an answer to save everyone and keep personnel together without whining to the Board of Trustees and being able to engineer his firing. Since his demise as president wasn't imminent, my only path was to do the best I could do in repairing the damage by replacing those who were leaving as quickly as possible. Their trust in the university and its mission had been shattered by the top leader, who could talk so callously about the geese who were laying the golden eggs. At the same time, I was hoping the new people would not be infected with the bitterness of those still hanging on.

A few years ago, Daimler-Benz decided that they were too reliant on their luxury car, Mercedes-Benz. They decided to expand, transform, and diversify themselves into four divisions: aerospace, financial services, automation and rail, and, of course, keep the prized brand, Mercedes-Benz. They made major investments and commitments. Yet they struggled with being pulled in too many directions. They were unable to live up to their expectations and commitments. They began to lose money at an alarming pace.

To try to repair the losses, the board promoted Jurgen Shrempp to CEO with the mandate: fix things. Turn things around, and do it quickly. Dismantle and then reassemble. But know this: Whatever you do will make headlines around the world.

If you were Shrempp, what would you do first? The color of the world is changing. What are you going to do about it? Where would you begin to turn things around and begin a restoration of profit? The business world is not like it was in earlier decades, and it will continue to change in the future. The information that follows will help you see what we might expect in coming years and why.

## LEADERSHIP CONCERNS

Our world is changing at a rapid-fire pace. It has been said, for example, that the top ten in-demand jobs in 2010 did not exist in 2004, the education our children are receiving today will be out of date in three years, we are trying to prepare students to solve problems that don't yet exist, and the average young worker will have ten to fourteen jobs by the time they are thirty-eight years of age. It is estimated that our knowledge doubles every six months and will continue to do so for the next ten years. The mid-1940s-1960s were nothing like this. You may have heard that time period referred to as Camelot. Change was something heard about but seldom experienced. We were able to look at the world, including the business world, through rose-colored glasses. No longer.

Perhaps you've heard the rumor that all followers resist change but all leaders like change. Not true. Think of all the uproar that accompanies changing any street name or paving a road in front of businesses. Changes in stationery or assignments of inconvenient parking places often get the tempers of both leaders and followers flaring. Leaders whom I know are reluctant to accept change, unless the change was their idea. Why? Change requires more work. So there may be some truth to another saying that "the only person who appreciates change is a wet baby."

Dr. David E. Morton, FACHE, regional executive with the American Hospital Association, once said, "Being a successful CEO in today's environment is like trying to change the fan belt on your car with the engine running. It is hard to do without getting bloody!" Several years ago, because of his leadership position, Morton established four theorems upon which he bases his leadership.

1. Consensus and compromise lead to mediocrity.

2. There is more than one way to skin a cat but none the cat likes.

3. Leadership is a learned behavior. It can be taught.

4. Empowerment without direction equals chaos.

Marcel Proust, French novelist, states, "The real voyage of discovery consists not in seeking new landscapes but in having new eyes." We must be able to see with new eyes and allow our minds to be flexible. We should not become fixed and settled in our thinking. We must be willing to entertain new ideas and contemplate new ways. Keep current with what the competition is doing without copying them. Even on talent shows, the judges pick winners who have something unique about them, some slight and pleasing change from the same ole, same ole.

Have you considered questions like the following: What are the costs monetarily in personnel, numbers, and work hours? What differences exist among people emotionally and ethically? What responses do changes demand? How can problems be identified and transformed for the good of all peoples? How can one modify personal thinking from the antiquated to the twenty-first century? How will people adapt? What are the leaders of today most concerned about? Are recent college grads more concerned about certain things than people were in the last ten, twenty, or thirty years?

Think about a really great organization that you have been associated with. What made it great? Was it the CEO or COO? If so, what were they doing that contributed to it being great? Could they let go of their egos? Did they build positive relationships? How did they add value? Did they share their power?

The questions are endless. So what are the things that concern leaders the most? See Table 2.1 for a sample of such concerns (with some overlap). At the same time, realize these concerns could be for a leader in any type of organization—education, religion, military, government, for-profit, or not-for-profit.

Table 2.1

| | | |
|---|---|---|
| Recruitment and retention | Shortage of qualified people | Appropriate balance |
| Productivity | Innovation | Professional development |
| Environmental changes | Ethics | Social responsibility |
| Technology | Globalization | New generations |
| Competition | Brand awareness | Creativity |
| Assurance of learning | Best practices | Differentiation |
| Return on assets | Maximum capacity | Auditing |
| Financial resources | Financial pressures | Value |
| Behavior | Motivation | Communication |
| Conflict | Coaching | Relationships |
| Measurements | Power | Politics |
| Negotiation | Culture | Diversity |
| Strategic changes | Spirituality in the workplace | Learning organization |
| Attitudes | Influence | Knowledge management |
| Leadership development | Succession planning | Satisfaction |
| Values | Groups | Teamwork |

The impact of each item listed could be experienced in every avenue of your life and in all organizations. For example, there are global changes that may forever alter the way business is conducted. World events such as the end of communism in Russia, the disintegration of the Eastern bloc, continuing problems in Iran, Iraq, Afghanistan, and Pakistan, the recent worldwide economical downturn, an earthquake in Haiti, BP's oil leakage and spill into the Gulf of Mexico, and other socioeconomic and political trends demand attention. The question is not, "Will change occur?" but rather, "When and how will change occur?" Or, "When will the next change occur?" It's often a surprise. So you and I will continue to have to wear several hats, experience being pulled in several directions, and get derailed, or at least be placed on a sidetrack, from where our destination was originally.

Someone once said that the last thing a fish notices about itself is that it lives in water. We cannot afford to be this oblivious to our environment. We cannot ignore the technical, political, and cultural shifts in thinking locally, regionally, nationally, and worldwide. To meet the challenges of a changing world, numerous questions must be addressed. The best answers come from the best questions, the right questions. One of those questions might be: Would you call your organization a high-performance organization?

In my experience, high-performance organizations are seldom the result of a specific action by a leader. They are the result of relentless pursuit of a new future. At times, we may feel like we're running a marathon by ourselves before others join in the endurance race to reach the point of a new organizational revitalization, a new revolution. If you're ever run or walked a marathon or a half-marathon, you know this is true.

## AN ORGANIZATIONAL REVOLUTION

Earlier I mentioned how our world, including our business world, was once referred to as Camelot. Change was something not expected. Once you had a job, you stayed with that job almost all your life. Loyalty was highly prized. It wasn't until the Vietnam War that our society began to realize something was wrong. Corporations began to be looked upon as "the man" who was keeping American down. Camelot was beginning to be dismantled brick by brick. Change in education, knowledge, and technology began to move forward at more rapid speed.

In corporate America, since the mid-1980s, a revolutionary shift has been in effect. Author Gwendolyn Cuizon has written that an organizational revolution "provides businesses with the means and actual 'goods' to begin thinking about the end of scarcity. Determining weak links in the organization, the causes of problems and acquiring new ideas from the environment all could contribute to radical change."

Two personal examples come to mind. Once I was asked to help turn around a church. The church was a new-plant congregation that had split off from a sister church. My wife and I had just moved into the area and placed our membership at that loving church. The church had been meeting for two years before we moved there, and it was struggling to fulfill what it saw as its mission. As I began working with the church's leadership, I discovered they had no written mission, core values, vision statement, or collectively shared goals.

I worked with the leaders of the congregation, held an all-day workshop on a university campus for all the church members, and was able to achieve a consensus of thought about the future. They took the lesson very seriously in that venue and worked like a graduate class to finalize their day with me. A ninety-word mission and vision became a driving force for them. The end result was a doubling of membership and the purchase of a new facility.

On another occasion, a university president asked me to help set a B-school on a different path. One of the specific charges he handed me was to establish and grow a graduate program (an MBA degree). When I moved to that university, the business faculty only numbered six people. They were a group much like the above church. They had no written mission statement, core values, vision, or shared goals. (This is not to say they had no vision or values as people.) But I sensed a major weakness. They displayed little belief in or respect for who they were and what they could potentially accomplish.

It took a year to get all the right things in place, but afterwards, they took their first steps to begin seeing themselves as a premier business school in the area. I helped by redecorating the building—new carpet, paint, and furniture—twice. That went a long way in effecting change in attitudes and outlooks. Within a year, I had jumped through all the hoops of on- and off-campus rules and expectations and implemented what became an extremely successful MBA degree. We added three undergraduate majors, doubled the number of faculty, and added five staff members. It's amazing what belief in oneself will do for people.

Lucius Annaeus Seneca (often known as Seneca the Younger), Roman philosopher and statesman, said, "It is not because things are difficult that we do not dare; it is because we do not dare that they are difficult." Thus, many revolutions or turnarounds are similar to a staged drama. There are protagonists, antagonists, dramatic themes, and a gripping plot played out over three acts. Noel M. Tichy, a University of Michigan professor and author, describes the drama accordingly:

Act 1. The *awakening*—when the need for change and revitalization is realized.

Act 2. The *envisioning*—when a vision is created and workers are mobilized.

Act 3. The *re-architecting*—when the design and construction of a wholly new organization are detailed.

The final act is exhilarating because it leads to rebirth. Try it. You will find, as I did, that successful dramas can change thinking, actions, being, and becoming. You might even wonder why you waited so long to do something. Why you weren't aware of the importance these acts were having on your business life. How you could have missed the impact they would have on corporate America. How you needed to be involved so that you could lead people with greater skills and confidence.

## RECOGNIZING THE NEED FOR REVITALIZATION

Act 1 is an *awakening*. It is a recognition that something needs to be changed, revitalized, or awakened. Please note, however, that some awakenings can be an emotionally wrenching process. I've been a Dallas Cowboys fan since their beginning. In Super Bowl XXVIII, the Cowboys found themselves trailing the Buffalo Bills 13–6 at halftime. However, a change in strategy at halftime resulted in a 30–13 win. It was a great victory for Cowboys fans.

Similarly, in organizational life, two steps are necessary to begin a revolution to be revitalized. Tichy offers the following two-step process:

1. *Kick-start the revolution.* Articulate why the change is necessary; make certain everyone is in agreement. (Of course, it's best to have all levels of the organization represented so a team decision can be made that will get everyone behind it. They will feel as though they had a say in the process.)

2. *Deal with resistance.* Provide the facts and the rationales for change; more often than not, followers will reach the same conclusions as the leaders.

Anytime I've been faced with the need or mandate to revolutionize a group, I've encountered sulking, fear, chaos, and unforeseen outcomes. Such fear breeds timidity and stifles proactive, forward movement. Sometimes the attempted revolution has been marked by conflict, denial, and resistance. Two examples:

Several times I've needed to make new assignments of teaching schedules. One particular person had been teaching a particular course for several years, but because of a change in department chairs, I needed him to start teaching in another business content area. Although he was willing enough to change for a year, anticipating that it was just for a year, when he was unable to get his "favorite" course back the next year, he was not very happy with the change. As a result I had to mentor him into a new awareness of needs in other courses for which he was well prepared. He actually became happier with this new venture than he had been with the previous "favorite."

In another instance, due to a particular policy change I had to introduce, one person apparently was infuriated. I walked into a meeting I had called to see that person sitting behind everyone with his chair turned in the opposite direction. I said something along the lines of, "Okay, well, it's time to get started, if I can have everyone's attention." Everyone quit talking and looked forward, but my comment didn't change the direction he was facing. I went ahead and held the meeting with him facing backwards and others glancing at him occasionally with bewildered expressions on their faces. I've forgotten now what that policy change was, but I guess he showed me! (He left for a different job the next year.) Several years later our paths crossed, and we were able to communicate about family, jobs, and sports as though nothing had ever happened between us. Funny how time works on the brain to make us realize that not everything in the future is as seemingly important as it once was.

*Conflict* may occur between those who have worked onsite for a long time and those who are new to the organization because of different need agendas. *Denial* may result in a refusal to even think about, let alone talk about, the issues. *Resistance* is common and may take many forms, but it will be strongest when the change is personal. It's amazing the reactions people have to things like insurance plan changes, bus routes, airline services, charges for food and baggage, no smoking policies in buildings, or name changes for a company or university. Thus, any negative thinking or acting must be dealt with. Unless a majority buys into the needed change, it will be difficult, if not impossible, to implement a transformation.

As Cuizon also says, "Organizational revolution … is necessary in order for the company to adapt to external and internal factors. Implementation of radical changes may be necessary in order to overcome some perceived failures and turn it into a success." Recognizing the need to do something is the first step in moving the organization forward. The next step is to work toward creating a vision that will have all followers desiring to be on board.

## CREATING A NEW VISION

Act 2, *envisioning,* is where the revolution comes into focus. Attention is directed toward the future. Emotion becomes a positive force. Frustrations and fears are channeled into positive, new directions. A vision is sought. Creativity is encouraged. President Obama ran on the magic word *change.* Young people and other Americans grabbed on to this mantra. They may not have been able to explain Obama's vision, but they knew they wanted whatever it was because of change. After years of presidential criticism, mocking, putdowns, and comics' pundits, the TV generation wanted a magical elixir because the proposed change looked exciting and beautiful, and it reeked of vitality.

An ancient writer once said that without a vision people perish. To amplify this thought, James Kouzes, author and executive fellow at the Center for Innovation, and Barry Posner, professor of leadership at Santa Clara University, wrote, "There's nothing more demoralizing than a leader who can't clearly articulate why we're doing what we're doing." If you've ever been put in a position where you have to follow such a person, you know how unmotivating that can be.

Theodore Hesburgh, a former president of the University of Notre Dame, said, "The very essence of leadership is that you have to have a vision. It's got to be a vision you articulate clearly and forcefully on every occasion." If the vision is something everyone in the organization buys into, they will support that vision regardless of the changes that will need to be made.

In every organizational revolution I've been involved, three organizational systems had to be addressed in order to create a new vision: the technical, political, and cultural system. For *technical systems,* I've been faced with organizing people, money, information, and technology. A more difficult aspect in one organization was the fear of new technology, especially in the early 1980s when personal computers were coming into offices. Training was a high priority to try to build an appreciation for such. Some of those who were hardest to sell on the idea later became the biggest fans for updating and exploring new software.

For *political systems,* I've had to allocate power, rewards, and growth opportunities. It is not uncommon to have to use intrigue or strategy to obtain any position of power or control in business, a university, a nonprofit organization, or a governmental institution. A key that has worked for me is to have the opportunity to provide professional growth and development opportunities for others. Sometimes one must use politics to overcome what seems unacceptable organizational politics. Other times it helps to have access to those up the ladder who are willing to listen and make necessary changes in the organization and in their other methods of dealing with followers.

For *cultural systems,* I've needed to share norms, beliefs, and values. In one particular organization, changes in leadership necessitated a regrouping, realignment, and restructuring that had the potential to undercut the organizational culture that had been built over the previous seven years. New norms, beliefs, and values had to be reemphasized, trust had to be restored, and relationships had to be tenderly solidified.

These technical-political-cultural issues can be thought of as three strands of a strategic rope. Remember though, a rope can unravel. An organization can come apart at the seams if it's not woven into a strong braid when its systems work at cross-purposes.

One thing I have come to believe very strongly is that a shared vision must be created and commitment formed in order to change an organization or to realign it. Donna Fitzgerald, research director at the Gartner Blog Network, writes, "With shared vision it no longer matters what we think but what thoughts and concepts we share with the team. In other words, shared vision is the point where we actually harness the horses so that we can get some work done." In the future, *you* must develop a technique for writing your own "movie script" and produce a new, revised future.

On a hot summer day in 1962, President John F. Kennedy made a speech in the football stadium at Rice University in Houston. He reaffirmed a commitment for NASA and the space program. In that speech, he said:

> We choose to go to the moon. We choose to go to the moon in this decade and do the other things, not because they are easy, but because they are hard, because that goal will serve to organize and measure the best of our energies and skills, because that challenge is one that we are willing to accept, one we are unwilling to postpone, and one which we intend to win, and the others, too.

The idea caught fire in the nation, and it was a goal that grew in power, strength, and national pride. A shared organizational vision that has been created and the commitment formed for changing an organization or realigning it can be met with the same enthusiasm as that first trip to the moon.

## BUILDING A NEW ORGANIZATION

Act 3, *re-architecting,* is the art of redesigning and rebuilding an organization. It evolves to meet the challenges it faces and to become a high-performance organization. The concern is often how to ensure the continuity of the organization and its people. In my consulting about achieving re-architecture or renewal, I've discovered three boundaries that must be taken down or creatively destroyed to avoid limitations.

1. *Vertical boundaries*—the ceilings of hierarchy (i.e., the power brokers).

2. *Horizontal boundaries*—internal walls (i.e., barriers between groups within an organization, such as functional, geographic, or product groups).

3. *External boundaries*—boundaries between the organization and its external stakeholders.

When attempting to work across such boundaries, I've heard people say such things as, "The challenges are too complex," or, "Our budget is too tight," or, "It's not worth the effort." The way I had to deal with such challenges was by designing paths for collaborating across these boundaries. As a leader, you will be expected to deal with such things, only to discover that no one unit or organization can address all of them fully. You'll have to discover how to deal with certain "speed bumps": turf and trust issues, lack of support by certain entities, the time required for a reconcilable solution, dealing with people who won't share information, and a lack of incentives. How will you circumvent such potentials for disaster?

To knock down these barriers, I have had to recommend that other leaders "de-layer" the hierarchy, broaden incentives, build partnerships, or create alliances. How people work together to get things done, who relates to who for what, and how decisions are made are always key areas to explore. President Ronald Reagan, as an example, was able to effect barriers being destroyed. In June 1987, Reagan gave a speech at the Brandenburg Gate on the west side of the Berlin Wall. The speaker system being used was loud enough to be heard on the east side of the Wall. His words were, "General Secretary Gorbachev, if you seek peace, if you seek prosperity for the Soviet Union and Eastern Europe, if you seek liberalization: Come here to this gate! Mr. Gorbachev, open this gate! Mr. Gorbachev, tear down this wall!" The key components were—and are—people, time, and space.

General Electric's former chairman coined the term *boundary-less organization* to describe what he wanted GE to become. He wanted to eliminate vertical and horizontal boundaries within GE and break down external barriers between the company and its customers and suppliers. He sought to eliminate the chain of command and replace departments with empowered teams. Although he did not achieve a boundary-less organization, he did make significant progress toward that end. Other companies such as Hewlett-Packard, AT&T, Motorola, and Oticon A/S also have explored what a boundary-less organization would look like. Is your organization doing anything to try to make it boundary-less?

Be aware, however, that once the three-act process is completed, it must be renewed and kept alive. An environment must be created where followers understand that change is not an event. Leaders may have to revitalize themselves as well as their followers. It is a continuing process that is living and dynamic, always moving forward with an exciting vision of hope and vitality. It should be like a bullet train—a beautiful sight of power and determination.

## LEADER AND FOLLOWER COMPETENCIES

Additionally, in any kind of revitalization effort, I've had to examine three competencies in an attempt to discover where the most positive competencies lie. First, how do the people involved identify, organize, plan, and allocate their resources (e.g., time, money, materials, facilities, and human resources)? Second, how are their interpersonal skills (especially regarding team members, participation, teaching and coaching, and ethnic diversity)? Third, what is their ability to acquire, evaluate, organize, maintain, interpret, and communicate information? In almost every circumstance, I have had to assist leaders in transforming self, others, and their organizations to meet their current challenges. I had to help them learn where their personal and organizational competencies were and how they could help in the transformation process.

Believe it. Followers depend on leaders for self-transformation and empowerment. They will be empowered when they view the leader as an ideal model. As writer Nanette Page and educator Cheryl Czuba have stated, empowerment is "a multi-dimensional social process that helps people gain control over their own lives. It is a process that fosters power in people for use in their own lives, their communities and in their society, by acting on issues they define as important." In fact, the primary objective of allowing empowerment is to enable people to achieve an inner strength or a set of beliefs about their capacity to pursue and realize a vision. They have to believe the Nike tee shirt they're wearing—that they really can "Just do it!"

## CHANGE IS NOT AN OPTION

To further amplify the necessity of change, consider two other things. First, I want you to experience the effect of attitude on what you do. Write the word *attitude* on a sheet of paper with your writing hand. Then write the word *attitude* again with your other hand. When you look at the two writings of the word, do you notice a difference? Chances are good that when you look at the word *attitude* written by the hand you do not write with, you get a picture of the kind of attitude you usually have when you are trying to do something new. If you're like most people, you probably hated doing the task and the result. Perhaps inventor Charles Kettering was right. "If you have always done it that way, it is probably wrong." Although such an exercise can reveal your attitude toward change, you must always remember that change (or the necessity of change) is not an option. Refusal to change may only prolong personal, departmental, or organizational pain.

Second, I want you to solve the following child's riddle. No doubt you've heard a number of riddles at one time or another, riddles such as: Two boxers are in a boxing match. The fight is scheduled for twelve rounds, but it ends after six rounds, after one boxer knocks out the other boxer. Yet no man threw a punch. How is this possible?

The answer, of course, is that they were two women boxers. (Did I hear you groan?)

Here's the riddle I want you to solve: On day one, a large lake contains only a single, small lily pad. Each day, the number of lily pads doubles, until on day thirty the lake is totally full of lily pads.

On what day was the lake half full?

(Pause for answer.)

Remember, the lily pads doubled each day.

(Another pause for answer.)

This doubling power of the lily pads accurately reflects the awesomeness of change. Lily pads and innovations are not going to stop multiplying. Former ways of doing things no longer guarantee the results they once did. Organizational life is not like it was in the 1980s, 1990s, 2000s, or any other decade. So why do we respond as Canadian-American economist John Kenneth Galbraith described? "Faced with the choice between changing one's mind and proving that there is no need to do so, almost everybody gets busy on the proof." Have they forgotten that change is not an option?

Each generation brings a broader understanding of thinking, serving, studying, and leading. The millennial or net generation is profoundly changing the way we have to interact with followers.

## CONCLUSION

Incidentally, it takes twenty-nine days for the lake to be one-half full with vegetation and only one more day to be completely full.

This much we know: Older models or frameworks of how things should be done are no longer appropriate. The negative aspect of recognizing such is that we may have to change the way we think about things, the way we approach problem-solving activities. To illustrate: John Maxwell, leadership expert and author, provides a way to go from thinking to a life change. His advice is cogent and provides a needed six-step process for making changes that may be needed in your life and mine.

1. When you change your thinking, you change your beliefs.

2. When you change your beliefs, you change your expectations.

3. When you change your expectations, you change your attitude.

4. When you change your attitude, you change your behavior.

5. When you change your behavior, you change your performance.

6. When you change your performance, you change your life.

Unfortunately, change seldom (maybe never) has a group of supporters. People prefer the status quo to the risk involved in change. That is why it is so difficult to move a person or an organization forward into a new dimension. It can happen, must happen, and does happen, but the leader must be the one to demonstrate the necessity for and the results of change—personally and professionally. In the words of Martin Luther King Jr., "The ultimate measure of a man is not where he stands in moments of comfort and convenience, but where he stands at times of challenge and controversy." Recommendation: Proceed with caution.

Bob Dylan, American singer and songwriter, captured the 1960s rock-and-roll generation with this poetic phrase: "And the times, they are a changin.'" Some fifty years earlier, William Butler Yeats, Irish poet and dramatist, wrote, "Things fall apart; the center cannot hold…" Few song phrases or poetic lines so accurately predict the future. The times, indeed, are ever-changing, and things are continuously falling apart.

If we cannot stop the lily pads of change from multiplying, then we must learn to expand the capacity to absorb change. We must learn to flourish in constant transition.

Welcome to day twenty-nine! Are *you* ready to double your efforts?

# WHAT IS IT GOING TO TAKE?
## LEADERSHIP TRAITS AND BEHAVIORS

Clearly understanding what traits and characteristics are exhibited by effective leaders allows us not only to match the right leader with the right situation but also to discover benchmarks for what we need to look for if we want to be (or train) the best leaders we can.

—Kristina G. Ricketts, educator and author

Guard the good deposit that was entrusted to you—guard it with the help of the Holy Spirit who lives in us.

2 Timothy 1:14 (NIV)

At an ethics conference in March 2009 at Oxford University, I delivered a paper to a group of leader-educators from all over the globe. While there, I had the opportunity to visit the Marlboro Castle, where Winston Churchill, former prime minister of England, was born. It was exciting to visit such a well-known place where one of England's great leaders had spent some of his early years. Perhaps you've toured homes of other famous or infamous leaders and imagined what formed their psyches.

Churchill was a man of wealth, family position, intelligence, integrity, inspiration, and energy. He was a person of courage, drive, and creativity. He was not blessed with good looks, but he had a magnetic, powerful personality and excellent communication skills. He became a member of Parliament in 1900. Then in 1940, he became prime minister and minister of defense at age sixty-five. He was in office for five years, and afterwards, he remained a member of Parliament until 1964. During that time, Queen Elizabeth II conferred on him knighthood and invested him with the Order of the Garter. In 1963, President John F. Kennedy made him an honorary citizen of the United States.

Early in his career, Churchill experienced failure and unpopularity, as well as distrust from members of his own Conservative party. He was not viewed as particularly charismatic, but through all those early years he maintained faith in himself. With good judgment and timing, he was able to overcome opposition and achieve memorable results. He communicated with assurance and purpose when he spoke publicly. Someone once said of him that when you listened to Churchill, you believed you could achieve anything.

What was it about Churchill that gave him the ability to influence and motivate others to action and achieve goals? How would you compare and contrast him to Adolph Hitler?

What would make you want to copy the characteristics of Churchill's leadership? What would allow you to build excellence? What kind of a leader are you becoming? What is it going to take for you?

Two decisions are critical to the survival of all organizations: *what* an organization wants to be and *how* it should get there. What the leader views an organization to be sets its direction. However, as Napoleon Bonaparte, military and political leader of France, reminded us, "Ability is of little account without opportunity." How leaders get their organizations to where they envision them requires forming a strategy (i.e., mission statement, core values, and vision statement) before setting goals and starting long-range planning and day-to-day decision making. Warren Bennis, organizational consultant and author, wrote, "Managers are people who do things right, while leaders are people who do the right thing."

Thomas Wolfe, American novelist, however, may have summed it up as well as anyone: "If a man has a talent and cannot use it, he has failed. If he has a talent and uses only half of it, he has partly failed. If he has a talent and learns somehow to use the whole of it, he has gloriously succeeded and has a satisfaction and a triumph few men ever know." With that in mind, let me briefly review for you some of the approaches to what makes leaders tick. (It is important to note that most researchers look to styles instead of traits to understand leadership. However, a style of leadership is a combination of traits and behaviors. That is why we'll begin with traits.)

## LEADERSHIP TRAITS

Are leaders born, or are they made by circumstances? Is character developed via nature or nurture? The nature-nurture debate has been going on for decades. Certainly nature influences us, but nurture normally determines our impact. For example: Konrad Lorenz, Austrian zoologist and animal psychologist, conducted studies on the imprinting that occurs in baby geese. He discovered they have it within them to imprint whatever is moving near them. In most cases, that would be their mother. As they imprint on their mother, she will have a major impact on their life. In this case, genes (nature) provide the goal, but the environment (nurture) provides the process. What happens during the process will determine the outcome.

Similarly, early leadership researchers summarized leaders' qualities and assumed certain *traits* were inborn. Thus, effectiveness was measured in terms of potential ability and personality characteristics of a leader and group members. As John Viney, founder of Zygos, said:

> If there is a trait which does characterize leaders it is opportunism. Successful people are very often those who steadfastly refuse to be daunted by disadvantage and have the ability to turn disadvantage to good effect. They are people who seize opportunity and take risks. Leadership then seems to be a matter of personality and character.

Both your personality and character would have been imprinted to some extent by those around you early in life, not unlike the baby geese.

Certain recognized leaders possess different traits from other leaders. For example, how many famous leaders had children who were famous leaders? Few. Analysis of trait research reveals that an attempt to select leaders based on traits seldom succeeds. Leader traits are different from follower traits, and traits vary from one person and situation to another. Some people like to lead in sport but not at work. Or they like to lead in their neighborhood social committee or on a school board but not on a church board. Of course, some people truly want to lead, but they don't desire or have time to lead everything. Others have a high need to control, but if they try to control everything, they're insane.

So if no one really agrees with leadership trait theory, are there traits that set people apart? Or are all leaders just mere mortals prone to the same mistakes that befall everyone else? The list of traits and characteristics drawn from various lists in current literature suggests there are characteristics that set leaders apart from anyone else aspiring to leadership. The list is practically endless. See Table 3.1. (Note: These are only a sample of leadership traits. Makes you think researchers can't really boil it down.)

Table 3.1

| | | |
|---|---|---|
| Positive attitude | Systems knowledge | Conceptual |
| Cooperative | Concern for others | Anticipatory |
| Inspiration | Self-knowledge | Consistency |
| Willingness to take risk | Persistence | Multidimensionality |
| Adaptability | Willingness to sacrifice | Decisiveness |
| Self-esteem | Aggressive | Initiative |
| Popularity | Humor | Intelligence |
| Alertness | Insightful | Responsible |
| Self-confidence | Creativity | Personality |
| Morality | High energy | Physical stamina |
| Tolerance for stress | Vitality | Communication skills |
| Experience | Trustworthy | Intuitive |
| Charisma | Hardworking | Determined |
| Witty | Good judgment | Vision |
| Integrity | Inspirational | Courage |
| Character | Honesty | Competence |
| Forward looking | Fair-minded | Broadminded |
| Straightforward | Imaginative | Justice |
| Judgment | Dependability | Comfort with ambiguity |
| Tact | Unselfish | Knowledge |
| Loyalty | Endurance | Cool under pressure |
| Maturity | Will | Assertive |
| Candor | Commitment | Self-discipline |
| Humility | Flexibility | Empathy |
| Compassion | Scholarship | Introversion-extroversion |
| Prestige | Political savvy | Emotional control |
| Biosocial activity | Physique | Health |
| Adaptability | Ambition | Economic status |
| Social skills | Control of moods | Optimism |
| Technical skills | Task motivation | Nurturing behavior |
| Articulate | Aloof | Administrative skills |
| Passionate | Credibility | Intimacy |
| Self-control | Efficiency-oriented | Logical |
| Comfort with uncertainty | Ability to receive criticism | |

With such a long list of traits, is there a way to narrow them down to a few characteristics that have the power to transform leaders and followers?

There do seem to be six traits the best leaders exemplify: *initiative, sociability, integrity, personality, thinking,* and *maturity.*

## INITIATIVE

Initiative is the willingness of an individual to start an action or a readiness to embark on a new business venture. President Abraham Lincoln clarified the importance of initiative when he said, "Things may come to those who wait, but only what's left behind by those that hustle." Therefore, on a scale of one to ten, with ten being the highest level, how would *you* describe your level of initiative? If you could change your initiative to be better, what could you do? Where could you start focusing?

Adolphe Monod, French Protestant churchman, said, "Between the great things we cannot do and the small things we will not do, the danger is that we shall do nothing." Thus, leadership requires an understanding of initiative. Great is the need to move forward, sometimes through chaos, to tackle major problems—to do something. To illustrate: European mountain climbers tell a story of passing a certain grave along the trail to a famous peak. On the marker is a man's name and the inscription: "He died climbing." Such a statement is the picture of a life moving toward a goal.

Initiative cuts to the nature and purpose of an organization and to the leaders' vision of what it should become. There is an implied assumption that no matter how strong an organization's present position, the status quo is on trial. An organization is subject to comparison of both leaders' and followers' expectations.

As a leader, I had to learn to snatch the moment, to not let it pass or be grabbed by someone in a competitive field. I came to believe in the motto the movie *Dead Poets Society* popularized,

*Carpe diem* ("Seize the day"). I had to learn to take a strategic initiative and move forward. In the words of David Mahoney, former co-CEO of McKesson HBOC Inc., "There comes a moment when you have to stop revving up the car and shove it into gear."

## SOCIABILITY (LIKEABILITY)

Leaders must also recognize and appreciate the work and dignity of each person. They must strive to understand human relations and respect others. They must understand their own feelings and frustrations and accept others' feelings and frustrations. That means leaders must also be open, friendly, and hospitable. Manipulation will never be an option. In the words of servant leader C. W. Perry, "Leadership accepts people where they are and then takes them somewhere else."

Leaders have to learn to exhibit expertise or competency in three areas that significantly improve their social skills. First, you will come to realize that people need to be needed. People have unlimited potential and value. You need to continually work on communicating this understanding by warmth to and openness with followers and being real about it.

David Seat, a friend who is senior vice president of BancFirst, shared an experience with me recently. He had been visiting with two entrepreneurs who were exceptionally successful. He asked them what they thought made the difference in their success compared to others of their same age. Their response was interesting. They said when they graduated from college, they noticed that everyone was smart, driven, and worked hard. The difference in success of leaders was likeability. How's your sociability/likeability?

Second, you will discover the importance of developing trusting relationships. Trust begins with you. Before followers can be trustworthy, you have to demonstrate trust (e.g., confidence, reliance, expectation, or hope), use the word *trust* with them (e.g.,

I trust you to make that decision), and when they do something well, tell them if they truly did something well (e.g., I knew I could trust you to do a great job). Don't overdo this, however, or it will become meaningless. Two points became especially important in demonstrating trust:

1. There are degrees of confidence bestowed on a trusted person, and trust levels increase with time and demonstrations of trustworthiness.

2. Minimal amounts of risk are involved in trusting another person. Sometimes it appears dangerous to reach out to others, but the effort usually results in growth.

Third, you must learn to provide proper recognition. People deserve credit and recognition for their accomplishments. Such recognition demonstrates an appreciation of their contributions. Sometimes a simple gift of a T-shirt, a book, an umbrella, or a pat on the back motivates people to continue their good work and affirms them. Or surprise them with a gift card for something they have been desiring or needing for their office. Or let them leave at noon on Friday afternoon.

## INTEGRITY

Someone once penned, "Some of the best fiction of our day can be found on the expense reports of organizational employees." If there is one trait that should distinguish you as a leader, it is the moral trait of integrity. Integrity is displayed via a consistency of actions, values, honesty, truthfulness, and virtue in regard to motivations for actions. The present ethical and moral crises in our society, and in fact the world, scream out for moral and ethical leadership, for character and integrity.

Organizations need those who make no compromises with wrong and who are not afraid to stand for truth. Henry Van Dyke, an American author, educator, and clergyman, said, "You have to live in a crowd, but you do not have to live like it, nor subsist on its food."

As a member of Rotary International, I admire their succinct four-way test for ethical behavior. It asks: (a) Is it the truth? (b) Is it fair to all concerned? (c) Will it build goodwill and better friendships? (d) Will it be beneficial to all concerned? Those are great questions for enhancing your integrity and testing a decision.

To illustrate: A CEO once told me about five young men his organization had hired. Four of those new employees drank heavily with some of the executives on the weekend. One did not. The one who demonstrated restraint was the one who received the faster promotions. The CEO knew he could trust this person to be sober, hold his tongue, and not get in trouble. I know that not everyone reading this illustration may choose to believe it, but this next statement you should have no problem believing. Our lives are a witness, even when we think no one is watching.

## THINKING

Some leadership research indicates that leaders have a somewhat higher intelligence than their followers. That is, they typically have greater analytical ability, skilled reasoning, and can see broad problems and complicated relationships. They also excel at communicating ideas, motivating others, and understanding what others are communicating. All these activities are highly dependent on mental capability, a capacity for differentiation, and a talent for integration.

What distinguishes leaders from followers might be simply called *thinking*. They have the vision to think two to five to ten to twenty years into the future. Such thinking enables leaders to accomplish great things. Lee Bolman, author and scholar, and Terrence Deal, lecturer and author, recommend that thinking leaders need a holistic framework that encourages inquiry, a palette that identifies a full array of options, the willingness to become more creative and take risks, and a passionate commitment to their principles.

Martin Luther King Jr.'s "I Have a Dream" speech caught the imagination of his listeners on August 28, 1963, and it still rings in the hearts of many Americans today. It was a catalyst replayed on TV so many times that most anyone can visualize the man saying this phrase and feel his passion and believe his principles.

One thing is for certain: Forward thinking is a desired strength in leaders. Unfortunately, organizational leaders today don't seem to be able to find the healthy balance between thinking strategically and acting tactically. Leaders of the future must find a balance between being a tactician and a strategist to avoid always being in a reactive mode to the unexpected. Maintaining a sense of collaboration with followers will help leaders to be able to think forward. The rewards may be incalculable.

## PERSONALITY

Leaders are also often described as driven. They are motivated to keep accomplishing. They enjoy responsibility and strive for intrinsic rather than extrinsic rewards. Seeing their organizations move smoothly and productively toward a goal motivates them to do more. Leaders work for success. They set an example of hard work. As they reach one goal, they aspire to a new one. One success becomes a challenge to achieve greater success.

The way leaders view themselves is the way they will view their followers. For example, consider yourself. Do you demonstrate self-confidence? Humility? Trustworthiness? Authenticity? Enthusiasm? A sense of humor? Have people told you that you are this way? Give this list to various people and ask them to rate you on these traits so you'll have confirmation. Or think of a time within the last year that you showed each of these traits.

I have come to believe that leaders who believe that followers are not very important must not have very much self-respect. If leaders view followers as cold and pessimistic, they are probably the same way. With the judgment leaders put forth on others, they themselves will be judged. Therefore, leaders and followers alike must analyze their self-image. Many are prisoners of their negative or distorted self-perception. They underestimate their potential. As a result, they are unhappy, unproductive, and dissatisfied. They work with misguided motives because they have no achievement motivation.

## MATURITY

Leaders must be emotionally stable and mature. They have a broad range of interests and abilities. They also have healthy self-concepts, are self-assured, and have respect for others. They can understand incoming data, convey ideas, and inspire others. They are neither defeated by failure nor go overboard with victory. However, they must continue to strive for unity among followers.

David Ogilvy, of Ogilvy & Mather, was a champion of professional standards. He smoked pipes and cigars and drank moderately. However, he never went to local bars with his colleagues. Instead, he registered disgust toward such behavior. He expected a higher level of maturity in those who worked for and with him.

Your emotional stability, as an example, is indicated in the way you deal with people. This stability is represented through understanding, trust, confidence, tolerance, loyalty, and empathy. Characteristics of immature leaders include tactlessness, difficulty getting along with people, resisting change, blaming others when things go wrong, inability to handle criticism and differences in others, and being overly critical of others. Leaders who evidence such immaturity (or perhaps a lack of control) usually fail.

## LEADERSHIP BEHAVIORS

Two pioneering studies of leadership behaviors were conducted at Ohio State University and the University of Michigan during the 1950s. You might wonder why I would refer to studies so old, and I understand why you might question it, since these studies were conducted before many readers of this book were born. The reason for doing so is that the form of research used some sixty years ago and the findings generated are still being confirmed and reinforced today. The findings identified in both studies are similar, but the Michigan study yielded a broader range of behaviors.

### THE OHIO STATE UNIVERSITY STUDIES

The OSU researchers identified 1,800 examples of leadership. They reduced these examples to 150 questions about functions of leadership. They then asked followers to describe their leaders by responding to a questionnaire. Leaders were asked to rate themselves personally on all the leadership dimensions. After all the data was gathered, two dimensions accounted for 85 percent of the descriptions of leadership behavior. Those two items were consideration and initiating structure. Would you have thought of these two items as dimensions of leadership?

## Consideration

Consideration is the degree to which leaders create emotional support, warmth, friendliness, and trust. They demonstrate these behaviors by being friendly, approachable, looking out for the personal welfare of their followers, keeping followers informed of new developments, and doing small favors for followers. Other examples include doing personal favors, finding time to listen, consulting with, being willing to accept suggestions, or treating followers as equals.

## Initiating Structure

Initiating structure is the degree to which leaders organize, define relationships, assign specific tasks, specify procedures to be followed, schedule work, and clarify expectations. Other examples include assigning tasks, maintaining definite standards, asking followers to follow standard operating procedures, emphasizing importance of deadlines, criticizing poor work, and coordinating activities of different followers. See Exhibit 3.1.

Exhibit 3.1:

| | High | |
|---|---|---|
| | Low Structure and High Consideration | High Structure and High Consideration |
| CONSIDERATION | | |
| | Low Structure and Low Consideration | High Structure and Low Consideration |
| | Low | High |

INITIATING   STRUCTURE

As you can well see, four combinations of consideration and initiating structure are possible: low structure and low consideration, low structure and high consideration, high structure and low consideration, and high structure and high consideration. All four dimensions are related to leadership outcomes. All four have been confirmed and reinforced in current, newer studies of behavior.

I have observed in almost all organizations that both initiating structure and consideration are important for team leadership. Without initiating structure behaviors, followers don't know what is expected, how to work with others, or the relationship of their work to organizational goals. The result is often frustration, which influences productivity. Similarly, a lack of consideration behaviors may leave followers unsupported, unrecognized, or bewildered. Leader feedback about team performance is of paramount importance.

## THE UNIVERSITY OF MICHIGAN STUDIES

The University of Michigan field studies focused on identifying relationships among leader behavior, group processes, and measures of group performance. Information about managerial behavior was collected via interviews and questionnaires. Objective measures of productivity were used to classify leaders as relatively effective or ineffective. A comparison of these leaders revealed three differences in managerial behavior.

1. *Task-oriented behavior*s. Effective leaders do not do the same work as their followers. Instead, they concentrate on task-oriented functions (e.g., planning and scheduling, coordinating activities, and providing supplies, equipment, and technical assistance). Effective leaders guide followers to set high but realistic performance goals.

2. *Relations-oriented behaviors.* Effective managers are more supportive and helpful with followers. Their supportive behaviors include showing trust and confidence, acting friendly and considerate, trying to understand follower problems, helping develop subordinates, keeping followers informed, showing appreciation for follower ideas, allowing autonomy to followers to do the work, and showing appreciation for the work done.

3. *Participative leadership.* Effective leaders use more follower supervision than supervising each follower separately. In a group meeting, effective leaders guide the discussion, keep it supportive, allow followers to participate in decision making and conflict resolution, are constructive, and are oriented toward problem solving.

## THE BRECKENRIDGE INSTITUTE STUDIES

There are other researchers, however, who have discerned some overlapping yet different dimensions. Recent research and field analysis compiled by the Breckenridge Institute and reported by Mark Bodnarczuk, director, indicate four interdependent dimensions of leadership. (The Breckenridge Institute is a research center for the study of organizational culture based in Boulder, Colorado.)

1. *Expertise, experience, and wisdom.* Education expertise, experience in specific industries and markets, and a track record of effectively leading

organizations with various numbers of employees and managerial levels.

2. *Problem-solving ability.* The appropriate level of "intellectual horsepower" to effectively perform the level of work and task complexity to which a person is assigned. "Work and task complexity" is defined as: (a) the number of variables operating in a situation, (b) the ambiguity of these variables, (c) their rate of change over time, (d) the extent to which they are interwoven so that they have to be unraveled in order to be seen, (e) the person's ability to identify and control the salient variables once known, and (f) the time horizon of the work in terms of days, months, and years.

3. *Personality, core beliefs, and values.* Patterns of behavior and interaction, tacit assumptions, intrinsic motivators, and underlying patterns of how leaders see themselves, other people, and the world around them. A key indicator that leaders possess this leadership dimension is the degree to which they avoid using "either-or" thinking or practice "both-and" thinking.

4. *Awareness of self and others.* Effective leaders know how to introspectively look into the mirror of personal responsibility when things go wrong. They also know how to attribute recognition to others when things go right.

These four leadership dimensions enable leaders, in the words of Mark Bodnarczuk, "to bring people together; to get them to work together effectively; to align them around a common purpose, goals, and objectives; to get them to cooperate and rely on each other; and to trust each other." Thus, the four dimensions must be viewed in a suitable context and applied to a real-life challenge a leader faces.

## CONCLUSION

All of the above leadership traits and behaviors should not be confused with leadership *styles*. In the above, we are talking about the characteristics of a leader, the things you might see in yourself or in others around you. This also is not to be confused with how to effectively lead others—leadership styles. In addition, recognize that while there are strengths in the trait approach to leadership, there are also limitations. The primary limit is that it does not tell us which traits work in which situation.

According to John Viney, if there is a trait that characterizes leaders it is opportunism. He also suggests that "leadership seems to be a matter of personality and character." Perhaps that is why researchers, scholars, and practitioners are beginning to weave leadership traits with leadership styles and emotional intelligence. (And that's what we will do in the next chapter.)

# WHAT'S YOUR EQ?

## LEADERSHIP STYLES AND EMOTIONAL INTELLIGENCE

The formula for a leader's success is really quite simple: The more leadership styles that you are able to master, the better the leader you will become. Certainly the ability to switch between styles as situations warrant will result in superior results and workplace climate.... That being said, it's not easy to master multiple leadership styles. That's because in order to master a new way of leading others, we may need to unlearn old habits.

—Bill Sharlow, editor of Money-Zine.com

But as for you, continue in what you have learned and have become convinced of, because you know those from whom you learned it.

2 Timothy 3:14 (NIV)

Is it possible that every organization has its share of unhealthy, immature (i.e., problem) people? Difficult people who are a nuisance and threaten the well-being of a group? Let me tell you about some people I know. You might recognize someone you know who resembles these people. Or you might even recognize yourself.

Through the years, I have had the misfortune of working with people who talk constantly and never listen. I've known people who spent their workdays talking from the time they entered the door until they left. They went from office to office all day, talking to people about endless items on their daily catalog of topics. If I hadn't known better, I would have thought they had been hired to bother people with endless chatter.

I've known those who criticize everything—technology, lighting, heating and air-conditioning temperatures, the wind, their car, the price of gasoline, food served in the cafeteria, the drive home, etc. They would criticize any label—clothes or food—that was not their favorite label. I've known a couple of people who are not only critical of everything, they are especially critical of people, even to the point of verbal and physical abuse (shoving when upset).

I've known a few who fail to keep commitments. They promise much but deliver little. They're bold enough to admit fault, but they do so by describing themselves as 80 percent people. That is, they start a task, are motivated to do it, but at about the 80 percent point of completion, they quit.

Are there really that many obnoxious people in the workplace? In church or temple? In civic clubs? In professional societies? Unfortunately, yes. Haven't you met some of these people? If so, how did you handle them? What was your style of interaction?

--------

Yes, there are difficult people in every organization, even in mine. I have a relative who is retired as a manager for DuPont. He said their general working philosophy was, "We hire only good people, and they can be changed to see the light." According to R. M. Bramson, consultant and author, there are seven patterns of difficult behavior that seem to be most disruptive or frustrating:

1. *Hostile-aggressive*—people who try to bully or overwhelm by bombarding others, making cutting remarks, or throwing tantrums when things do not go their way.

2. *Complainer*—individuals who gripe incessantly but never try to do anything about the situation, either because they feel powerless to do so or because they refuse to bear the responsibility.

3. *Silent-unresponsive*—people who respond to every question or plea for help with a yes, a no, or a grunt.

4. *Super-agreeable*—individuals who are always very reasonable, sincere, and supportive but either do not produce what they say they will or act contrary to the way you expected them to act.

5. *Negativist*—people who respond to any project proposal with an "It won't work" or "It is impossible" can effectively deflate others' optimism.

6. *Know-it-all expert*—"superior" people who believe and want others to recognize they know everything about everything.

7. *Indecisive*—individuals who stall major decisions until the decision is made for them or who will not let go of anything until it is perfect (which means never).

Such difficult people are alive and well, although those who complain don't always complain and those who are indecisive sometimes make decisions. Sometimes a few of these problem employees are encouraged to quit. Recognizing such behavior patterns of these people sets the stage for taking effective action. But it raises a very important question. What leadership style should you use with difficult people? Do all seven of these difficult people require a different leadership style? Or can you use the same leadership style for all seven?

## LEADERSHIP STYLES

Most researchers look to styles to understand leadership. A style of leadership is a combination of traits and behaviors. As we observed with the number of traits discussed in leadership literature, there are also a number of styles available. See Table 4.1.

Table 4.1:

| | | |
|---|---|---|
| Autocratic | Bureaucratic | Laissez-faire |
| Democratic | Coaching | Pacesetting |
| Affiliative | Coercive | Visionary |
| Participative | Situational | Emergent |
| Transactional | Transformational | Charismatic |
| Strategic | Team | Influence |
| Cross-cultural | Level Five | Servant |
| Leader-centered | Contingency | Possibility |
| Consultative | Group-centered | Value-based |
| Path-goal | Normative | Tell |
| Sell | Managing | Delegative |
| Motivational | Entrepreneurial | Reengineering |
| | Bridge-building | |

This much seems clear: Whatever leadership style is preferred, researchers seem to all agree that four components are involved—the leader, the followers, the context, and the results. Thus, leadership is a social influence exerted on individuals and/or groups to achieve goals, and the style of the leader determines the results.

## AUTOCRATIC (AUTHORITARIAN)

Those interested in a stylistic approach have been concerned primarily with autocratic or leader-centered behaviors (e.g., Hitler, Stalin, Mao, Hussein, Castro) and democratic or group-centered behaviors (e.g., Aristide, Thatcher, Clinton, Blair). Autocratic (or authoritarian) leaders have been labeled with many terms: directive, Theory X, coercive, task-oriented, and outcome-centered.

In 1755, on All Saints Day, Lisbon, Portugal, experienced an earthquake (9.0 on the Richter scale) that killed 90,000 people and leveled the city. A tsunami followed the earthquake, and if that wasn't enough, fires burned for five days and destroyed 85 percent of the capital city. The energetic Marquis de Pombal, prime minister of Portugal, took control of the situation, put out the fires, and buried the dead. Within a year, thanks to the autocratic and dictatorial style of leadership, he got construction underway. Because rebuilding required an almost dictatorial leader, Pombal's popularity with the nobility sunk like a stone in the lake. An attempt was made on his life, but he was able to respond quickly and terribly and crush his opposition. Today, he is regarded as one of Portugal's greatest statesmen. A large statue of him was erected in downtown Lisbon.

The authoritarian approach contributes to order, consistency, and conflict resolution. For example, sometimes followers may be working on a project that is derailed because of poor team organization or the inability of the leader to set deadlines. In such cases, an autocratic leader can take charge, assign tasks, and set deadlines. There are some team members who actually prefer an autocratic style. However, it should normally only be used on rare occasions. If time is available and I want to gain commitment and motivation from followers, my personal preference is to use a participative style. Although I can't use that style all of the time, it is most likely to yield positive results in particular situations.

## PARTICIPATIVE (DEMOCRATIC)

Participative leaders include one or more followers in the decision-making process. The leader still has the final decision authority. This style of leadership also has been classified several ways: Theory Y, considerate, consultative, participative, consensual, employee-centered, supportive, facilitating interaction, and relationships-oriented.

The democratic style contributes to commitment, loyalty, involvement, and satisfaction of followers. It should not be viewed as a sign of weakness. Rather, it is a sign of strength that followers respect. For example, I have particularly found the participative style useful when I have part of the information and knowledgeable and skillful followers have other parts of the information. Using this style is mutually beneficial to both them and me. The followers are part of the team and assist me in making better decisions.

Participative leaders are often more likely than authoritarian leaders to get a buy-in from group members on changes and important decisions. Why? Because participative leadership is targeted toward solutions, efficiency, and productivity. Participative leaders possess a strength and skill that followers respect. How often should it be used? You will know the answer the next time you are deep in a particular challenging situation.

## DELEGATIVE (FREE-REIGN)

When a leader delegates, followers are allowed to make decisions. The leader is still responsible for the final decisions made, however.

Knowledgeable and skillful followers have the ability to analyze the situation and make a decision. The leader sets priorities and delegates tasks. This style is also known as free-reign leadership or laissez-faire leadership. Both terms suggest the noninterference of the leader.

This style can be used when the leader fully trusts followers. I personally believe in delegation of authority and responsibility. However, I abhor the terms *free-reign* and *laissez-faire* because of the negative connotation each portrays. They suggest the leader is lazy or abandons the process of leadership and leaves all decisions up to the followers. What is the leader's responsibility when decisions made by followers go awry? Delegative leadership is not a style to use for blaming others when things go wrong.

Delegative leaders know that empowering others in the work environment can be a positive force for good. To take advantage of this empowerment, you will need to recognize the individuals who have the competency for the job to be assigned, have access to the needed resources for this position, and provide the necessary authority to get the job accomplished. Delegative leadership will certainly require more time than autocratic leadership, but the outcome may be more meaningful to all those involved.

## POSSIBILITY

The traditional emphasis on leadership style centers on how to handle obstacles. Possibility leadership focuses on opportunities. As Josh Billings, humorist, said, "Occasions are rare; and those who know how to seize upon them are rarer." Thus, the implications are clear. Leaders must have a transforming dream—the ability to envision possibilities. If so, they will be heard to say something like, "The future is always more interesting than the past." They will promote organizational health and longevity.

For example, despite partisan affiliation, most people would agree President Ronald Reagan was a visionary leader. He is credited with restoring the image and vitality of the role of president, of rallying the American people, of restoring pride. Think of all the voters—Republicans, Democrats, Independents—who endorsed his bid for the presidency. He may not have shared *all* of his fellow Americans' beliefs, but Reagan had the foresight, the ingenuity to gain broad support that transcended party lines.

## SITUATIONAL

Because there is no one best leadership style or behavior, different situations call for different leadership styles. Each situation involves varying personalities, interest levels, motivation, physical setting, or group size. Sam Walton, owner and founder of Walmart, bought into this approach: "Outstanding leaders go out of their way to boost the self-esteem of their personnel. If people believe in themselves, it's amazing what they can accomplish."

In my experience, the characteristics of a situation specify the need to match traits and behaviors. Thus, situational leadership is a style that matches the leader to the incident. It reveals what type of person would be suited to lead in a given situation. For example, if you're working with a group that has high need for control and direction, you should not attempt to be a democratic leader. On the other hand, if you're working with a mature, well-functioning group, you should not be an autocratic leader.

There are three primary conditions that seem to define the situational leader: power of the leader, nature of the task (i.e., mission), and human relationships with the group (i.e., followers or community). Thus, you are expected to meet the following expectations of followers: communicate effectively, respond creatively and innovatively, and set priorities. In addition, you will need to possess a results orientation, an empathetic attitude, and a supportive attitude. In the words of Bruce Barton, American business executive, "Nothing splendid has ever been achieved except by those who believed that something inside of them was superior to circumstance."

## VISIONARY

Fred Smith, founder of Federal Express, said, "We will deliver the package by 10:30 the next morning." His vision changed the basis of competition in that industry. Would a similar inspiring vision do the same for your own organization? Absolutely. In the words of former first lady Rosalynn Carter, "A leader takes people where they want to go. A great leader takes people where they don't necessarily want to go, but ought to be going."

All who have accomplished great things have had a great aim; they have fixed their gaze on a goal that was high and sometimes seemed impossible. So leaders must create a compelling picture of the future. The absence of vision leads to stagnation and decline. Where there is no hope, there can be no vision. When visionaries stop dreaming or allow others to squelch their dreams, their organizations suffer and, in some instances, die. Success is the distance between one's origin and final achievement.

True leaders "dream the impossible dream." They remember the Red Queen's advice in English author Lewis Carroll's *Alice in Wonderland.* When Alice protested there was no use in believing impossible things, the Queen replied, "I daresay you haven't had much practice...when I was your age I did it for half an hour a day. Why sometimes I've believed as many as six impossible things before breakfast."

All great leaders have an unusual ability to envision the future and imagine possibilities (Washington, Adams, Ghandi, Sadat, Begin, Byrd, Shackleton, Roosevelt, Churchill, Walesa, Salk, Carter, Bush, Obama). They possess a sense of what could be.

They are willing to risk their lives to accomplish their dreams. Thus, to dream or inspire people to perform, leaders must leave the security of the status quo with its predictable environment. They risk entering uncharted territory. After all, as someone once said, "A task without vision is drudgery. A vision without a task is a dream. A task with a vision is hope."

Unfortunately, I have noticed that the world does not always appreciate such dreamers. Typically, they are not taken seriously—especially those with limited connections, financial backers, or big names in their address books. However, their vision—whatever it may be—is the ideal for which to strive. It must be strategic, able to capture the imagination and spirit of organizational members. Vision motivates an organization to action. It provides a framework for day-to-day decisions and priorities.

A number of possibilities exist for understanding visionary leadership. The classical approach suggests that leaders schedule time for reflection. A leader must get away from the urgent and unimportant distractions in the work environment and spend time alone, thinking and planning. A second and similar approach involves meditation on both the current reality as well as the new goal state. The intended result is an aligned organization where group leaders and followers do their best to achieve a common vision. A third approach gets into the idea of imaging—a way of picturing how one would most likely behave that goes beyond positive thinking.

The motto at Disney's Epcot Center in Florida is, "If you can dream it, you can do it." Thus, the leader's vision must describe the present and determine the future. The leader grasps the vision's challenge, commits to the mission, and implements the goals that will accomplish the mission and fulfill the vision. In fact, few things are more valuable to a leader than vision. Effective leaders are able to see something out there in the future, vague though it may be, that followers don't yet see.

Clearly, there is an imperative to dream and be creative. However, it is not enough to dream alone. Visions are always future-oriented. You must discover ways to involve others in creating dreams for the future. Others help develop the dream about the future, at least how the situation will be different in two, five, and ten years down the road. In the words of Jonas Salk, American medical researcher and discoverer of the polio vaccine, "I feel that the greatest reward for doing is the opportunity to do more."

## FORCES THAT AFFECT LEADERSHIP STYLE

In most cases, a leader will use a combination of styles. For example, you might use a (friendly) authoritarian style with followers who are new on the job. When working with a team of followers who know the job, you might use a participative style. If followers are well trained and have very strong technical and interpersonal skills, you might use a delegative style. Depending on the situation, you will reach into your leadership style bag and select the one that will work best on this occasion.

Forces that influence your leadership style (like the choices above) include the following circumstances:

1. Time available

2. Strength of relationships

3. Information needed for a decision

4. Internal politics and conflicts

5. Task involved

6. Laws or professional procedures

7. Stress levels of all involved

Depending on the forces at work, and you have enough insight and *panache,* you might approach your followers by using either a possibility or visionary style. If rewards or reprimands seem to be needed, you may choose the situational style. As you might suspect, you do not stringently use one or another of the styles. Instead, you work off of a continuum of leadership styles, choosing the most appropriate style for the issue at hand. The wrong choice of a style could be damaging to organizational performance.

## GENDER DIFFERENCES IN LEADERSHIP STYLES

A few researchers are highly interested in whether males choose a particular leadership style more often that a style chosen by females. This research is based on the assumption that women are more likely to be relationship-oriented, cooperative, and nurturing. Men are thought to be more commanding and control-oriented. One researcher, Judy Rosener, professor emeriti at the University of California, Irvine, concluded there *are* gender differences in leadership styles. Based on self-reports, Rosener found that men do indeed tend toward a command and control style. Women tend toward a transformational style and rely on interpersonal skills.

In contrast, Jan Grant, educator and author, concluded in her research that there are few, if any, behavioral differences between men and women. In fact, as women climb the traditional corporate ladder, they identify with the male model of leadership and reject some feminine traits they had earlier endorsed. Thus, corporate culture affects which styles are encouraged and which are not.

## EMOTIONAL INTELLIGENCE

Based on research in a number of companies, Daniel Goleman, author and psychologist, has suggested that effective leaders can move among styles, adopting the one that best meets the needs of the moment. For example, which style would give you the ability to understand someone else's feelings, have empathy with them, regulate emotions, and enhance their quality of life? He discovered that effective leaders were alike in one primary way. They all had a high degree of "emotional intelligence" (EQ). There's an IQ (intelligence quotient). Why *not* an EQ?

If leaders do not have emotional intelligence, their full potential may not be achieved. Goleman and fellow researchers Richard Boyatzis, professor at Case Western University, and Annie McKee, founder of the Teleos Leadership Institute, say, "The message sent by neurological, psychological, and organizational research is startling in its clarity. Emotional leadership is the spark that ignites a company's performance, creating a bonfire of success or a landscape of ashes."

Leaders with high levels of emotional intelligence will develop an organizational culture of information sharing, trust, healthy risk-taking, and learning. Those with low levels of emotional intelligence will create a culture of fear and anxiety. Followers will demonstrate tension and terror because their leaders don't "feel their pain."

Goleman, Boyatzis, and McKee designed a five-part process to rewire the brain toward more emotionally intelligent behaviors. These five components involve leaders asking themselves the following questions:

1. Who do I want to be?

2. Who am I now?

3. How do I get from here to there?

4. How do I make change stick?

5. Who can help me?

The answers will vary by person.

Goleman, Boyatzis, and McKee also suggest that the process begins with imagining your ideal self and then coming to terms with your real self, as others experience you. The next step is creating a tactical plan to bridge the gap between ideal and real, and after that, to practice those activities. It concludes with creating a community of colleagues and family—call them change enforcers—to keep the process alive.

The answers and actions thereafter may prevent an emotional train wreck in the office.

## EMOTIONAL MOODS

In addition, if leaders do not have emotional intelligence, they may not be able to develop the ability to manage personal moods and the moods of followers. For example, my mood and behavior drives the moods and behaviors of followers. If I am bad-tempered and ruthless, I could cause a meltdown and create a toxic organization. If, on the other hand, I am inspirational and inclusive, I should be able to create an organization of people able to meet any challenge. Dr. Phil has shared his experience in high school after he decided he wanted people to feel better after talking to him—to demonstrate inclusiveness. Such an attitude makes a world of difference in relationships and is not unlike the Golden Rule.

If emotional moods are such powerful drivers in organizational life, you must ensure you are regularly optimistic and authentic and, when appropriate, demonstrate high energy. Obviously, it is difficult to be that way all the time. However, if you are upbeat, reliable, and cheerful, your actions should generate a performance-oriented organization. Such emotions are caught by others. I once worked with a person who was unbearable in the mornings—surly and crabby. You had to tiptoe around him until he got that first cup of coffee. No doubt you have heard someone say or seen it on a sign at Cracker Barrel, "If Momma ain't happy, ain't nobody happy." A cheerful mood, on the other hand, swiftly spreads among followers.

This dynamic of how moods affect people and organizations is called *resonance*. Thus, as Goleman, Boyatzis, and McKee say, "An emotionally intelligent leader can monitor his or her moods through self-awareness, change them for the better through self-management, understand their impact through empathy, and act in ways that boost others' moods through relationship management." Goleman has set forth four key factors about emotional moods:

1. *Self-awareness*—the ability to understand your own emotions, know your strengths and limitations, and have high self-esteem. Self-awareness helps to measure personal moods and understand how they affect others.

2. *Self-management*—the ability to control emotions and act with honesty and integrity in consistent and adaptable manners. Self-management helps prevent temper tantrums when things don't go as planned. The occasional bad mood does not ruin the day.

3. *Social awareness*—empathy for others and intuition about organizational problems. Social awareness allows leaders to show they care and to accurately size up political forces in the organization.

4. *Relationship management*—the ability to communicate clearly and convincingly, disarm conflicts, and build strong personal bonds. Relationship management helps leaders spread their enthusiasm and solve disagreements, often with kindness and good humor.

Thus, if you wish to discover the most effective leadership style, perhaps you should first look at the key role that mood plays in what you do first and best. Moods—good or bad—apparently matter just that much.

## CONCLUSION

With all that has been said about the various styles of leadership, emotional intelligence, and moods, effective leaders are able to take a portion of each theory and mold it into a style that works for them at the moment a certain style is required. As John Kenneth Galbraith, a Canadian-American economist, said, "All of the great leaders have had one characteristic in common; it was the willingness to confront unequivocally the major anxiety of their people in their time. This, and not much else, is the essence of leadership."

A few years back, there was a particular high school in a rural setting in Texas that adopted the practice of saying to their students when bad attitudes needed an adjustment, "Watch your EQ."

How about you? Have you checked *your* EQ lately?

# II. LEADERSHIP CHALLENGES

The challenge of leadership is to be strong, but not rude; be kind, but not weak; be bold, but not bully; be thoughtful, but not lazy; be humble, but not timid; be proud, but not arrogant; have humor, but without folly.

—Jim Rohn, American speaker and author

5. Does Right Seem Wrong Seem Right? Ethics and Integrity

6. Has Greed Become Legal? Ethics and Cheating

7. Can Only a Dead Person Keep a Secret? Communication Flows, Networks, and Feedback

# DOES RIGHT SEEM WRONG SEEM RIGHT?

## ETHICS AND INTEGRITY

Adversity is a test of our stability—our ability to endure, to survive. But prosperity is a test of our integrity. Like nothing else, it reveals the honest-to-goodness truth regarding our most basic value system. Difficult though it may be to grasp this fact, integrity is hammered out on the anvil of prosperity … or it fails the test completely.

—Charles R. Swindoll,
author, chancellor of Dallas Theological Seminary

For I have walked in my integrity … I will walk in my integrity … Joyful are people of integrity, who follow the instructions of the Lord.

Psalm 26:1, 11; 119:1 (NKJV)

In Frank Capra's 1946 classic movie *It's a Wonderful Life,* George Bailey (James Stewart) has a chance to make his dreams come true. His longtime nemesis, the rich, powerful, and mean Henry Potter (Lionel Barrymore), offers him a job with a lucrative salary. But there's a catch in the job offer. If Bailey accepts the position, Potter gets to shut down Bailey Brothers Building and Loan—a business that has been serving the working people of Bedford Falls for many years.

The job offer is tempting, and Bailey asks for twenty-four hours to think about it. It was a deal that would allow him to travel the world with his wife, Mary (Donna Reed). Then, as he is shaking Potter's hand, he changes his mind. He says, "Wait a minute here. I don't need twenty-four hours. I don't need to talk to anybody. I know right now. The answer is no, no, no."

Bailey could live in the nicest house in Bedford Falls, buy his wife new clothes, and travel the world. But when he arrives at this ethical intersection in his life, when he is faced with an ethical dilemma, he draws from a well-stocked pantry of convictions he has been storing up since childhood. He checks his moral compass, makes the right decision, and says no.

If the movie had had a 2006 date instead of being sixty years earlier, would George Bailey still turn down the job? Or would he be more like Gordon Gecko (Michael Douglas) in the 1987 movie *Wall Street* and the 2010 *Wall Street: Money Never Sleeps* and give in to greed?

---

Business history indicates that leaders, followers, and organizations engage in questionable, dishonest, unethical, and even illegal acts. I understand any guilt that a person might feel in such situations if they understand what is happening. When I was working on my master's degree, I was employed at a Colorado bank as a teller. I had been invited out of state to interview for a job. The night before my wife and I were to fly out for the interview, I balanced out my cash drawer and discovered I was exactly $100 short. I had been short some change a few times before, but nothing like this. (At that time, each teller would keep any extra change of an overage to the side to handle the small under balances.)

Who had I given the extra money to? One person? Several people? You can imagine my guilt of being short with my boss knowing I was leaving on an out-of-state trip the next morning. (I was never treated any differently upon my return, however. Incidentally, I did get the job—not another bank, fortunately.)

Worldwide corruption has become a serious problem, and it needs to be understood and combated. Enron, Tyco, WorldCom, and others have taught us through vicarious experience about dishonesty in the workplace. Few professions are immune from public embarrassment of ethical misconduct. Cheating is commonplace, and there is no reason to expect that it will cease to exist. Ethical misconduct has become a conspicuous part of corporate life. Leaders, followers, and organizations have yet to achieve an enlightened state where all behaviors are governed by the very highest ethical standards.

If we had achieved such a heightened state of behavior, we wouldn't have situations like reported in May 2010 of a University of Kansas ticket scandal. The KU report alleged that Tom and Charlette Blubaugh, Rodney Jones, and Brandon Simmons inappropriately sold or used 2,181 men's football tickets worth $122,000 and 17,609 basketball tickets worth $887,000 for personal reasons. The tickets were disguised as complimentary and inventory tickets or other categories with limited accountability. Any decision on legal action is pending at the time of this writing.

In your opinion, is there anything we can do about this? Are there times when right seems wrong and wrong seems right? Can we find answers for ethical dilemmas in the workplace? Is it possible to improve ethical behavior? Is there even such a thing as "business ethics"? In this chapter, research will tell all. I will show what my research has revealed about our beliefs in business ethics.

## ETHICS

Imagine the following scenario: You and I are negotiating. You own a bank, and I agree to give you some of my money. Okay? What if I give you someone else's money? It's not illegal. Is it ethical? Or how about this: We're buying goods from Bangladesh. There are people in sweatshops starving. What's a fair wage? What are the ethics in such a situation?

The study of ethics is an ancient tradition, rooted in religious, cultural, and philosophical beliefs. However, it is obvious that not everyone agrees as to what is ethical and what is not. What causes such disagreement? Is it the complexity, dynamism, and interdependence of business? Is it because business operations are often tainted with compromise? Is it that judgment is clouded on questions of what's right and wrong, unethical or ethical? Or is it that we have ignored (or denied) the importance of values and morals for ethical decisions?

To illustrate: Some salespeople might not curse in front of a Christian if they knew it would offend and cost them a sale. On the other hand, some might curse because they feel it is their freedom to speak as they wish and they want to be themselves with everyone. Similarly, some businesspeople might not steal office supplies because they don't want to be seen doing it, be reprimanded, or go to jail. In contrast, some might steal office supplies because they view these items as perks or as adjusted compensation.

In the country of Ghana, it is perceived to be unethical to drag your own parent to courts, regardless of the circumstances. However, it is perfectly legal and ethical in the United States to do so in some cases, if not all cases. The Ghanaian society doesn't condone the actions of some parents, but they still believe family issues can be best resolved by family elders. At what time in our society did we lose that respect for family elders?

A number of arguments have been cited in favor of business morality and social responsibility. Questions have been raised about the policies and competitive strategies adopted by corporations and how such policies and strategies are to be implemented. Ethical theory has been linked to leadership behaviors. The major philosophical, ethical, and moral theories have been classified.

Two points, however, need to be agreed on by leaders and followers. First, our business ethics cannot be separated from our personal ethics (or all ethics). Second, business will never be any more ethical than the people who are in business. Seem simple enough? In the long run, ethics has to stand on its own. Decisions have to be based on company values and ethics.

## DEFINITIONS OF BUSINESS ETHICS

Definitions place limits on how we think about and work with concepts. Therefore, there can be no answers to ethical problems without precise definitions. We need an internal understanding to make sound decisions about ethical or unethical behaviors. Based on this need, I engaged in a research study to address three questions.

1. How is *business ethics* defined in the literature and by businesspeople?

2. What are the points of agreement on a definition of *business ethics?*

3. Can a definition of *business ethics* be synthesized from the available definitions?

Data was gathered from both primary and secondary sources. A total of 158 textbooks were reviewed, and fifty articles that had the words *ethics* or *morality* in the title were reviewed. A brief questionnaire was distributed to a random sample of both blue-collar workers and white-collar executives, asking simply, "What is your definition of *business ethics?*"

I received 185 responses. These responses were analyzed by a panel of two judges. Content analysis by the judges proceeded in two stages. First, each response was examined to identify those concepts expressed. Second, an attempt was made to group the concepts into a small number of definitions. Then the judges' categorical groupings were compared. On concepts that did not match (i.e., where the judges disagreed), I made the selection of fit.

A synthesis of definitions from textbooks, articles, and workers and executives resulted in the following definition: *Business ethics is rules, standards, codes, or principles that provide guidelines for morally right behavior and truthfulness in specific situations.*

Concentration on the major concepts in this definition yielded the following rewards:

1. *Rules, standards, codes, or principles*—moral guidelines that, if followed, will prevent unethical behavior.

2. *Morally right behavior*—individual actions that conform to justice, law, or another standard; individual actions in accord with fact, reason, or truth.

3. *Truthfulness*—statements and/or actions that conform with facts or that have the appearance of reality.

4. *Specific situations*—occasions of personal moral dilemma calling for ethical decisions.

Based on the above definition, business ethics is broader than just virtue, integrity, or character. It involves the application of our understanding of what is morally right and truthful at a time of ethical dilemma. There may be another dozen bits and pieces of a definition of business ethics. However, this synthesized definition is broad enough to cover the field of leadership in a sense as full as most leaders might conceive of it.

## ETHICAL PRINCIPLES

Because of the pervasive impact organizations have on all of us, an ethical focus has shifted from individuals to leaders. This shift raises questions of whose ethics or which ethical principles should be adopted. Few disagree that standards of ethics are needed and desirable. Ethics deals with behavior and with standards of right and wrong.

Recognized authorities of Western tradition agree that there are appropriate sets of ethics that apply to all and in the same fashion. Experience suggests that people cannot work together without at least tacit, if not, overt, agreement concerning customs of standards of conduct that they hold in common. The absence of these will promote incoherence and lack of consensus. The problem, of course, is that there is no consensus on the right set of ethics. Ethics concerns not only the behavior that *is* in society but also the behavior that *ought* to be customary in society.

Because of the mass of ethical ideas, issues, and systems, I engaged in other research projects to try to identify the ethical principles that should be used as guidelines in business. There were three separate studies conducted. In the first attempt to gather data, seventy-eight executives from Fortune 500 companies responded to a fourteen-item questionnaire. In the second, 160 middle-level leaders responded to the fourteen-item questionnaire. In the third, one hundred individuals from various walks of life and business responded to the fourteen-item questionnaire. See Table 5.1.

Fourteen ethical conduct principles were used in the three studies. These principles were cataloged by George and John Steiner (two educators and researchers). A chi-square test was used to determine whether any of the items were statistically significant between any of the three groups.

Table 5.1:

1. Act in a way he or she believes is right and just for any other person in a similar situation. (Kant's Categorical Imperative)
2. Bluff and take advantage of all legal opportunities and widespread practices or customs. (Carr's Conventionalist Ethic)
3. Ask how it would feel to see the thinking and details of the decision disclosed to a wide audience. (Disclosure Rule)
4. Look at the problem from the position of another party affected by the decision and try to determine what response the other person would expect as most virtuous. (The Golden Rule [Matthew 7:12])
5. Do whatever she or he finds to be in her or his own self-interest. (Hedonistic Ethic)
6. Go with his or her "gut feeling" or what he or she understands to be right in a given situation. (Moore's Intuition Ethic)
7. Take selfish actions and be motivated by personal gains in business deals. (Smith's Market Ethic)
8. Ask whether some overall good justifies any moral transgression. (Machiavelli's Means-End Ethics)
9. Seize what advantage he or she is strong enough to take without respect to ordinary social conventions and laws. (Nietzche/ Marx's Might-Equals-Right Ethics)
10. Ask whether actions are consistent with organizational goals and do what is good for the organization. (Organization Ethic)
11. Do whatever she or he wills if there is a proportionate reason for doing so. (Garrett's Principle of Proportionality)
12. Do only that which can be explained before a committee of his or her peers. (Professional Ethic)
13. Pray, meditate, or otherwise commune with a superior force or being. (Revelation Ethic)
14. Determine where the harm in an action is outweighed by the good. (Bentham/Mill's Utilitarian Ethic)

## ETHICAL SHOULDS AND SHOULD NOTS

Based on comparisons of the three groups, I was able to discover two sets of conclusions as to what a leader *should do* to make ethical decisions and what a leader *should not do* to make ethical decisions.

First, there was high agreement on how a decision maker *should* behave when faced with a moral choice. In fact, there is almost a step-by-step sequence. A person should:

1. *Look* at the problem from the position of the other person(s) affected by a decision.

2. *Try* to determine what virtuous response is expected.

3. *Ask*—How would it feel for the decision to be disclosed to a wide audience?

4. Is the decision consistent with organizational goals?

5. *Act* in a way that is right and just for any other person in a similar situation and good for the organization.

Second, there also was high agreement on what a decision maker *should not* do when faced with an ethical choice. Specifically, a leader should not:

1. Be motivated by selfish gains or take selfish actions.

2. Bluff or lie.

3. Depend on principles easily explained to one's peers.

4. Take undue advantage of a situation, even if law or social practices permit it.

In the majority of situations, some moral standard could be applied with no further thought or research required by the decision maker. Leaders know almost reflexively what to do or what not to do. However, it is those situations that they don't know clearly and readily what to do where help is needed. It is those dilemmas that are not reducible to common methods of decision analysis, that exist outside clearly defined systems of corporate ethics, that need a step-by-step procedure, something practical and concrete in nature. If not, we are relying on the leader's integrity and character to make the right decision. Of course, that may be enough.

## INTEGRITY

Peter Drucker, author and consultant, has written:

> The final requirement of effective leadership is to earn trust. Otherwise there won't be any followers ... A leader is someone who has followers. To trust a leader, it is not necessary to agree with him. Trust is the conviction that the leader means what he says. It is a belief in something very old-fashioned called *"integrity."*

Are you and your colleagues demonstrating trustworthiness?

Benjamin Franklin, a founding father of the United States, wrote, "It is a grand mistake to think of being great without goodness; and I pronounce it as certain that there was never yet a truly great man that was not at the same time truly virtuous." Henry David Thoreau, American author and philosopher, penned, "How often must one feel as he looks back on his past life that he has gained a talent but lost a character ... Society does nominally estimate men by their talents, but really feels and knows them by their character."

On December 11, 1995, a fire burned most of Malden Mills to the ground and put three thousand people out of work. Most of those out of work assumed they were out of work permanently. However, CEO Aaron Feuerstein said, "This is not the end." Then he spent millions of dollars keeping all three thousand employees on the payroll, with full benefits, for the three months it took to get another factory up and running. Why? In his own words, "The fundamental difference is that I consider our workers an asset, not an expense." Does that sound like the leadership at your organization?

Emmerling Communications recently conducted a poll of 101 alumni of Young & Rubicam, a leading advertising agency, about the way things were in the advertising field in the late 1950s and 1960s. If you are a fan of AMC's television show *Mad Men,* you will not be surprised by the results.

1. Fifty-eight percent smoked.

2. Sixty-eight percent had at least one drink at lunch.

3. Thirty-nine percent had two or three drinks at lunch.

4. Five percent had four drinks at lunch.

5. Seventy-five percent agreed there was a hiring bias toward good-looking women.

6. Forty-five percent agreed that women were subjected to male chauvinism, sexual innuendo, and off-color jokes.

7. Fifty-five percent gave a resounding "definitely yes" to office sex taking place.

8. Eighteen percent said they heard "strong rumors" about office sex occurring.

Some would say that business hasn't changed much in the last fifty years. Many of the things that were happening back then are still occurring. Is it possible that the *Mad Men* have no principles, no integrity? If they are not building their advertising business on integrity, what hope can they really have for long-term income? Ethical conduct must be the primary basis upon which their business is based.

Jack Welch, former chairman of General Electric, said:

> Integrity is the rock upon which we build our business success—our quality products and services, our forthright relations with customers and suppliers, and ultimately, our winning competitive record. GE's quest for competitive excellence begins and ends with our commitment to ethical conduct.

Such a statement doesn't seem to resonate at all with *Mad Men*.

Unfortunately, our world seems to have lost its emphasis on integrity, considering it to no longer be an issue for our leaders. To highlight this general understanding, Richard Breedan, former chairman of the Securities Exchange Commission, stated, "It is not an adequate ethical standard to aspire to get through the day without being indicted."

This mentality reminds me of the "Toddler's Rules of Ownership" that made the rounds via e-mail a few years back. Perhaps you saw it.

1.   If I like it, it's mine.

2.   If it's in my hand, it's mine.

3.   If I can take it from you, it's mine.

4.   If I had it a little while ago, it's mine.

5. If it's mine, it must never appear to be yours in any way.

6. If I'm doing or building something, all the pieces are mine.

7. If it looks just like mine, it's mine.

8. If I think it's mine, it's mine.

9. If it's yours and I steal it, it's mine.

Whoever the unknown author was, he or she then tried to add a humorous ending to the rules. "Whoops! These aren't a toddler's rules. They're just part of Microsoft's business plan." (I doubt Bill Gates found it all that funny.) Such sentiment could apply to many chain franchises today. For example, you may have noticed after McDonald's has added something new on their menu, Burger King seems to add something similar to their menu. After the success of Starbucks, McDonald's decided to enter the coffee scene and even converted the interior of some of their stores to look more like a coffee bar. Did Burger King and McDonald's act ethically when they decided to copy their competitors, or is this just "doing business"? Were they making changes with integrity in trying to appeal to more customers and please their current ones? Or are they just depending on the forgiving nature of the American consumer? Perhaps it is time for all corporations to act ethically in all their dealings in the marketplace.

On a related but different note, I am fascinated at how the Old Testament of the Bible (Exodus 20) sets forth Ten Commandments for us to follow in order to keep us out of trouble all our lives. However, it is estimated that US legislators have passed 35 million laws designed to enforce those Ten Commandments. Still, it is estimated that only 13 percent of our population feel the Ten

Commandments have relevance. And Americans feel the number one cause of business decline is low executive ethics. What a cyclone of confusion. Do we think the rules are irrelevant for ourselves but not for others? To illustrate:

1. If you say something in particular, it's another disgusting lie; if I tell the same thing, it's a justifiable, reasonable explanation.

2. If you break it, it's sneaky and stealing; if I borrow it, it's needed for my job and no big deal.

3. If you have a love interest, it's a rotten affair; if I have one, it's at long last love found.

4. If you dress like that, you're unprofessional and letting yourself get slovenly and need a talking to; if I dress like that, I'm being business casual and young and in style.

5. If you're late, you are unorganized and undependable; if I'm late, there's a horrible or humorous story about why.

Part of our dilemma may be that we don't take a hard, honest look at our inner person to determine the condition of our integrity. Another part of our problem is that we fail two revealing and effective tests—the tests of adversity and prosperity.

## THE TESTS OF ADVERSITY AND PROSPERITY

Adversity shows how strong (or weak) we are. The survivors of Haiti's earthquake had a test of strength in 2010. It was a true test of strength and character for those who survived. Those who survived the towers crashing in New York on 9/11 were put to the test of adversity. The ultimate limits of their stability were tested. For others, adversity tests come via inflation, cancer, unemployment, racial tensions, etc. Has adversity surprised you lately? (It's always a surprise. Right?) How did you fare? Did you pass the test?

A second test is equally as revealing as adversity. Prosperity reveals the truth about our basic values. Charles Swindoll, author, educator, and evangelical Christian pastor, says, "Integrity is hammered out on the anvil of prosperity...or it fails the test completely." Those who have integrity possess a well-respected virtue. They can be trusted. Their words and convictions reveal the truth. Think in what way the test of prosperity has surprised you lately. How did you fare? Did you pass the test?

In my experience, hardly anyone will admit to or wants to think of prosperity. In reality, however, it could be any number of things. Examples: An expense account arranged by parents while a son or daughter is in college; a recent increase in salary; birthday gifts; a cool breeze on a hot day; sunrise and/or sunset; rain during a dry season.

## LEADERS OF INTEGRITY

At one time, Goldman Sachs said, "Integrity and honesty are at the heart of our business. We expect our people to maintain high ethical standards in everything they do both in their work for the firm and in their personal lives." After the fiscal fiasco of 2009–10, of course, we might question how closely they affirmed that philosophy.

While I was working in Los Angeles County, an article in the *San Gabriel Valley Tribune* by Charley Reese caught my eye. He was celebrating the birthday of George Washington accordingly:

> What distinguished Washington, aside from his courage and competence, was his integrity. A British historian said of him, "In Washington, America found a leader who could be

induced by no earthy motive to tell a falsehood, or to break an engagement or to commit any dishonorable act."

Reese also quoted Thomas Jefferson as saying about Washington, "He errs as other men do, but errs with integrity." In addition, Reese wrote, "An artist, Gilbert Stuart, remarked...'All his features are indicative of the strongest passions; yet his judgment and great self-command make him appear a man of a different cast in the eyes of the world.'"

Reese also wrote:

> The narcotic effect of power, fame and adulation had no effect on him...Daniel Webster said, if nothing else, America can always be proud of Washington...Few if any humans can be said to be indispensable, but Washington probably was. There were others who could have handled the political chores of the Revolution, but they could not have held together the ragged army that ultimately defeated the British. No one else could have welded the federalists and the republicans into one administration. No one else could have assured ratification of the Constitution simply by endorsing it. He was an indispensable man.

How many men and women can you say that about today who serve in our government?

He and Martha were said to never turn away any traveling visitor who stopped by their farm after his presidency. Visitors would be offered a cup of punch and conversation before the visitors were on their way again. He was both a role model and leader. Stuart caught those qualities in his many paintings of Washington. In fact, by all accounts, Washington loved to pose for those paintings.

A second leader of integrity is one in my own state. Lee Keeling, at age eighty-six, still goes to work every day. He is the owner of the state's largest oil and gas appraisal firm, has twenty-five employees, and is located in Tulsa. Although he has been a cornerstone in Oklahoma's oil and gas industry, many would think there is nothing special about Keeling. He hasn't been a part of any corporate scandals and has spent no time in jail. He doesn't believe in bribes, favors, or perks. Instead, he has fired those individuals at indications of impropriety and stepping over the line.

What Keeling and his family do believe in is an old-fashioned work ethic, honesty, and integrity. According to *Senior News and Living Oklahoma,* Keeling says, "We provide a service based on total competency and honesty and when we sign a report it must be accurate and honest." His concerns are to keep a distance from undue influence and to maintain a high degree of honesty and integrity. Sounds like great advice.

## BELIEF CHALLENGES IN A WORKING WORLD

A survey conducted by *Personnel Journal* of Costa Mesa, California, found that middle-level leaders aged forty to forty-five are more likely than other employees to be dishonest because of the intense pressure to get ahead. People midway through their careers are the ones most likely to steal, bend the truth, and cheat on their expense accounts.

Authors James Patterson and Peter Kim conducted a survey of more than two thousand Americans over a one-week period of time. Those surveyed were given the opportunity to express what they believed about things that mattered. Each of them answered over 1,800 questions. Thousands more answered a shorter version of the questionnaire or cooperated in telephone interviews. It is the most massive, in-depth survey that has ever been conducted of what Americans really believe. Sometimes we are amazed what we learn about people when we are able to look behind the scenes. Here are some of the highlights of the study:

- Sixty-eight percent don't believe that America has a single hero right now.

- Eighty percent believe that morals and ethics should be taught in our schools again.

- Ninety percent said that they truly believed in God, and yet when they make decisions on right and wrong, they do not turn to God or religion for help.

- Women are morally superior to men. They lie less, are more responsible, far more honest at work, and can be trusted more. (These factors were the conclusions of both men and women.)

- Fifty percent of high school students and 30 percent of college students cheat on exams. (A study by the Institute of Ethics found that these students believe "it is not unethical to do whatever you have to do to succeed if you don't seriously hurt other people." Many people believe that since the information was self-reported, the percentages may ever be higher than they seem to be.)

- Thirty percent of high school students lie on their job application.

- Twenty percent of students falsify reports to keep their jobs. Worse yet, their parents are the examples they are following.

The Josephson Institute of Ethics says that many Americans ache to do the right thing but feel that there are no outlets through our current institutions.

In Patterson and Kim's book, *The Day America Told the Truth*, various professions were graded for integrity. Firemen were number one, Catholic priests were number seven, college professors were number ten, and Protestant ministers were number nineteen. The president of the United States rated number twenty-eight, which is a notch below the average plumber and construction worker. The TV evangelist was number sixty-nine, which was third from the bottom, barely nosing out drug dealers and crime bosses. Three (TV evangelists, drug dealers, and crime bosses) failed to match the moral standards of prostitutes.

A cartoon in the *New Yorker Magazine* depicts two clean-shaven, middle-aged men sitting in a jail cell who capture our ethical plight. One inmate turns to the other and says, "All along, I thought our level of corruption fell well within community standards."

Robert Bork, American legal scholar, in *Slouching Toward Gomorrah* offers a prophetic and unprecedented view of the United States as a nation in such serious moral trouble that its foundation is crumbling. He describes America as "a monster of decadence, a plague several generations in gestation," and cites that "we are now slouching, not toward Bethlehem...but toward Gomorrah, the biblical city burned to the ground for the sinfulness of its people."

If Bork is correct, leaders have a tremendous challenge to make a difference in this mixed-up world where Elvis is alive and God is dead. We have the unique challenge of working in a world in which integrity seems to be a thing of the past. Ralph Waldo Emerson was correct: "Every great institution is the lengthened shadow of a single man. His character determines the character of his organization."

## CONCLUSION

Our communities still need those like George Washington, leaders who are trustworthy and neither corrupt nor negligent, leaders on whom the "narcotic effect of power, fame and adulation" have no effect. Our communities, businesses, and agencies still need integrity! Billy Graham, evangelist, said, "*Integrity* is the glue that holds our way of life together. We must constantly strive to keep our *integrity* intact. When wealth is lost, nothing is lost; when health is lost, something is lost; when character is lost, all is lost." If you've not given it any thought, you should consider developing an integrity checklist and action plan before you get into a crisis.

On what is your ethical base founded? Do you have a moral compass? If, during a job interview, you were asked to comment on your moral compass, how would you answer? It's been asked before. For example, once during a job interview, I was asked to describe my spiritual walk. How would you have answered such a question?

Remember this: Doing the right thing is always right. Guard your integrity as you would any precious possession. It will get you far in life! As Samuel Johnson, a British author, said, "Integrity without knowledge is weak and useless, and knowledge without integrity is dangerous and dreadful." In addition, Guy Anthony, assistant treasurer for mergers and acquisitions for Intel Corporation, says, "I believe a clear conscience unleashes maximum creativity. Weak character is preoccupied with win-low competition with your neighbor, energy-sappy paranoia and ego-driven compromise."

George Bailey got it right! How about *you?*

# HAS GREED BECOME LEGAL?

## ETHICS AND CHEATING

Those who fall out of leadership roles during adversity often are too weak, too corrupt, or too mercenary to stand firm against the storms of uncertainty or the temptations of their own desires.... So when wealth, fame, or power creates a temptation or the boat is rocked by change and chaos they fall with no credibility. Clearly history shows us that credibility is one of the most difficult attributes for a leader to earn and then sustain.

—Coaches@Work, White Paper

I don't really understand myself, for I want to do what is right, but I don't do it. Instead, I do what I hate. But if I know that what I am doing is wrong, this shows that I agree that the law is good. So I am not the one doing wrong; it is sin living in me that does it. And I know that nothing good lives in me, that is, in my sinful nature. I want to do what is right, but I can't. I want to do what is good, but I don't. I don't want to do what is wrong, but I do it anyway. But if I do what I don't want to do, I am not really the one doing wrong; it is sin living in me that does it.

Romans 7:15–20

In December 2007, John Quinones and ABC's *Primetime* set up hidden cameras in a New Jersey diner and gave the cashier a stack of extra $10 and $20 bills to dispense along with the customers' change as if by accident. Over the course of two days, they watched as forty-six different people were given too much change. The question they were seeking to answer was, "What would these people do when they noticed they had received extra money?"

Some who received an extra $10 noticed and returned the extra change then because they thought the cashier had made a mistake and returning the money was the right thing to do. One person who received an extra $20 with her change said her motivation to return the money was that she was Irish-Catholic and her mother always told her if she stole anything she'd go to hell.

In all, eighteen of the forty-four (41 percent) subjects in the experiment returned the money at the cash register; twenty-six (59 percent) people walked out of the restaurant with the money. So *Primetime* decided to up the ante and have the cashier give out extra $100 bills as if by accident. This time, sixteen of the twenty-five (64 percent) people who left the restaurant with the extra change returned the $100.

What do we learn from these two experiments? Does this tell us anything about the general ethical behavior of Americans? If you had noticed the extra change, what would you have done?

Worldwide personal and organizational corruption has become a serious problem, especially as it relates to cheating. Cheating has become commonplace, and there is no reason to expect that it will cease to exist. In fact, ethical misconduct has become a conspicuous part of corporate and political life. Men, women, children, and organizations have yet to achieve an enlightened state where all personal and business behaviors are governed by the very highest ethical standards. Why else would Dell Inc. CEO Michael Dell propose a settlement with the SEC in 2010 by setting aside $100 million to cover the cost of settling charges that employees misled auditors and manipulated results to meet performance costs?

R. Edward Freeman, academic director of the Business Round-table for Corporate Ethics, has written, "The upside of the recent scandals is that they have led to widespread public concern about ethical business practices. This heightened level of engagement creates a moment—a unique moment—to make a lasting difference in corporate practice." If those in our organizational world would only take note.

We know that moral standards vary from person to person and are influenced by our family, culture, norms, beliefs, values, and traditions. Furthermore, our morals influence our perception of the intensity of a moral dilemma. Those values also influence our propensity to act in a moral or an immoral manner. Unfortunately, not everyone's ethical standards meet our personal criteria. Instead, we are witnesses to the fact that we have become a nation—a world—of cheaters.

## CHEATING

In our research study about ethics, a colleague (Dr. Jeffrey A. Simmons) and I focused on *why* businesspeople choose to cheat. The cheating urge was examined via literature and a survey of business professionals. A general review of articles on cheating provided a taxonomy of why individuals and organizations cheat. You might even be able to think of more reasons. See Table 6.1. The reasons were interesting, even exciting. Tiny risks bring a high to some people, a laugh to share, a secret to cherish against "the enemy," or the opportunity to fool someone.

The self-reported survey of 251 full-time business professionals at entry-level, manager, and upper-management classifications in the Oklahoma City area yielded a real-life perspective on cheating in business, government, health care, and the military. The individuals completing the questionnaire came from a variety of ethnic (national and international) and religious backgrounds—Christian, Muslim, Hindus, Buddhists, and non-religious. Our goal was to discover the answers to four questions:

1. What are the reasons individuals cheat?

2. What are the reasons organizations cheat?

3. Why should people be ethical in a culture that idolizes material success and the lack of values?

4. How can a person be ethical in business?

Table 6.1:

Pressure—peer, personal, organizational, others

To get up, get by, get ahead, stay afloat

Rationality that immoral behavior is accepted practice, ability to rationalize dishonesty

Normal expectation, everyone else is doing it, casual acceptance of such behavior, expectation of corruption, expectancy theory

Laziness

Can't get everything done that needs to be done, taking shortcuts, to save time

Have to be competitive, high need for achievement

No shame, resistance to perceived accountability, there's always going to be dishonesty

Easy to get away with it, extremely remote possibility of being caught

Spur-of-the-moment situation, it will only be for this time

The rush of getting away with something

Incompetence, no purpose in life, no honor

Pathological immaturity, mentally unbalanced, confusion

Special circumstances outweigh ethical concerns, "the ends justify the means"

Born to be bad

Choice of a course of action that least infringes on a person's basic human rights

Preemptive strike, do unto others before they do it to you

Self-image—low, high

Mood—feel like it

Insecurity—financial, the future

Not to do so is foolish, quaint, not practical

To win, to come in first not last, mentality to succeed at all (or any) cost

Following examples of role models, people of authority, corporate scandals

Focus on getting the job done vs. how to get it done

Cynicism, skepticism, irrationality

No personal relationship with God

Allowing society to shape and mold behavior, conforming to patterns of the world

Emotional needs, personal problems

Self-importance, fame, too much pride in one's attitudes and beliefs

It demonstrates great entrepreneurial acumen

It's good training for the real world, for business

Cultural expectation (i.e., different races/cultures)

To gain an advantage that would be more impractical, difficult, or impossible to obtain by more honest means

Member of a pampered and overindulged generation

Instant gratification, need to be satisfied now, quick-fix, instant results, quick solutions

Fear of, embarrassment of, or to avoid failure

Desire for sense of fairness, loss of fair play, situation is inequitable

Temptation too strong to overcome

Easy money

Risk of penalty is negligible, possible rewards outweigh possible punishments, it's only wrong if (when) you get caught

Increase chances for bonuses

Loss of moral compass, loss of fundamental integrity, lack of sense of guilt, forsaking belief in principles, lack of personal ethics, loss of ethical judgment

Freedom to do what one wills, wishes, wants, or can do

Unhappiness

Intellectual dishonesty

Desire to be rich, accumulation of wealth, need for lots of money

Forgotten golden rule of integrity, compromised values

Blaming situations, others

"The devil made me do it"

Greed, economic self-interest

Uneducated, ethically challenged, moral or ethical dummy, stupidity

"The greatest benefit for the most people"

All is fair in love, war, and business

Power, eagerness to gain more power

Lack of understanding of standards of right and wrong

The greatest benefit for the most people

123

The questions were asked in an open-ended answer format, and the survey resulted in numerous answers that, at first, appeared unique. We looked for relationships among the items by content analyzing the responses for overarching principles. This consolidation led to nine categories of influences associated with reasons for individual or organizational cheating behaviors. See Table 6.2.

Table 6.2:

| | | |
|---|---|---|
| Competitive (desire to succeed) | Financial (monetary concerns) | Lazy (disinclined to work hard) |
| Unconfident (unsure of self) | Extrovert (outward concern) | Social (interpersonal) |
| Morals (trust, honor, values) | Consequences (result, outcome) | Fugitive (avoid punishment) |

## COMPETITIVE

Respondents reported that people turned to cheating in order to "keep up with the pack" or "to be the best." Others simply said that greed drives people to cheat. Associated with the concept of greed were the concepts of acquisition and a zero-sum game point of view. That is, if one person is to acquire something, another must lose. Thus, greed corresponded to competition.

When considering organizational behaviors, respondents attributed a desire to "gain an advantage," "get ahead," and "be number one" to cheating behaviors. These reasons implied the presence of competition. Even responses such as "to look good," "gain prestige," or "appear more profitable" indicated a desire to enhance the competitiveness of an organization. For example, the reason a company wants to "look good" or "gain prestige" is so it can either gain more investors (i.e., have more capital with which to compete) or gain more customers (i.e., obtain a more beneficial competitive position).

## FINANCIAL

Respondents also reported that cheating behaviors can be attributed to a "love of money," "to make more money," or to "make the company rich," which suggested a concern for financial status. A more pessimistic financial concern was evidenced in responses such as "to avoid losses or penalties that may be incurred" or "to cut costs." Finally, even the mention of a desire to meet quotas can be attributed to financial concerns since production quotas (especially when related to sales production) are correlated to financial outcomes.

## LAZINESS

Several items related simply to people not wanting to put forth much effort to succeed (i.e., laziness). "It's easier to cheat," "they want the easy way out of a difficult situation," and "poor work ethic" were items clearly associated with the concept of laziness. However, some responses related to a lack of time or preparation. Typically, those were symptomatic of people not willing to put forth more effort to properly plan. Even a response such as "can't make a good (review) rating on their own and keep up with the pack (i.e., others)" had a connotation of laziness, since it suggested that people would rather rely on cheating as opposed to earning positive results.

## UNCONFIDENT

It appeared that some people resorted to cheating because they lacked confidence in their own ability. Representative items included "lack of pride in their perceived abilities," "no other option to succeed," and "inability to provide for family or self." Self-confidence was lacking.

## EXTROVERT

Some people's personalities were such that they placed much value on and were concerned with others. Typically, these people are referred to as extroverts. One aspect of extroversion related to a concern for the manner in which individuals were perceived by other people. A desire to avoid negative perceptions appeared to lead some people to cheat. For example, some respondents attributed "embarrassment of not knowing the answer" or "being afraid to ask for help" as reasons for cheating behaviors.

Extroversion also pertained to a simple concern for others (e.g., what are the actions of others or what effect one's actions will have on others). Thus, such responses as "everyone else is doing it" and "thinks (their actions) will not hurt anyone" were included in this category.

## SOCIAL

Other responses were similar to those categorized as *extrovert* but were not included because they related more with interpersonal dynamics (i.e., social aspects) rather than personal psychological qualities. These items were primarily associated with the impact one's actions have on society as a whole or on one's immediate social circle. Items such as "ethical people always give the world hope" and "cultural consistency is the backbone of society" are primary examples.

## MORALS

Some responses were based on moral philosophy and suggested people's behavior is guided by their moral worldview. For example, respondents suggested that people's actions are influenced by their "faith in God," "considering how to act when no one can see," and moral virtues such as "trust, honor, and values." Our personal, professional, and societal behaviors are based on the values we have adopted. Those values guide our moral and ethical behavior in all settings in which we find ourselves. If one's virtues include honesty, that moral will guide a person safely away from the temptation to cheat. Should one have no such virtue, cheating is an easy trap in which to fall.

## CONSEQUENCES (OR REWARDS)

Many items were associated with the outcomes of one's behavior or the effect of cheating behaviors on the person cheating or on his or her organization. For example, respondents suggested that people who choose not to cheat "get further in life" or "sleep better at night." Some cheaters, of course, might cheat off someone they feel is smarter so they can be proud of their work. Others suggested that people can "build self-esteem and self-respect" by not cheating. Several respondents equated non-cheating behavior with better long-term business results.

## FUGITIVE

Finally, some people were influenced by the prospect of having to deal with the personal consequences of their actions and whether they would be caught. One respondent suggested that some people cheat for the thrill of getting away with it. Another respondent said that people should obey any set of laws or rules. Since these items related to whether one chooses to follow the "law," we referred to this category as *fugitive*—as in someone whose actions either caused them to "be on the run" (like a fugitive from the law) since they broke the rules or to avoid having to suffer any punishment from breaking the rules. This category differs from the *consequences* category since the items included here focused on dealing with or avoiding negative personal consequences.

## REASONS INDIVIDUALS CHEAT

What are the reasons people cheat? Five categories (see Tables 6.3 and 6.4) relate to reasons individuals cheat. The associated categories are the same for males and females. However, the percentage of responses attributed to the *competitive* category—the largest category—is higher for males than for females. This could be attributed to the general belief that males tend to be more oriented to competition than females, and males may resort to cheating behaviors in order to succeed.

Interestingly, though *competitive* is the largest category, *lazy* comprises the second largest category of reasons individuals cheat. On the surface, one might view this as contrary to a competitive nature. However, being lazy or not willing to put forth the effort is not incompatible with a desire to succeed. It is indicative of one's work ethic (or mode of operation), not one's desires. Thus, it is possible for someone to *want* to succeed and at the same time *not want* to work for it. They would prefer to think of it as taking a creative shortcut; they are used to this well-known temptation.

Table 6.3:

| | | |
|---|---|---|
| Competitive (41.8 percent) | Lazy (28.6 percent) | Unconfident (12.6 percent) |
| Extrovert (8.5 percent) | Fugitive (8.5 percent) | |

Table 6.4:

| | | |
|---|---|---|
| Competitive (28.2 percent) | Lazy (24.6 percent) | Unconfident (19.0 percent) |
| Extrovert (19.0 percent) | Fugitive (9.2 percent) | |

The two categories of *competitive* and *lazy* captured a majority (70.4 percent male and 52.8 percent female) of responses for the reason individuals cheat.

David Ogilvy, the most celebrated advertising executive of his day, built Ogilvy & Mather into a global enterprise. He held deep beliefs in honesty and respect for others. One of his favorite sayings was, "The consumer is not a moron, she is your wife. You wouldn't lie to your wife. Don't lie to mine." In contrast, Dan Draper and his colleagues on the TV show *Mad Men* show little respect for the interests of their clients or workforce. In fact, there is little evidence they adhere to any professional standards. If it is true they live and work without professional standards, it should be no surprise to learn that cheating behaviors are guiding their work. There would be no reason for them not to cheat their clients and even their colleagues.

Another example: In spring 1999, San Diego State University reported what they considered the worst cheating scandal in their history. Twenty-five students were caught cheating on a quiz. The quiz counted for only two percent of the semester grade. All twenty-five students were given a failing grade in the course. The lecturer of the class, Brian Cornforth, told the *San Diego Union-Tribune,* "This is just too egregious, it's too heinous a cheating scandal, and hopefully it will have positive ripple effects not only in the class but other classes throughout the university."

The class?

Business ethics.

You would think that if there is any class in which students would not cheat it would be a course in business ethics. We might wonder what in the world is being taught in that course. Perhaps these students have found that cheating is so easy in college, why should an ethics course deter them from behaviors they have practiced in other classes. If they do it now, they are quite likely to do so in a corporate setting.

## REASONS ORGANIZATIONS CHEAT

What are the reasons organizations cheat? Four of the five categories (see Tables 6.5 and 6.6) associated with individual cheating behaviors were related to organizational behaviors. Furthermore, as with individuals, *competitive* issues topped the list of reasons organizations cheat for both males and females. (The reason for asking this question was to separate any distinctions people sometimes make between individuals and organizations. Obviously, it is the people within an organization who cheat and not the organization itself.)

Since the context of this research involved ethics in a business environment, it was expected that respondents would be more likely to attribute competitive reasons for organizational cheating behaviors. A significant difference between respondents' perceptions of individual and organizational cheating was the presence of *financial* reasons to cheat. This category encompassed 30.9 percent of male responses and 26.7 percent of female responses. Given the importance of financial matters in business, this too made intuitive sense.

Table 6.5:

| | | |
|---|---|---|
| Competitive (48.0 percent) | Financial (30.9 percent) | Unconfident (9.8 percent) |
| Extrovert (6.6 percent) | Fugitive (4.7 percent) | |

Table 6.6:

| | | |
|---|---|---|
| Competitive (56.1 percent) | Financial (26.7 percent) | Fugitive (6.7 percent) |
| Lazy (6.7 percent) | Unconfident (3.8 percent) | |

*Competitive* and *financial* categories captured 78.9 percent (male) and 82.8 percent (female) of the reasons given for why organizations cheat. This suggested that, regardless of increased focus in the media on social responsibility, society still views the primary focus of business to be: Make the most money.

For example, consider the situation where Merck Pharmaceutical discovered that an adaptation of a veterinary drug has the potential to kill the parasite that causes river blindness in Africa and Latin America. Unfortunately, none of the sufferers could afford to pay for the medication. The company executives had to decide how to balance their obligations to shareholders with the duty to save lives. Eventually, they decided to give the drug away, even though it would cost them $20 million a year to do so.

Many large corporations find themselves entangled in the pursuit of money because of greed. At times it may seem they don't have any concern for the "little man." Fortunately most of them begin to see the fallacy in such thinking and make more honorable decisions. If they didn't do so, we might wonder why anyone should be ethical.

## WHY PEOPLE SHOULD BE ETHICAL

Why should people be ethical in a culture that idolizes material success and the lack of values? Given the different explanations and justifications of why people should be ethical, it was not surprising that the responses differed from those explaining why people and organizations cheat. See Tables 6.7 and 6.8.

Both males and females suggested that people should consider the consequences of their behavior and behave in a more ethical manner. It should be noted, however, that this response did not differ much from those associated with the reason people and organizations cheat. The primary reason people cheat is to achieve a desired outcome, which correlated to respondents suggesting that people consider the outcomes (i.e., consequences) of their actions.

Table 6.7:

| | | |
|---|---|---|
| Consequences (56.9 percent) | Social (20.1 percent) | Morals (14.4 percent) |
| Other (8.6 percent) | | |

Table 6.8:

| | | |
|---|---|---|
| Consequences (43.0 percent) | Morals (37.5 percent) | Social (12.5 percent) |
| Other (7.0 percent) | | |

Males and females differed with regard to the ranking of the other reasons people should behave more ethically. Males reported people should be guided by the effects of their actions on society (20.1 percent) more than the moral consequences (14.4 percent). Females, on the other hand, suggested that moral consequences (37.5 percent) take precedence over social concerns (12.5 percent).

Consider the following as an example that required a recognition of right and wrong and the consequences associated therewith. In spring 2007, thirty-four first-year MBA students at Duke University were accused of cheating on a take-home final exam. Duke officials called this the most widespread cheating episode in the business school's history.

The final was an open-book test in a required course. The students were told to take the exam on their own. Many students collaborated, however, in violation of the Fuqua School of Business honor code. Nine of the thirty-four students faced expulsion; fifteen were suspended for a year and given a failing grade in the course; nine were given a failing grade in the course; one got a failing grade on the exam. Four students accused of cheating were exonerated.

Would their actions have been different if they had been caught on camera? On TV? On video? If their pictures were going to be on the front page of the newspaper? Perhaps this is why we are finding more and more ethics officers in organizations. Cheating is such an easy activity that if one learns it well in college they will be tempted to continue such activities in the organizations for which they choose to work after graduation. Perhaps we need college courses on how to be ethical rather than on nebulous discussions of case studies about ethical situations.

# HOW A PERSON CAN BE ETHICAL

How can a person be ethical in business? One interesting finding was the fact that when asked how a person can be ethical in business, males, more than females, said people should allow morality to guide their behaviors. See Tables 6.9 and 6.10. Females placed the most emphasis on social effects. Also, when the two categories (*moral* and *social*) for both males and females were combined, the percentage of responses captured were 78.1 percent and 68.8 percent, respectively, which accounted for a large majority of all responses.

Table 6.9:

| | | |
|---|---|---|
| Moral (42.2 percent) | Social (35.9 percent) | Fugitive (7.3 percent) |
| Other (14.6 percent) | | |

Table 6.10:

| | | |
|---|---|---|
| Social (36.1 percent) | Morals (31.9 percent) | Fugitive (19.3 percent) |
| Confident (5.4 percent) | Effort (4.2 percent) | Other (3.0 percent) |

Furthermore, relative to the male responses (7.3 percent), more female responses (19.3 percent) suggested that one should consider the personal (i.e., *fugitive—running away*) consequences of one's behavior.

To illustrate: Innovator and entrepreneur Philipe Kahn tells a story about how he tricked a salesman for *Byte* magazine into extending credit for an ad space during the company's early days. On the day of the appointment with the salesman, Kahn hired extra workers to scurry about and had the phones ringing in order to make the office look busy. He also prepared a media plan, crossed out *Byte*, and made sure the salesman inadvertently saw the plan. When the salesman asked if Kahn wanted to advertise in *Byte*, Kahn said he couldn't afford it. The salesman pleaded and finally extended terms of credit that would allow the ad to run once. Kahn sold enough software to get his startup venture on the road. No personal consequences of behavior were ever considered.

Kahn achieved what he set out to do, but was he being ethical? Or was he just "doing business"? Perhaps a consideration about personal consequences would have led him in a different direction and wouldn't resemble "running away" from the more ethical path.

## MAKING THE RIGHT DECISIONS

Whatever the causes of cheating may be, a need exists for an orderly, systematic, and quantitative process by which we can make the kinds of analyses and applications business ethics requires. Such predicaments may need a step-by-step procedure for understanding, correcting, or making decisions. As leaders, you and I are called upon to make tough decisions, particularly during times of economic stress. One of the models I prefer is provided by the Center for Business Ethics at Bentley College. They recommend six steps for ethical decision making:

1. *Is it right?* This question is based on the theory of ethics that there are certain universally accepted guiding principles of rightness and wrongness. "Thou shall not steal" is one of those principles.

2. *Is it fair?* This question is based on the theory of justice that certain actions are inherently just or unjust. For example, it is unjust to fire a high-performing employee to hire a less competent person who is a relative by marriage.

3. *Who gets hurt?* This question is based on the notion of attempting to do the greatest good for the greatest number of people. For example, should our gov-

ernment be judged by whether policies benefit the majority?

4. *Would you be comfortable if the details of your decision or actions were made public in the media or through e-mail?* This question is based on the principle of disclosure. For example, any and all information that affects the full understanding of a company's financial statements must be included with the financial statements (e.g., outstanding lawsuits, tax disputes, company takeovers, etc.).

5. *What would you tell your child, sibling, or a young relative to do?* This question is based on the principle of reversibility, which evaluates the ethics of a decision by reversing the decision maker. Is it possible to rebound from an unethical decision so you can come back from the harm the decision caused?

6. *How does it smell?* This question is based on a person's intuition and common sense. For example, counting a simple product inquiry over the Internet as a sale would "smell" bad to any sensible person.

Although ethical decision making will never be easy, the above model is an organized way to think through the situation to decide whether a given act is ethical or unethical. There are issues in our work where we are faced with the necessity of asking these questions regarding a potential ethical dilemma. Using these questions will not only help your decision making go smoother but also produce the best results. Wouldn't it have been swell if the leaders at Enron, Tyco, MCI/WorldCom, Credit Suisse First Boston, Hyundai, Goldman Sachs, and many more had asked themselves these six questions? A lot of people's lives would be happier today.

## CONCLUSION

In the 1987 movie *Wall Street,* Michael Douglas, as Gordon Gekko, made one statement famous worldwide: "Greed is good." In the 2010 movie *Wall Street 2: Money Never Sleeps,* he references that statement, but he adds, "Now it seems it's legal." Do you agree or disagree?

Any way you choose to view it, business ethics is a complicated field of study. We do know several things, however. Sound ethics is good business, and profit is not the sole motive of business. Pressure to compromise personal standards is felt keenly at the middle and lower leadership levels, and competition can cause persons to ignore ethical considerations. The person most likely to act ethically is one with a well-defined personal code. Also, people are likely to behave ethically if they have an ethical leader. However, pressure from higher up the organization to achieve results can cause unethical behavior. Thus, the more leaders and followers are taught to identify with their organizations and have loyalty to the same, the more they are encouraged to abdicate personal responsibility for their actions.

Opportunities for cheating exist at all organizational levels. Persons who practice "small" unethical practices have a tendency later to attempt more serious unethical practices. Since no repercussion occurred when something little was done (e.g., you didn't get caught), there is no threat in attempting something more serious. In the long run, since most people seem to depend upon cultural consensus or upon their religious and philosophical beliefs of what is right or wrong, perhaps we should all just accept the Golden Rule. In fact, what would the business world be like if we all followed the Golden Rule—"Ask yourself what you want people to do for you, then grab the initiative and do it for them" (Matthew 7:12, MSG).

# CAN ONLY A DEAD
# PERSON KEEP A SECRET?

## COMMUNICATION FLOWS,
## NETWORKS, AND FEEDBACK

Years of language dilution by lawyers, marketers, executives, and HR departments have turned the powerful, descriptive sentence into an empty vessel optimized for buzzwords, jargon, and vapid expressions. Words are treated as filler—"stuff" that takes up space on a page. Words expand to occupy bank space in a business much as spray foam insulation fills up cracks in your house. Harsh? Maybe. True? Read around a bit, and I think you'll agree.

—Jason Fried, cofounder and CEO, 37signals

Hear this, you elders; listen, all who live in the land. Has anything like this ever happened in your days or in the days of your forefathers? Tell it to your children, and let your children tell it to their children, and their children to the next generation.

Joel 2:2–4 (NIV)

Anytime I consult with a company or do programs for them, I always wonder what I'm going to learn about them. I was invited into a sales-service company several years ago that had several thousand employees in its US plants. All the plants had decentralized operations with strong leadership authority.

The company communicated with everyone through publications, newsletters, bulletin boards, and slick audiovisual presentations. Normally, the employees liked these media. However, by the 1990s, the employees found them neither timely nor candid in communicating important information. Most, in fact, believed that official publications only confirmed what the grapevine had been saying anyway.

I conducted a systematic survey of the leadership team in the home office and discovered that the ones with the most information seldom communicated with the rank and file. At the next level down, I learned that the supervisors lacked time and motivation. Some of them shared an unspoken belief that information equals power; therefore, information should not be disseminated. If they had information, they perceived they had power, and they liked that feeling—a perk of that job level (one-upmanship!). It reminded me of the children's ditty, "I have one, and you don't."

The highest-level people in the organization did not insist that the supervisors and leaders communicate important information in a timely manner. Neither did they evaluate managerial communication behavior. Much of the information invariably traveled through the company grapevine (not to mention e-mail, Facebook, Twitter, blogs, etc.), which saved them money, time, and talent for production. Yet, my survey results indicated that employees preferred to hear official information from their managers. It was more professionally reassuring, and it built trust and layers of calmness and confidence in the system—all the way to the top. Trust up the ladder.

If you had been a member of that company, how would you have felt?

In a similar situation at a different facility, one person I know felt mad, sad, alone, unimportant, not educated. Had this person been younger, she would have sought another job with a different company. However, she was fearful because she felt she had no power in the situation and was willing to ride out her misgivings.

What kind of a communication system would you recommend be installed? A centrally directed one? Or a uniform but flexible one? The company had not done anything about their communication system because the president did not believe in its importance.

What remedies would you recommend for the morale of the employees?

---

Everyone eventually becomes involved in a situation where communication fails. However, the effective leader recognizes the importance of communication and learns to use it as a tool to respond to challenges. Communication is one of the least understood processes of interpersonal relationships. You'd think that in today's advanced society, we should be able to solve problems by talking to one another. The truth is twofold: communication is incredibly complex, and little attention has been paid to the question of what is or what is not being communicated.

As a leader, you must build a community of communication with others, a climate for the sharing of messages, ideas, or attitudes. You must establish a *commonness* (a sense of belonging) with others. You must allow communication to flow not only from you to them but also from them to you. None of us can exist very long without good communication. Your followers and you both fulfill your task roles and responsibilities by speaking, listening to, and observing one another's verbal and nonverbal expressions. There can be no doubt that communication involves the intentions of the speaker and the impressions of the hearer.

Two examples come to mind. First, on a few occasions, my wife and I have been invited out to dinner by a follower who said they'd like to talk to me informally over dinner. A hidden agenda I've often suspected was that the informal, private matter they wanted to talk to me about was intended for my wife to hear. That way, she could talk to the follower's wife about it, or my wife could "nag" me about the problem the person was needing help with, especially if my wife already had a high opinion of this person. In all honesty, however, some problems are not easily solved, even if my wife does know about them.

Second, a former football player I know once described the tactics of his high school coach. Before the game, the coach would inspire the team. He would talk to them about the smell of victory. Then he would describe what it was like to win and hear the roar of the crowd, to see the sparkle in a girlfriend's eye, to be congratulated by classmates in the hallway at school. My friend said at the end of these pep talks, they not only imagined victory, but also they could smell, feel, and taste it in their very cellular being. They were ready to respond and do what they had practiced. And they would go out to win the game.

If there is a foundational activity for all planning, organizing, directing, and controlling, it is communication. Communication plays an important role in both individual and organizational achievement. Without communication, decisions cannot be made or implemented. Achievement is impossible. In an organization that markets goods and services, a new sales strategy can only be implemented if it is clearly articulated (along with the rationale behind the shift) to company associates. "Because I said so" doesn't work well with anyone—even two-year-olds—without pouting and stiff-necked resistance. Adults just aren't allowed to scream, "I don't want to!" for five minutes at the top of their lungs in the company dining room without security hauling them away or getting canned.

## A DEFINITION OF COMMUNICATION

Someone once said that only a dead man can keep a secret. Why? Because humans talk. Even when they have promised not to say a word to anyone, they talk. Thus, like many leadership and social behavior components, there are many definitions of communication. For our purposes, communication is the sending and receiving of messages, the sharing of ideas and attitudes. Ideas stress an intrapersonal view of communication. Messages emphasize the interpersonal side of communication. Attitudes overlap both and suggest the importance of nonverbal communication.

Through communication, people process information, test ideas, exchange opinions, and achieve consensus on decisions. They develop interpersonal relationships and form subgroups from a large number of individuals. Communication is *the* organizing medium for the leader. For communication to be productive, therefore, those involved must see some reason for interaction.

First, gain the attention of the receiver. Imagine the frustration you would experience if you were speaking before a group who was not paying attention. You might as well be talking to a wall because the results will be similar. There are any number of ways by which you can get someone's attention. The three most common ways might be to smile, exude self-confidence, and make eye contact. It also will be helpful to look relaxed and happy. Your positive attitude will win personal rewards.

Second, achieve understanding. Present ideas or messages in a manner acceptable to the needs of your followers. Make sure the followers structure ideas in their minds the same way you originally framed them. Communication is basically a process of exchanging meanings. Thus, to attain understanding, you and your listener must perceive the purpose of the exchange, recognize whether the purpose is being achieved, and help one another achieve the purpose. Otherwise, there is no real need to communicate.

Third, gain acceptance of one's ideas. Although such acceptance is not essential to getting others to do what one wishes, it is helpful for the long-run life of the group. Clearly, followers are inclined to maintain satisfying relationships if they believe in their leaders and what they are doing. If either acceptance or agreement is impossible, a corollary goal should be to prompt the listener to think.

Fourth, gain productive action. Not only do you want followers to listen to you, understand what you say, and accept your ideas, but you also want followers to do what you suggest. Action is one way to check communication results. It is, in fact, the main criterion for speaking or writing. For example, in an advertising campaign, an ad is written to produce results (e.g., increase sales, promote an event, win a vote, secure prospective customers, etc.). A successful ad increases those numbers. Little or no response indicates a failure to communicate (especially if market research has indicated an unfulfilled need).

Finally, strive to maintain good relationships with others. Friends seldom have the problem understanding one another that opponents do. When a leader develops satisfying relationships, followers are more likely to listen to what the leader says and respond as desired.

Unfortunately, some leaders operate as a board of directors. They think they can meet like politicians in "smoke-filled" back rooms, making policy decisions and handing down edicts to follow. The problem with this approach is that there has been no participation or input from the membership, and often, their suggestions are ignored or even rejected. Leaders must avoid their nonproductive behavior and devise organizational settings where communication and planning can take place.

Some leaders may be responding in this manner because they think they are more educated or liberated. Certainly, sweatshops didn't expect any different behavior. Even my mother and mother-in-law were content with the way their bosses kept them in the dark. On the other hand, nurses want doctors to listen to them. The nurses have been in the hospital all day and have ideas as to what the patient needs.

## THE NATURE OF COMMUNICATION

It is impossible to discuss communication without relating it to task situations. Every organization has tasks to perform. Consequently, communication should be explored in terms of flows, networks, interactions, and feedback. For example, contrasts are made between one- and two-way flows of information. An important advantage of two-way communication is its role in decision making (e.g., sales calls, conference calls). People who have to carry out a proposal have an opportunity to react to it and contribute to the decision. There are also advantages to one-way communication, such as speed, simplification, and orderliness (e.g., departmental memos, letters). Nonetheless, two-way communication is more valid since it allows for more accurate transmission of information, especially with face-to-face or person-to-person communication.

In addition, communication is often described as information flowing vertically or horizontally—upward (follower to leader), downward (leader to follower), or laterally (leader to leader or follower to follower).

### VERTICAL COMMUNICATION

Vertical communication involves messages flowing upward and downward in an organizational hierarchy.

## Downward Communication

Downward communication is probably the most frequent communication flow in an organization. It involves directives, policies, procedures, instructions, goals, or objectives. For example, if I tell others what to do or pass on information needed to perform a job or service, I might use announcements, memorandums, post-it notes, or voice mail. However, if the communication is unclear, followers will not respond in the way I wish. And if my communication is limited (e.g., I don't talk to them enough or see them often), followers will give only minimal compliance. Downward communication is a one-way process and can be stifling since people feel they have no say about how things are done. No feedback is allowed, although it might be needful.

As a leader, you must provide clear channels for funneling information, opinions, and attitudes up through the organization. You should be willing to adopt a communication training program for all leaders. You should make sure you get out of the office and talk to individuals on "the firing line." You should conduct regular supervisory-employee discussions (i.e., use participative interaction to identify, analyze, and solve problems). At the same time, you need to know that too much faith in downward communication may blind you as to the actual rumors abounding in the organization and thereby create problems instead of solve them.

## Upward Communication

Upward communication involves followers relaying information to their leaders. This type of message flow provides feedback, and it is probably the more needed communication flow. Therefore, it is two-way and, as a general rule, improves morale. People feel as though they have a voice in how things are done, that they are heard. So if you listen and observe followers more, you will find many implicit messages being sent upward. From such information, you can rectify ineffective practices, jump-start lifeless activities, and take other important steps to breathe new life into tired practices.

To illustrate, a young team of seven salespeople for a financial organization was asked at their yearly meeting to provide feedback of how the organization could help them do their jobs better. After putting their heads together, the spokesman for sales recommended the company purchase iPads for their use, instead of just Blackberrys. One part of this particular presentation referenced how the accountants and support staff always send Excel spreadsheets to update information and how difficult it was to read those when out in the field. Most of the salespeople work out of their cars during the daytime. At the end of the presentation, top management thanked the presenter for the insight and recommendations of the sales team and promised to take their recommendation under advisement. Six months later the sales team had not heard a word about whether the company would purchase iPads. The sales team concluded they would have to purchase their own iPads if they wanted to use one during the workday. While upward communication had been attempted, it did not reap the benefits hoped for by the sales team.

Upward communication can probably only be beneficial if you will ensure that communication lines are open, encouraged, frequent, and that the communication is followed up on. You must not only keep your ears to the rail but also keep your eyes open for the train! You must provide for continuity of information. It is not something that can be turned on and off. You need to encourage a free flow of upward information that will yield an improved picture of the work accomplishments, problems, plans, attitudes, and feelings of followers. In addition, individuals, policies, ideas, and help of followers can be tapped, better answers to problems can be received, and responsibility can be eased. You need to also make sure you model good active listening. Good listening makes for good listeners.

Both upward and downward communication are related to formal structures. Lines connect the various units within an organization's hierarchy. Systems of responsibility and explicit delegations of duties are clearly drawn. Exact statements of the nature, content, and direction of communication are provided. Because of this high formality, some leaders try to establish more informal atmospheres, like casual Fridays, birthday celebrations, or brief speeches of appreciation. They try to create a climate of acceptance, warmth, team playing, and listening rather than communicating authority and power.

## HORIZONTAL COMMUNICATION

Horizontal (or lateral) communication is usually the strongest flow of information because it allows for message exchange among people on the same level of authority. It tends to focus on joint problem solving and coordination of workflow. Typically, it leads to better understanding among members than vertical communication does. Good horizontal communication includes task coordination, problem solving, information sharing, and conflict resolution. Additionally, horizontal communication provides a good opportunity to banish certain communication barriers by downplaying status.

Because business and industry need a large amount of horizontal communication, a basic principle has been introduced to guide communicators. That principle is called a "bridge" and connects hierarchical lines. (If you've viewed an organizational chart lately that shows a straight line connection hierarchy, you might also have noticed some dotted lines going from one part of the organization to another. Those dotted lines are the bridges.) A bridge is often necessary for followers near the bottom of a chain of command.

As much as two-thirds of the communication in an organization may be horizontal. My experience suggests that people who work very closely together on the same levels seldom have trouble understanding one another. The reason is that horizontal communication furnishes emotional and social support, and it also provides task coordination.

One fault I've noticed with horizontal communication is that an overabundance of horizontal communication can weaken the authority structure because too many messages are flowing in all directions without screening or filtering. Another is that even though people are at the same level, a few will have seniority or more years of service and think they should be heard more. They view themselves as the leaders, the pets of the organizations, and more mature. At times, younger followers must watch out for mothering, snide remarks, being ignored, receiving only "dog jobs" to do (e.g., assignments or hours to work that no one wants), or snarky attitudes. A third fault is that someone may be purposely left out of the loop and is the last to know. Thus, when you question what is happening, they say something like, "Oh, didn't we tell you about that?"

## THE GRAPEVINE

Vertical and horizontal communication are considered formal types of communication because they follow a chain of command on most organizational charts. A communication system that does not follow the chain of command and therefore has no official sanction is referred to as the *grapevine* (i.e., rumors and gossip). In 1968, American singer and songwriter Marvin Gaye made a hit with the song "I Heard It On the Grapevine." And we all know that's the way most information flows. Perhaps you've been amazed at how quickly something can travel on the grapevine.

The grapevine creates an informal structure that departs from formal tasks and hierarchy and develops its own twisting and turning vines as channels of communication and dependence. It is eye-popping to hear that five out of six messages in an organization are carried by the grapevine instead of by official channels. Therefore, the grapevine is fast, selective, versatile, and influential. It is doubtful it could ever be destroyed. Watch any prison movie or TV show, and you will see inmates who have many ways of communicating through the prison system.

The reality is this: the "I-heard-it-through-the-grapevine" communication lines are undeniably strong. It is estimated that 70 to 90 percent of the information carried via the grapevine contains correct *bits* of information but is incomplete and sometimes false. At this time of writing, for example, Bill Cosby, actor and comedian, has had to use TV, Facebook, and Twitter five times to deny the gossip that he has died. Apparently this keeps him quite busy.

If you understand how the grapevine works (i.e., who passes on information), you can influence and use the grapevine network by supplying accurate data. You can open all channels of communication, fight rumors with a positive presentation of facts, prevent employee idleness and boredom through better job design, and develop long-term credibility. You can also use the grapevine to keep current on what followers are thinking and saying.

## COMMUNICATION NETWORKS

Every group develops its own unique structure and pattern of communication. These patterns connect the sender and receivers to a functioning social organization and are called networks. Networks show who talks to whom. A factor affecting communication networks is group size. For example, the time available per person for communication during a committee meeting decreases as committee size increases. Followers have fewer chances to speak in groups of twelve than in groups of five. In addition, people feel threatened and inhibited in large groups. Similarly, discussion diminishes as group size increases. The distribution of participation also varies. The gap between leader and followers tends to grow proportionately as size increases.

Leaders can evaluate the results of their communication performance through the various networks within an organization. There are four major communication subsystems, according to consultant and author Howard Greenbaum:

1. The *regulative communication network* seeks to secure conformity to plans and assure productivity. It is concerned with controls, orders, and other forms of direction. It focuses on feedback between followers and leaders in task-related activities. Three examples of regulative communication are policy statements, procedures, and rules.

2. The *innovative communication network* strives to ensure organizational flexibility. It helps the organization adapt to varied internal and external influences (i.e., technological, sociological, educational, economical, political). It is concerned with problem solving, adaptation to change, and the implementation of new ideas. Two examples of innovative communication are suggestion systems and participative problem-solving meetings.

3. The *integrative (or maintenance) communication network* is concerned with feelings for self, associates, and work. It is directly related to employee morale. It also involves acceptance of the organization by

nonmembers, such as community and governmental units. It is manifested by supportive, self-maintaining behavior leading toward self-realization and human fulfillment. Examples of integrative communication are gossip, praise by a superior, highly visible rewards, and public relations.

4.  The *informative-instructive communication network* is concerned with getting and giving information not associated with the other communication networks. It includes the instructions that enable subordinates to properly execute job requirements Therefore, it is also concerned with conformity, adaptiveness, and morale. It constantly works for higher levels of productivity and effectiveness. Three examples of informative-instructive communication are bulletin board notices, company publications, and training activities.

Each of these networks consists of specific communication rules. So one of the challenges you face as a leader is to recognize who does or does not get information and then fill those gaps. Such recognition allows you to supply good information to the liaisons and avoid excessive gate-keeping tendencies. Thus, you must develop a one-on-one network with various individuals. This involves visiting with them professionally or socially, doing activities with them, going with them to watch their kids (e.g., little league, soccer, football, or cheerleading), volunteering activities, and speaking with them at meetings. Some leaders try to sit by different individuals at meetings, walk with various ones to a meeting, or stop by various offices on a MBWA approach to visiting. Other leaders invite people to lunch. If you choose to do that, be sure to include both sexes and a variety of ages. Take two or three people with you. People notice.

As a leader, you must ensure that everyone who needs information should have access to it. Whatever the situation, you must allocate significant time to developing "a network of cooperative relationships."

## COMMUNICATION INTERACTIONS

Your behavior affects those in the group. If you choose not to be an active member of the group or communicate, you may, by example, encourage others to remain uninvolved. If, on the other hand, your behavior influences others to participate actively, group interaction can be improved.

Two styles of interaction that can influence a group either positively or negatively are those of the *peacemaker* and the *democratic group member*. A peacemaker gets a consensus and keeps people together. A democratic group leader tries to include everyone in a discussion. By learning to be sensitive to the participation and interaction level of a group, you can contribute by spotting potential trouble areas. Since the interaction skills of group members vary, you should emphasize brevity, objectivity, and listening. Such communicative behavior results in solving problems, soothing hurt feelings, increasing effectiveness, and building bridges.

## COHESIVE PATTERNS

Cohesiveness is the ability of organizational members to work and stay together. As followers develop a higher level of cohesion, they communicate more because they are open, supportive, and trusting. They feel pressure to interact and communicate because everyone else is involved. Cohesion grows out of commonality, understanding, and trust. This process is the result of gradual and proactive attempts by leaders and followers to nurture the relationships that exist and foster the building of bridges to those people who feel outside the loop. And oddly enough, you may be surprised that even the majority may feel out of the loop, even many extroverts. So be kind.

# FEEDBACK

In communication, feedback determines levels of understanding. Perhaps that is why the Tibetan Dalai Lama (Tenzin Gyatso) said, "Our prime purpose in this life is to help others. And if you can't help them, at least don't hurt them." If feedback is discouraged or hurtful, an organization's vitality and problem-solving ability suffers. The terms *interaction* and *communication* are often used synonymously. Group interaction is the communicative feedback provided by and for leaders and followers. Therefore, feedback refers to the responses a person makes to others. For example, if I ask a question and someone responds to that question, makes a face, rolls his/her eyes, guffaws, snorts, slams a fist on the table, or expands with another suggestion, both the follower and I influence one another.

The examples above illustrate two basic types of feedback: positive and negative. Positive feedback reinforces and stimulates. Negative feedback counteracts and neutralizes. Groups use both types of feedback to regulate their progress toward consensus decisions. That is, groups tend to reinforce other's acceptable behavior but punish deviant behavior. Such "punishments" may be in the form of harsh words, giving unpleasant assignments, or removing someone from a group. I've heard some leaders say things like, "Oh, Rob, come on!" or, "Shut up, you jerk," or, "Just drop it; it's no big deal."

For verbal feedback to be useful, it must be helpful. That is why your feedback to followers needs to be very specific. If your followers are to be helped, they need to understand what you said, be willing to accept it, and be able to do something about it. Trust must exist between you and them before a message is accepted. The same is true of nonverbal feedback. It is possible a leader's nonverbal behavior may seem vague and nonspecific but is very relevant to the real meaning of what is or has happened. The TV show *Lie to Me* makes that point very clear!

## FEEDFORWARD

While giving and receiving feedback has long been considered essential, there is one fundamental problem. Feedback focuses on the past. That is why some leaders and trainers have adopted the communication technique *feedforward*. Whereas feedback requires knowing about the speaker or listener, feedforward requires having good ideas for achieving a future task. According to Marshall Goldsmith, a top executive coach, there are ten reasons to try feedforward:

1. We can change the future. We can't change the past.

2. It can be more productive to help people be right than to prove they were wrong.

3. Feedforward is especially suited to successful people.

4. Feedforward can come from anyone who knows about the task. It does not require personal experience with the individual.

5. People do not take feedforward as personally as feedback.

6. Feedback can reinforce personal stereotyping and negative self-fulfilling prophecies. Feedforward can reinforce the possibility of change.

7. Face it! Most of us hate getting negative feedback, and we don't like to give it.

8. Feedforward can cover almost all of the same material as feedback.

9. Feedforward tends to be much faster and more efficient than feedback.

10. Feedforward can be a useful tool to apply with managers, peers, and team members.

If you are one of those individuals who feels feedback causes negative feelings and responses, you might wish to try feeding information forward. Some leaders report that feedforward not only works, it is also fun. To feed information forward does not require personal knowledge about another individual. You might even be amazed at how much you can learn from someone you don't know. For example, if you want to be a better listener, a fellow leader can provide ideas on how you can improve. Feedforward only requires having good ideas for achieving a task.

## CONCLUSION

It should be obvious by now that good communication is essential to success. If you don't know what's expected of you, you will seldom be able to perform to your potential. Leaders who communicate effectively are far more likely to report high levels of high performance than those organizations that do not communicate effectively. As a writer for *Inc.* magazine, Fred Holloway said, "You can tie back almost every employee issue—attendance, morale, performance, and productivity—to communication."

Therefore, as a leader, you must understand how communication flows and how people are connected to one another into a network. You must create a culture for communication, make sure messages are heard, and use all flows, networks, and available feedback to enhance your communication skills and abilities. As information moves throughout the organization, it has certain implications for the persons sending and receiving the messages. You must keep the information flowing from you to them and from them to you in order to successfully understand one another.

Are *you* listening?

# ARE YOU READING HIM (HER) RIGHT?

## COMMUNICATION BARRIERS AND NONVERBAL COMMUNICATION

When you are listening to somebody, completely, attentively, then you are listening not only to the words, but also to the feeling of what is being conveyed, to the whole of it, not part of it.

—Jiddu Krishnamurti, East Indian author and speaker

A fool finds no pleasure in understanding but delights in airing his own opinions.... He who answers before listening—that is his folly and his shame.

Proverbs 18:2, 13 (NIV)

Three Floridians work in the same organization. The executive vice president typically dresses in well-tailored, subtly colored suits, sans vest, and muted ties. He occupies a corner office with low, indirect lighting. He makes direct eye contact with others and comfortably calls others by their first names. He is generally relaxed in communication situations and feels free to interrupt others or allow long periods of silence.

The financial officer also dresses in well-tailored clothing but wears tightly buttoned blouses under her jacket. Her accessories include fancy pins, a large diamond ring, and gold-buckled shoes. She has a large office crowded with furniture, which is located halfway down the hall from the executive vice president's office. Her office walls hold an array of certificates she has received over the years. She typically quotes lawyers and accountants in her conversations.

The production manager dresses in colorfully patterned shirts with dress slacks. His desk is in a well-lit, open-space area with several coworkers. He walks with rounded shoulders and doesn't look at others when he talks. He is often interrupted when he speaks.

What nonverbal messages can you decode about these three leaders? Who has power, who is pretending to have power, and who doesn't have power? How do these three leaders deal professionally and personally with others?

Now answer those questions about the nonverbal messages you send, about how you interact with others, how much power you have, and how you use it.

---

Nonverbal communication is important. Both leaders' and followers' potential for success cannot be enhanced without improving their communication knowledge and skills but also nonverbal behaviors. The leader's objectives should be to search for and use communication skills *and* actions that will enhance understanding. Unfortunately, many problems can arise along the way.

When listeners fail to understand the speaker's intended meaning, that person often replies, "That's not what I meant!" The listener's response is often more colorful in description. Such situations have led many researchers to conclude that communication may be the biggest problem in human relationships. As the old saying goes, "I know you believe you understand what you think I said. However, I'm not sure you realize that what you heard is not what I meant." The reason for misunderstanding is often that the leader's verbals don't match the nonverbals.

A communication barrier is anything that blocks the message flow so that leaders and followers do not get the intended message. When a breakdown occurs between leaders and followers, nonproductive communication is the cause. New and better communication is needed to correct the problem. However, correction usually transpires only after the problem is recognized. The leader identifies communication barriers and works diligently to overcome them—verbally and nonverbally.

I hear you. I see you. I'm reading you right, right?

## RECOGNIZING BARRIERS

Nonproductive communication may occur because people do not want to communicate, they do not provide feedback, they fail to listen, or they try to show off their knowledge. Becoming aware of potential communication barriers is the starting point in coping with breakdowns. Anticipating, preventing, or easing them is the next logical step. Some common communication problems include allness, bypassing, ambiguity, and status.

## ALLNESS

*Allness* is a tendency leaders have when they believe that whatever they say about a particular subject is all there is to say about that topic. For example, the leader who says, "Don't confuse me with the facts; I already know what I want to know on this subject," is suffering from allness. This malady happens when either leaders or followers fail to remain objective and open-minded. It is a common affliction. Many particulars are left out of everything they say, hear, read, or write.

Therefore, as a leader, you must remember that there is always more information than what a follower has presented. There is always an *et cetera*. There is always more to say and learn. Knowing there is always more information to gain, ask questions.

It is sometimes said that men seldom ask questions. They are comfortable giving and receiving the bare facts; they are uncomfortable discussing feelings. If true, they need encouragement and no doubt training to ask questions in order to learn more, especially on the job when results are so important.

## BYPASSING

*Bypassing* is the tendency to not recognize that one word can have different meanings and that different words can have the same meanings. For example, when someone refers to death, a whole gamut of words or phrases might be used. We might hear "passed," "left this mortal life," "asleep in the Lord," "gone on before," "ceased to be," "singing with the angels," or "dead as a doornail." Yet all these words and phrases describe the same concept.

On a lighter side, to further illustrate this point, Monty Python had a famous skit with John Cleese (Mr. Praline) and Michael Palin (shop owner) about a dead parrot. Notice the euphemisms for death used by Cleese in the skit (dialect corrected by the author):

He's not pining! He's passed on! This parrot is no more! He has ceased to be! He's expired and gone to meet his maker! He's a stiff! Bereft of life, he rests in peace! If you hadn't nailed him to the perch he'd be pushing up the daisies! His metabolic processes are now history! He's off the twig! He's kicked the bucket. He's shuffled off his mortal coil, run down the curtain and joined the bleeding choir invisible! *This is an ex-parrot!*

If a leader assumes a follower is using words the same way the leader would, misunderstandings could result. Whenever leaders project their meanings into a follower's words, a communication breakdown is likely. When possible, a leader should find the most precise term to communicate meaning (i.e., avoid euphemisms). In the 1988 presidential debates, both George H. W. Bush and Michael S. Dukakis accused each other of "questionable judgment." What they really questioned was the other's competence and patriotism, yet they each employed vague language to cloak their accusations.

Thus, to be an effective leader, you have to look to people for meanings instead of to words. You must be sensitive to the way words are currently used. Meanings are in people, not in words.

## AMBIGUITY

*Ambiguity,* like bypassing, results from words meaning different things in different contexts. Consider the following: What do leaders really mean when they recommend a colleague serve on a committee by saying, "I know this person very well and cannot recommend him too highly"? Or what about a new follower's young child whose mother asked her to say grace at the noon meal?

She answered, "I don't know what to say."

"Just say what Mommy says," replied the mother.

Bowing her head, the little girl prayed, "Dear God, why did we ever invite these people to lunch?"

Leaders constantly have to deal with uncertainty and unpredictability. It is therefore imperative they develop the ability to manage ambiguity. If they do so, they can reduce project ambiguity and help teams achieve or remain productive. Managing ambiguity involves establishing ground rules, fostering communication about needs and solutions, prioritizing issues, reducing distractions of unknown factors, and solving conflict.

To be effective, you have to learn to spot statements that can have several meanings and ask the follower to clarify, paraphrase, or confirm. You must ask for specific, concrete examples to avoid conflict and confusion. You must listen without prejudice for complete understanding.

## STATUS

Communication problems also result from an involvement of different people's egos, status relationships, or positions. Status can be measured by job/profession, titles, offices, desk sizes, parking spaces, home location, car, degrees, spouse's position, and so forth. For example, a company I once consulted with had four status achievement levels. One was the type of desk a person had. A wooden desk with a glass top was better than a wooden desk without a glass top, which was better than a gray metal desk with glass on it, which was better than just a gray metal desk.

A second status level was the use of acronyms in communication. The group with the highest number of acronyms that no one else knew the meaning for was more important than those without acronyms.

In most organizations, the two primary major status determinants for leaders or followers are probably the nature of their work and the size of their paycheck. Dissatisfaction ensues when either perceives another is out of line. Therefore, as a leader, you must make sure the status ladders are aligned properly to reduce the perceived inconsistencies and get communication back on the right track. You must actively work toward overcoming anything that interferes with your relationships with followers.

## COPING WITH BARRIERS

Good communication is, at best, a difficult process. Although there are many barriers to communication, the situation is not hopeless. In fact, almost any serious effort to improve communication will have beneficial results. One of the best ways for the leader to start improving communication is to become aware of communication problems. Normal communication, as an example, often results in partial misunderstanding. Thus, decisions will be made as to how large a margin of difference in understanding can be tolerated. The leader must then learn to cope with the problems. There are at least three ways leaders and followers can cope with barriers: recognize the others' frame of reference, use feedback, and reinforce words with actions.

When overcoming most barriers, very few verbal or nonverbal communication tools rival effective listening. In fact, if more leaders were aware of the need for effective listening, they could probably double their knowledge and success. Consider the difference, for example, between hearing and listening. Someone once said that *hearing* deals with noise, whereas *listening* deals with meaning. Unfortunately, many leaders and followers seem to have trouble paying attention to one another.

Have you considered how much time you have spent developing the skills you use each day? How much time have you spent developing the skill of listening? Research indicates most people experience a 75 percent loss of information within forty-eight hours. And what is worse, as ideas are communicated from one person to another person, to another, to another, the messages are distorted by 80 percent. Based on these figures, a leader might question a follower's memory. However, it is difficult to remember what was not heard in the first place. Perhaps that is why sometimes followers seem to invent stories to tell others (while others take notes). Or why many cannot remember the name of a person they were just introduced to five minutes ago.

If you wish to be an effective listener, you must demonstrate genuine interest in what a follower is saying. If you are successful at doing that, you usually will be seen as a motivator. Followers are usually more committed to leaders who are interested in their ideas and in them personally. Most people want to be heard. If you show a willingness to listen to a follower's ideas, the follower will reciprocate. There is, after all, a time to be silent and a time to speak. And sometimes silence speaks louder than any words.

## ACTIVE LISTENING

Effective listening requires practice. Active listening relates to hearing, understanding, and responding to the message as the sender intended. Unfortunately, both leaders and followers often pretend to pay attention when they are not really listening. Research conducted in a bank and hospital in the Midwest by Dr. Marilyn Lewis, retired university professor, unveiled a difference in listening among men and women. Male managers assumed they have been heard if their listeners did what they had been told to do. Female managers assumed they had been heard if their listeners looked them in the eye.

You may have experienced similar situations. The listeners may make eye contact, smile, and nod their heads knowingly, but their minds are on another subject. Sometimes they listen to every word until the follower uses terminology that causes them to become so detached that they lose contact with what is actually being said. They become emotionally deaf.

Some leaders let their egos get in the way. They think only about what concerns them. They are not interested in a statement unless there is something in it to enhance their status. Other leaders are just lazy. They do not want to take the time or expend the energy it takes to listen.

Listening is the key to solving ethnic tensions between the Arabs and Israelis, Protestants and Catholics in Northern Ireland, the Serbs and Croats in former Yugoslavia, or the Tutsi and Hutu in Rwanda. But warring factions are so wrapped up in their own agendas that they turn a deaf ear to the valid objectives of the opposition. True leaders understand the messages they receive.

It is possible to hear but not actually receive a transmitted message. Two simple tools, however, can be used to improve active listening skills immediately: confirmation and clarification.

## Confirmation

*Confirmation* helps a leader understand exactly what was said and why. If you work on advertising projects, know these projects are becoming increasingly complex; they also involve deadlines and budgets. In such situations, a confirmation of needs, dreams, and plans are imperative. Or you may find yourself involved in a situation where there is a misunderstanding and feelings seem to be reaching a boiling point. Confirmation is needed. For example, you might say something like the following: "So are you saying you would be willing to … ?" Or, "It sounds like you are feeling some anger over this situation."

Clarification is especially helpful to a leader who disagrees with the message or is being asked to become committed to a particular program. Whenever there is doubt about what is being sent or meant, therefore, you should confirm the message. You should make sure you know what was said and why before taking action. After all, if you do not have time to get it right the first time, when will you have time to do it over?

## Clarification

When you do not understand a message or am not certain about a follower's motives, you should ask for *clarification*. It helps the speaking/listening environment if you will maintain eye contact and rephrase what you hear or ask questions about what you think was said. For example: "I do not believe I understand what you are saying. Tell me more," or, "Why do you think that?" or, "Why do you feel this way?" or simply, "Oh?" You must make sure you understand what your followers mean. That way, you will have more motivated, committed followers than those leaders who do not listen. And you will be more apt to have needs met or problems solved.

Do you remember a particular job interview during your senior year of college? Perhaps the interviewer asked a question and you were unsure as to how to respond to a question. You were afraid to ask a clarifying question because you did not wish to seem unsure or that you had something to hide. However, if you had answered minimally, you could have then asked for clarification. Who knows, perhaps the interviewer intended to make you uncomfortable to see if you would ask for clarification.

## PRESCRIPTIONS FOR BETTER LISTENING

Many opportunities arise every day to listen, confirm, respond, question, and clarify thoughts not understood. Effective leaders work to become better listeners. They concentrate, work at listening, keep an open mind, take advantage of thought speed, listen for total meaning, and are sensitive.

The first mandate for more effective listening I've discovered is to concentrate, to force attention, to focus on the subject. You must neither yield to distractions nor tolerate or create interferences. If interruptions do occur, you should take them in stride and return attention to the speaker. You must not pretend to pay attention. Instead, you must try to develop a sincere interest in the ideas being communicated. You must find purpose in every listening situation. You must learn to adjust to various listening situations and to different speaking rates. In short, you have to work at listening and get actively involved with what is happening.

An active listener can aid the speaker by creating a nonthreatening climate. You must attempt to not be critical, evaluative, or moralizing. Instead, you must try to develop a climate of equality, understanding, acceptance, and warmth. An open attitude is also important. It is possible to become overly emotional by reacting to certain words, but it is possible for a leader to learn to temper enthusiasm by not getting overstimulated about certain subjects. Avoiding arguments and criticizing a speaker's delivery before the idea has been fully developed will also help to maintain emotional stability.

We think as much as six times faster than the average person speaks. Thus, you must take advantage of the thought-speaking time difference to make mental summaries and increase attention span. You should also review what is heard and seen, focusing on the nonverbal as well as the verbal by noticing all cues. You must use thought speed for productive listening, not daydreaming or texting.

In short, you must listen for total meaning. Both the content and tone of a message are necessary for complete understanding of what a follower means. At least three skills are important: listen for main ideas as well as facts, identify supportive elements, and analyze the message's basic elements. It also helps to find a natural link between the questions asked and the responses received. The primary objective of listening is to listen in depth. You must learn to respond to the feeling or attitude underlying the message and become involved with the follower's message and actions.

Sensitive listening can assist your relationships with followers. When tone is more important than content, you should respond in a manner that is sensitive to the feelings of the followers communicating. Sensitivity can be thought of as the ability to predict what others will feel, say, or do. Your expression of sensitivity creates a supportive climate. It allows you to detect and cope with communication barriers. It also provides the followers and you with greater satisfaction.

Closely tied to active listening is a technique that will help improve the listening/speaking process: Avoid speaking in an abrasive manner. Abrasive language evokes distrust in listeners and instills fear. It results in listeners not being eager to follow the leader speaking. King Solomon wrote, "Rash language cuts and maims, but there is healing in the words of the wise" (Proverbs 12:18, MSG). And he followed that thought with another gem: "A gentle response defuses anger, but a sharp tongue kindles a temper-fire" (Proverbs 15:1, MSG). Or as my mother used to say, "Keep a civil tongue in your head!"

## NONVERBAL COMMUNICATION

Nonverbal communication has much to do with the way leaders perceive and respond to followers. Since a leader's ability to communicate goes far beyond the ability to speak, understanding the nature of body language provides another technique to achieve understanding. Success depends, in part, on sensitivity to the feelings of others and on competence, sincerity, trustworthiness, and interests. A leader's nonverbals must match the words expressed. No one can accept an apology from someone who is saying it grudgingly. To illustrate: When Judge Lance Ito made lawyers Marcia Clark and F. Lee Bailey apologize to one another during the O.J. Simpson trial for yet another angry confrontation in the courtroom, did either of them really believe the other's apology?

Some of those nonverbal cues included crossed arms, typically implying resistance. There were nose rubs, which is often linked to deception. There were instances when hands were placed on chins, signaling a decision is being made. There also were back-of-the-neck scratches, which can suggest there are still questions and concerns in someone's mind.

The conclusion from nonverbal communication research suggests people are constantly communicating information about themselves. Tone and inflection of voices, facial expressions, body positions, and gestures speak very clearly. Such nonverbals significantly affect sending and receiving messages. The specific signals that alert individuals as to what to send or how to receive are cues. On a basic level, consider the role of a mime. Without uttering a single syllable, such an actor can communicate a message and a variety of emotions. Communication that incorporates verbal and nonverbal elements is chock-full of meaning at many different levels.

## CUES

Nonverbal cues are signals that do not require a person's concentrated efforts. These cues may be intentional or unintentional. The expressions of feelings, emotions, and attitudes are nonverbal and can rarely be concealed from others. Messages frequently consist of intentions that are logically inconsistent with the verbally professed statements. That may be why some leaders, for example, practice cues and even include hand motion comments in their outlines of speeches they will give. Sincerity is probably the key to all communication cues. Forgetting yourself and focusing on others helps you to make natural, graceful cues.

If, for example, I have difficulty communicating my thoughts and feelings by verbal symbols, I will communicate by means of nonverbal symbols (e.g., body language). Two concepts are especially pertinent.

First, leaders cannot *not* communicate. Nonverbal cues go out constantly: face muscles tighten, eyes dart, arms are crossed, bodies turn away, nostrils flare, lips curl, etc. Second, if a leader says one thing and the nonverbals signal something else, people will pay more attention to the nonverbals. It is similar to the follower who is coerced into compromising over a conflict but whose body language sends a defiant message that says, "I'm right, despite what I'm saying!"

Only a very small portion of a message is transmitted by words (perhaps 10 percent or less). The majority of a message is non-verbal—tone of voice, facial expression, and body motion. It is no wonder followers pay more attention to what leaders do than what they say. Leaders are aware of the nonverbal ways of reacting to situations. They understand what others are experiencing and their circumstances. Through nonverbal communication, they discover when to communicate and what to say, as well as when to listen. American philosopher and poet Ralph Waldo Emerson's statement is still true: "What you are speaks so loudly I can't hear what you say." With that in mind, consider how the following areas of nonverbal communication provide cues.

## BODY MOTIONS

The study of body motions (kinesics) concerns five primary areas: the face, gestures, posture, body shape and type, and physical attractiveness. Each of these areas provokes certain actions from others and may assist or impede communication.

### *The Face*

The face is the most visible indicator of emotions and feelings. With more than a hundred possible expressions, the face accurately reflects one's feelings toward others and provides feedback on others' comments. My wife claims that when I'm angry about something, my language may be controlled, but my nostrils flare.

### *Eye Contact*

Perhaps the part of the face most likely to yield information is the eyes. Rolling one's eyes, for example, says a lot, and it may be different in different situations. When communicating with followers or establishing or maintaining relationships, you must attempt to increase eye contact—but not stare. Contact at the eye level needs to be broken every so often. Sometimes I look at a follower's forehead if it is difficult to keep focused on the eyes.

## Gestures

Gestures can express one message or an entire language. Although the hands are most prominent, the whole body can send a message. Successful leaders confirm that followers send nonverbal messages of acceptance or reflection of messages by folding or unfolding their arms, leaning forward or reclining in their chairs, crossing or uncrossing their legs, or checking the time. Gestures can be large, expansive, assertive, and outgoing, or they can be limited, self-protective, and close to the body. But, as with mimes, every movement has meaning.

## Posture

Posture also provides information. The way one sits, stands, walks, or lies down expresses feelings, interest, involvement, or tension. Body language, as well as physical barriers, can be used to get rid of time-wasting office guests. For example, I may rise and remain standing when a follower enters my office (making the visitor reluctant to sit), signaling this visit will have to be short. Holding a pen or pencil at the ready implies I am about to write something important and am eager to get on with it. If I raise an eyebrow, I may be signaling irritation, disbelief, a desire to get back to the business at hand, or a tell-me-more attitude.

My posture tells whether I wish to include or exclude others in my thoughts or conversations, whether I am open or closed to certain ideas. My posture expresses whether I am warm toward certain people, whether I like or dislike certain ideas, and whether

I can become emotionally involved. My posture also says something about my role and status in certain groups. Standing erect or slouching may indicate an appropriate pecking order in U. S. culture.

## Body Types

There are three general body types: ectomorph (frail, thin, and tall), endomorph (fat, round, and short), and mesomorph (muscular, athletic, and tall). Most people stereotype one of these physiques. For example, research suggests that ectomorphs are tense, suspicious of others, nervous, pessimistic, and quiet. Endomorphs are talkative, old-fashioned, sympathetic, weak, dependent, and trusting. Some researchers contend endomorphs encounter negative prejudice in job interviews and promotional decisions. And, in fact, a number of endomorphs are taking their employers to court and charging them with job bias. Mesomorphs are stereotyped as handsome, adventurous, mature, and self-reliant. Look at the models used in advertising to help you understand this stereotype. At least 90 percent are mesomorphs. Anyone can exhibit characteristics of all three groups. Leaders do not let societal attitudes affect the way they relate to each of these types of people.

## Physical Attractiveness

In today's world, physical attractiveness is a factor in nonverbal communication. Body color, smell, hair length, and clothing influence the quality and quantity of communication that occurs among people. Based solely on physical appearance, many people will make decisions regarding dating, courtship, and marriage, not to mention hiring and firing. For example, it is believed many leaders put people through testing programs during interviews to weed out weak candidates and then hire the tallest person. However, one does not have to be physically attractive to be either an effective leader or follower. Albanian catholic nun Mother Theresa (Agnes Gonxhe Bojaxhin) was not physically beautiful, but she was an excellent communicator.

Americans tend to overemphasize the externals. President Abraham Lincoln, for example, would not have looked good on television with his deeply lined face. President William Howard Taft's weight exceeded three hundred pounds. How would he appeal to today's voters? How would voters today react to President Franklin Delano Roosevelt in a wheelchair? We know how the left-wing media reacted to President George W. Bush and presidential candidate Sarah Palin. All you had to do was watch Tina Fey and the *Saturday Night Live* cast to see what a job they were doing on those two individuals, funny though it was intended to be. The effective leader does not relegate people to the desk and keep them out of leadership opportunities because of their appearance, mannerisms, physical limitations, or ungraceful words.

## SPACE

Spatial relationships (proxemics) also affect the quality and quantity of communication among people. Distances between leaders and followers (arrangement of furniture in homes, classrooms, and offices) may enhance or stifle understanding. A leader sitting behind, beside, or away from the desk may convey different messages, depending on where that person is sitting.

Personal space varies among nationalities. Americans, who tend to talk at arms' length, mark off a generous amount of personal space in which to operate. However, members of other nationalities customarily interact within inches of each other. That is why you may find Americans backing up when speaking to Latinos or Arabs.

Space is often referred to as territory, which assumes certain ownership rights of an area without any legal basis. Examples of territory might include a certain chair in a classroom, a parking space, an easy chair at home, a pew at church, and so forth. Any invader of territory is apt to be treated with suspicion or exasperation. For example, my wife once seated herself on a certain pew at a church where I had been invited to speak. We were early, and my wife found what she thought would be a perfect spot to hear (and later critique) me. About five minutes before the service started, a petite older lady walked down the aisle to the pew where my wife was sitting and stood at the edge of the pew, shuffling and looking lost. My wife noticed her and said, "I'm sorry. Did I get your seat?"

The elderly lady responded, "I've been sitting there for twenty years." My wife apologized and found another seat. Apparently no one could sit on that pew except that lady.

Territory can be employed to convey an aura of power. Some leaders' offices may be viewed almost as shrines by easily impressed visitors or followers. I once worked with an individual who had a small stage built in his office for his desk and chair. That way, when someone entered his office, they had to look up at him on his throne. All the chairs in the room were below the desk so he could look down on everyone who came to visit and sit in a chair.

Of course, such attempts to demonstrate superiority may have a boomerang effect—some visitors or followers may see a quest for power and/or a waste of budget. The effective leader uses space to enhance communication, not to indicate power.

## CONCLUSION

Communication is similar to every other leadership topic or issue. It begins with the speaker's and listener's values. In fact, you can usually judge the values held by the way a person says certain things or the outcome of the person who heard what was said. Communication flows smoothly from an effective leader.

By now, you understand that we communicate meaning not only verbally but also nonverbally, in symbolic ways. You will need to possess an understanding of the various nonverbal social and cultural differences on the job. You also must have knowledge of body motion and kinesic behavior, chronemics and the use of time, proxemics and spatial relationships, paralanguage and the human voice. Because we associate certain roles with certain body types, our transmission and reception of information can be enhanced or distorted by our stereotypes. The way people dress, cut, or brush their hair often determines the amount of information shared. Sending, receiving, and understanding messages between an "insider" and an "outsider" are likely to be quite different than if both were communicating to the group in which they hold membership. In one sense, dress is an exercise in status display.

If you are aware of these nonverbal messages, you have another technique for more effective communication with followers. In fact, body language appears to be the basis for communicating effectively with others. Understanding this area of communication should aid your attempts at decoding both nonverbal and verbal messages.

You must remember: You cannot *not* communicate. And meanings are in people, *not* words.

# ISN'T IT GOOD TO BE THE KING?

## POWER AND INFLUENCE

[Nelson] Mandela believed that embracing his rivals was a way of controlling them: they were more dangerous on their own than within his circle of influence. He cherished loyalty, but he was never obsessed by it. After all, he used to say "people act in their own interest." It was simply a fact of human nature, not a flaw or a defect … Mandela recognized that the way to deal with those he didn't trust was to neutralize them with charm.

—Richard Stengel, managing editor of *Time* magazine

His dominion is an eternal dominion; his kingdom endures from generation to generation. All the peoples of the earth are regarded as nothing. He does as he pleases with the powers of heaven and the peoples of the earth. No one can hold back his hand or say to him: "What have you done?"

Daniel 4:34–35 (NIV)

One of those things that surprises me in working with business leaders over the years is how few of them have a theory of influence. They are paid to some extent to change the behavior of a large group of people and get them aligned to execute the decision. That process means influence. Unfortunately, too many leaders have confused influencing people with talking them into doing something. After all, it's good to be the king.

Can you imagine what it would be like to discover that your heart surgeon is working off a "gut hunch" about how to conduct the bypass you need? Do you think you could talk a smoker or drinker into quitting by making a verbal presentation? Or what about the leaders I've seen who make a few speeches and think they've done all they need to do to influence their followers? What about those who publish platitudes as their mission and values statements and file them in a filing cabinet, assuming they've influenced everyone to do what was written? "I said it, so let it be so."

Who do you know who has power and influence? Is it the big, handsome guy in the Armani suit with a cigar in hand or the short, trim guy in a Sears suit with a cigarette in hand? Is it the short, dumpy woman from Pepperdine University or the tall, statuesque woman from Baylor University? If you have viewed them in action, would your opinion change? How much power do you have? How much do you want?

---

Power is central to the study of leadership. If a group exists, there is a power structure. High-status people in a group influence behavior. Nineteenth-century German philosopher Friedrich Nietzsche observed, "Wherever I found the living, there I found the will to power." But power is usually thought of as one of people's less attractive characteristics. It connotes self-serving, manipulative behavior. "Power corrupts, and absolute power corrupts absolutely" and "He who has the gold makes the rules" are sayings often heard in discussions of power.

According to Suzanne Kryder, the following statements describe the most common one-hit wonder power styles. Does one of these sound like you?

- "I'm very participative. I want input from everyone on my staff, even if they don't feel comfortable giving it."

- "I tell people what to do. That's my job. My boss expects me to run the show and get results."

- "I care more about my employees than their work. I'm always available to help, even with their personal problems."

- "I'm hands-off. My people know what they're doing. They don't want me meddling in their work."

When Thomas Phillips was CEO of Raytheon, he says he observed that power was displayed in three distinctive forms: military power generated by high tech, personal power exerted in a leadership context, and spiritual power exhibited in the transformation of people's lives. Concerning his own power, he says, "I wanted to create an atmosphere in which people could come and talk with me about any failures they had without fear of being fired."

Power can be used to influence behavior, and some types of power are more likely to produce compliance and commitment than other types. If you have that power, you should be able to connect with people, handle difficult people and situations, know how to overcome unusual situations, change other people's behavior, influence others intentionally, and create win/win outcomes.

Once you understand that leadership is a function of power, you will recognize that the components of power can influence the behavior of others.

Gary Yukl conducted a scholarly analysis of leadership, power, and effectiveness. His summary of that research indicates the following:

> Descriptive research on the use of different forms of power by leaders suggests that effective leaders rely more on personal power than on position power. Nevertheless, position power is still important, and it interacts in complex ways with personal power to determine a leader's influence on subordinates. The potential to use position power for influence attempts with peers of superiors is much more limited, and her personal power is clearly the predominate source of power.

The amount of power—personal or positional—will depend on the leader, type of organization, task to be accomplished, and followers. A leader's successful outcomes often depend on the way she or he uses power and influence on others.

## POWER

*Power* is the capacity to influence others to do something they would not have done without having been influenced. It is intangible, multifaceted, elusive, and invisible. Yet it can be felt in a person, a group, an organization, or a country. For example, I was once in a room full of young Republicans waiting for a presidential candidate to arrive. I could literally feel the power of this man as he walked into the room with his entourage. It was a heady moment, even though he wasn't the most popular of US presidents. The power was almost palpable. I've experienced those same feelings when a governor entered a room.

*Influence* is the ability to change someone's behavior through words or actions. *Power* is the ability to positively or successfully exert that influence, which, in turn, enhances one's status. *Status* is the ability to exercise power, to influence decisions and outcomes. Some people know how to *acquire* power. They are able to know where power exists, use their abilities to obtain it, and avoid actions that will decrease it. Their *use* of power depends on their status, influence, situation, or need to exercise that power (for good *or* evil). Effective leaders use their power to *empower* others. They do not tie people's hands. Instead, they provide members with the knowledge, skills, information, resources, and support to accomplish goals. They give people credit for being able to think, reason, plan, and implement those plans. As a result, followers will take a more vested interest in their work and its impact.

Most people do not like to admit they want power. Those who have it often go to endless lengths to mask the fact. Some US presidents, like Lyndon Johnson, Bill Clinton, or Barack Obama, seemingly relish the trappings of power. But the American style of power is to pretend that you have none. To confess that you *have* power is to make yourself responsible for using it. Safety lies in an artfully contrived pose of impotence, behind which you can do exactly as you please. Most organizational members do not admit to seeking power. Once they have it, though, few willingly give it up. Most elected officials tend to run again or go on to other higher offices if they keep their noses clean. The possession of power is one of the surest roads to promotion and success.

Power is inherent in all organizations. It can be exercised vertically, horizontally, or circularly. *Vertical power* is represented by hierarchy—up and down the organization, top management to the lowest employee, or vice versa. Hierarchical power is perhaps best represented in the Catholic church, with its system of members, priests, monsignors, bishops, archbishops, cardinals, and the pope.

The focus is on position and dominance, control, its outcome, and submission to authority.

*Horizontal power* pertains to relationships across the organization—vice president to vice president, manager to manager, department to department. The focus is on joint problem solving and coordination of workflow. It typically relates to task coordination, information sharing, decision making, and conflict resolution.

*Circular power* views the leader as a resource member or enabler of a team. To illustrate: Formal and informal relationships are recognized and appreciated. Differences are valued and respected. Although leaders are expected to be knowledgeable and competent, followers are viewed as having skills and important abilities also. The focus must be on people, purpose, renewal, and growth. Such a structure depends on a trusting relationship between leaders and followers.

## INTERPERSONAL SOURCES OF POWER

Nobel Peace Prize recipient Henry Kissinger called power the supreme aphrodisiac. Such stimulating discussions of power perhaps explain the downfall of many a leader. Consider the twenty-five-year president of a Christian college in Mississippi who was considered a quiet, humble, rock-solid moral authority. Yet he was also said to have full, complete, and absolute power over the college and its board of trustees. Labeled by the media as a modern-day "Bible Belt Jekyll and Hyde," he apparently believed he *was* the college and could do *whatever* he wanted. Details of an alleged secret life indicated offshore bank accounts, far-flung liaisons with prostitutes, pornographic literature in his files, and a vial of strychnine. Power offers such subtle temptations, especially when one is able to wield virtually unchallenged authority.

How much does one really know about power and powerful people? For example, is it possible to understand why the trappings of power would lead to the arrest of Galleon founder Raj Raja-ratnam, who was involved in a network of back-channel dealings between prominent hedge fund managers and senior executives in the high-tech industry? He was charged with masterminding the largest insider-trading racket in decades. Why would Mark Kurland, cofounder of New Castle Funds, a $1 billion hedge fund investment firm, engage in conspiracy and securities fraud and be sentenced to more than two years in prison?

Why would Hector Ruiz, the former CEO of Advanced Micro Devices (AMD), provide insider information about the spinoff of the company's manufacturing business, Global Foundries? Ruiz resigned. No charges have been filed. Why would Robert Moffat, senior vice president at IBM, get involved in conspiracy and securities fraud? Why would he provide inside information about deals in the works and about financial results at AMD, Lenovo, and IBM to the woman he was sleeping with? Why would he become ensnared in one of Wall Street's largest hedge fund insider trading cases? Power is entrancing and can lead to erroneous decisions, affairs, insider trading, and fraud.

The classic model for understanding such interpersonal power is referent, legitimate, expert, reward, and coercive power.

## REFERENT POWER

*Referent power* is that power granted to a leader because the group accepts that person's influence. They identify with and admire the leader who serves as a reference point of how to think and act. People respond voluntarily to her or his requests, perhaps because of charisma. They place power in this person to make the right decisions about behavior standards, attitudes, or values. You can increase your referent power by being fair, developing credibility, building a high *esprit de corps,* and communicating informally.

Referent power may be used by the leader of only a few people, or it could be demonstrated by someone like Gandhi. Such power is gained if you have strong interpersonal relationship skills. You will revoke desired responses because of the trust existing between you and others. You will have the ability to influence followers because of respect, loyalty, admiration, and affection.

## LEGITIMATE POWER

*Legitimate power* involves an authority relationship whereby leaders have the right to make certain decisions because of their position. Formal organizational mechanisms have invested power in these individuals. These leaders are authorized (i.e., delegated the authority) to make decisions by law, a higher status level, or a group. The recipients of their influence view such decisions as right (e.g., the president of the United States, CEO and/or president of a company, chancellor of a university, or director of a non-profit organization). I've known college professors who see their role as teaching to fail students and grading subjectively so there can be no student recourse.

You can increase your legitimate power through a climate of trust, respect, and honor. You also can strengthen your legitimate power base via compassion, consistency, integrity, kindness, openness, and patience. Legitimate power does, however, require agreement on both.

## EXPERT POWER

*Expert power* comes into recognition as workgroups mature and someone becomes competent in a given area. That person possesses special knowledge to solve a problem, perform a task, or decide on a future course of action. Others see this person as someone with superior ability because of specialized knowledge, information, or skills. Whether by college major, hobby, experience, or apprenticeship, and so on, they look to this person as an expert. Expert power is especially important in our information age.

Although a football quarterback may gain legitimate power when the coach says, "You're it!" he must demonstrate ability on the job to have expert power. Teammates must see that he reads defenses and calls plays accurately. He then becomes a leader in fact as well as in name. Such was the case with Super Bowl wins by Steve Young, San Francisco 49ers, 1995; Troy Aikman, Dallas Cowboys, 1993 and 1994; and Drew Brees, New Orleans Saints, 2010.

## REWARD POWER

*Reward power* is a person's ability to obtain desired responses by offering payoffs. The rewards may be formal, such as pay raises, promotions, pats on the back, enticing prizes, or gold stars. Or they may be informal, like special recognitions, the granting of a favor, or dinner for a job well done. "Payments" are usually determined by position. The individual with reward power has control over the distribution of rewards and negative sanctions. But this type of power is useful only if others value the rewards offered. For example, the power to determine a course grade has aspects of both reward *and* coercion if students see an *A* as reward and *D* or *F* as penalty. The question is, do you want "the carrot or the stick?"

## COERCIVE POWER

*Coercive power* results from the belief that failure to follow directions will result in punishment, reprimand, suspension, demotion, or dismissal. Thus, while some followers increase productivity to gain a higher salary (i.e., respond to reward power), others may also increase productivity to escape being fired (i.e., respond to coercion). Coercive power, like poor parenting, produces fear and often provides no way to escape what a leader desires. Uncontrolled, coercive power is seldom a pleasant sight and often results in ostracism. An exception might be during an emergency when you must insist an employee evacuate the building "now" or give you their keys and leave the building with security. There is no discussion.

A leader's coercive power is contingent on the follower's perceptions of how probable it is that the leader will exact punishment for noncompliance and the degree of negative consequences such punishment will entail. It should be noted, however: Coercive power will gain compliance, but it will not create motivation. If, for example, you insist on enforcing your authority and neglect things like organizational mission, goal achievement, empowerment, and open communication, you shouldn't be surprised to see followers leave for other, more "user-friendly" jobs.

## THE FIVE POWER SOURCES

Of these five power sources, referent and expert power are thought to best support a positive work climate. However, any of the five can get the job done, depending on the situation you may be in at the moment. Note:

1. Expert power is more strongly and consistently related to satisfaction and performance than is any other type of power.

2. Legitimate power, along with expert power, is ranked as important but is an inconsistent factor in determining organizational effectiveness.

3. Referent power is of less importance for complying with leader directives but is positively correlated with organizational effectiveness.

4. Reward power is also of less importance for complying with leader directives and has an inconsistent correlation with performance.

5. Coercive power is the least valuable in bringing about compliance and is negatively related to organizational effectiveness.

Power-hungry leaders seldom recognize the needs of others. The others are necessary only for increasing their personal power. The president of a nonprofit organization in Texas, for example, was notorious for running over people, using their talents as long as it met his needs, and then getting rid of them when they were no longer useful for his purposes. Is it any doubt that the followers felt powerless in the face of such a leader? They were without the informal power that their formal roles demanded.

## STRUCTURAL AND SITUATIONAL SOURCES OF POWER

Most discussions of power center on its interpersonal nature. However, power may also be determined by the situation and the design of an organization's structure (e.g., division of labor or departmentalization). That is, decisions are made as to *who* does *what*. Not everyone involved in a job can or should do the same thing. Followers behave more productively as their tasks become specialized. They increase their effectiveness when they have a single, planned, and directed activity to move toward (i.e., a unity of direction).

Structural and situational power sources include information, knowledge, resources, and decision making.

## INFORMATION

The person who possesses information also possesses power. Leaders or followers who control information about current operations, possess information about alternative possibilities, or acquire knowledge about the future have enormous power to influence others. The leader who has information that may be of use to the followers and decides to withhold that information exerts a controlling power over the followers. Children know this instinctively. Remember triumphantly saying something like, "I know something you don't know," "I'm not telling you my secret," "Guess what? Guess! Nope, not it"?

## KNOWLEDGE

If information is power, it follows that knowledge is power. The speed and rate of the growth of knowledge have been phenomenal over the last two decades. However, the knowledge explosion places pressures on today's leaders that their predecessors only fifty years ago did not have. Witness all the thrillers in the bookstore dealing with espionage and all the arrests for political and industrial spying. Organizations that depend on highly sophisticated databases can easily become obsolete, unless planned change efforts are continuous. Thus, while knowledge is important, wisdom is crucial.

Greek historian Herodutus said that the bitterest pain is to have much knowledge but no power, yet to have knowledge without wisdom may be bitter indeed. A leader's power is the product of legitimate power multiplied by the ability to use knowledge competently. The competent use of knowledge, however, implies wisdom. As poet laureate Alfred Lord Tennyson wrote, "Knowledge comes, but wisdom lingers."

## RESOURCES

A number of resources affect power in an organization (e.g., financial, physical, human, intangible, structure, culture). Which resources are most important depend on the leader, followers, and situation. Typically, the most effective and best-liked leaders are those who command more of an organization's resources, who bring something valuable from outside into the group, and who have access to information affecting the group.

## DECISION MAKING

Decision making is choosing between alternatives. The way problems are solved affects what happens not only to the decision maker but also to those who are led. To the extent that followers can affect some part of the decision process, they acquire power. That is why some followers want the right to make a decision or have some say in it, and others shirk the risk and responsibility. Does "no taxation without representation" make you want a cup of British tea for some reason? The colonists wanted some input in their own taxation process, you'll recall.

Most models of decision making include defining the problem, analyzing the problem, establishing criteria for a solution, proposing possible solutions, evaluating the alternatives, selecting a solution, and plotting a course of action. Because decisions involve risk, it should be noted that mistakes are seldom final and devastating. Often, they are effective teachers.

Thomas Edison, inventor, tried at least six thousand vegetables, 1,600 minerals, monkey's hair, and even the hair from a mustache until he hit upon the answer—a carbon-impregnated cotton thread that had been baked in a furnace—for a lightbulb filament. If a decision was wrong or it did not work, Edison was willing to admit failure and cut losses. Leaders do not compound a bad decision with blind determination to make it work. Recalls of a product and negative publicity or articles in the media are such examples. Our slips are always available for the world to see in any given twenty-four-hour period. That is why some people recommend the servant-leader model of leadership as an alternative to the power model.

## THE SERVANT-LEADER MODEL

A *servant leader* is someone who helps followers by working on their behalf for goal achievement. Mother Theresa was such a person. In a *Life* magazine article, she said she was but "a little pencil in the hand of God." The servant-leader model and movement was formulated by Robert Greenleaf. It was his view that leadership derives naturally from a commitment to serve others—followers, customers, and community. Key values of a servant leader's behavior normally include integrity, humility, empathy, fairness, and empowerment.

Servant leadership is based on a high level of selflessness. The leader becomes the follower at the lowest rung of the corporate ladder in order to serve others. It is successful if followers become wiser, healthier, and more autonomous. The end result is positive performance and longevity.

Four basic guidelines make up the foundation of servant leadership:

1. *Help followers discover the strength of their inner spirit and their potential to make a difference.* Servant leaders acquire empathy for the circumstances of others and are willing to show vulnerabilities.

2. *Earn and keep followers' trust.* Be honest and true to your word. Servant leaders need no hidden agendas, and they are willing to give up power, rewards, recognition, and control.

3. *Help others rather than attain power and control over them.* Doing what's right for others takes precedence over protecting personal position. Servant leaders make decisions to further the good of their followers rather than promote their own interests.

4. *Listen effectively.* Do not impose your will on followers. Instead, listen carefully to the problems others are facing and then engage the group to find the best course of action. Servant leaders affirm their confidence in others.

The servant-leader framework is based on stewardship. Historically, stewardship was the responsibility of taking care of someone's needs. It also referred to planning for and taking care of the environment and all things pertaining to it. Notably, stewardship was taking care of something owned by someone else. The term then began to be used as a follower-focused form of leadership that embodied allowing followers to make decisions and having control over their jobs. The key to stewardship, according to Springfield College professor Robert Lussier and University of Virginia professor Christopher Achua, is based on four supporting values:

1. *Strong teamwork orientation*—self-managed teams of core employees and the leader work together to formulate goals and strategies for a changing environment and marketplace.

2. *Decentralized decision making and power*—authority and decision making are decentralized down to where work gets done and employees interact with customers.

3. *Equality assumption*—there is perceived equality (i.e., a partnership of equals) between leaders and followers; honesty, respect, and mutual trust prevail.

4. *Reward assumption*—the compensation system must be redesigned to match rewards to actual performance. Those with more responsibility and authority are compensated accordingly.

Servant leadership is based on a strong ethical viewpoint that we all have a moral duty to help and support each other. It values service from the bottom as well as the top and involves coaching followers to do the leading. Followers are empowered by leaders.

It should be noted, however, that there are some limitations to the servant-leader theory—organizational incompatibility with the welfare of followers, use of drastic measures in times of economic turndowns, and competition for high performance, productivity, and wealth creation. There is some evidence to indicate servant leadership may be more appropriate in health care, education, religious organizations, and government organizations than in business corporations. However, the potential benefits of servant leadership may outweigh its limitations.

## CONCLUSION

The true measure of you, as a leader, is not in terms of the power you wield. It is the power released in others—the power to decide and accomplish goals and grow. Follower satisfaction is increased when you empower your followers, not subjugate them. Power is a two-edged sword. Used properly, it motivates; used improperly, it creates problems.

You should consider the use of a servant-leader model when appropriate to get others to accept ownership and accountability for the well-being of the organization. If you are a believer in the Bible, you might find it interesting that the word *servant* or its derivative can be found 794 times, depending on which translation is used. The word *leader* or its derivative can only be found 372 times, depending on which translation. (I used *Young's Concordance of the New International Version* to capture these numbers.)

Are you a fan of power leadership or servant-leadership?

# ARE WE ALL IN THIS TOGETHER?

## TEAMS AND TEAMWORK

The main ingredient in stardom is the rest of the team.

—John Wooden,
former UCLA basketball coach,
winner of ten NCAA National Championships

Jesus went upon a mountainside and called to him those he wanted, and they came to him. He appointed twelve—designating them apostles—that they might be with him and that he might send them out to preach and to have authority to drive out demons. These are the twelve he appointed: Simon (to whom he gave the name Peter); James, son of Zebedee and his brother John (to them he gave the name Boanerges, which means Sons of Thunder); Andrew, Philip, Bartholomew, Matthew, Thomas, James, son of Alphaeus, Thaddaeus, Simon the Zealot and Judas Iscariot, who betrayed him.

Mark 3:13–19 (NIV)

There I was, standing in a circle with fifteen other men and women who were attending a four-month city leadership program. That day was the final exercise before we "graduated" from the program. The facilitators were holding a dozen beanbags and telling us that we were going to learn how to juggle. I was thinking, *I'll believe that when I see it.*

One of the facilitators threw a bag across the circle to me. I was then to toss the bag up and over to another participant and so on until everyone had "juggled" the bean bag. That bag was then thrown up and back to the facilitators. This process was repeated a number of times, adding more and more bags each time, until bags were flying up everywhere. We were unable to predict where the next bag was coming from because there were so many being thrown at the same time. Lose attention for even a moment and you were apt to get hit in the face or some other part of your anatomy. It was chaotic.

The goal was to juggle the bags without dropping any and completing the exercise as fast as possible. As we were continually challenged to improve our performance, people kept dropping bags. Gratefully, an end to this madhouse experiment was called, and another of the facilitators began a discussion of what we had learned from that exercise.

What did I learn that morning? Trust among participants was enhanced. Bonding was hastened. There was no attempt to humiliate anyone, and no one was angry because of missing a bag thrown at them. It was possible to have fun while making fun of others or them making fun of me. We were ready for the next exercise.

Have you ever participated in a group that did something similar? What did *you* learn? Were you able to take anything back to the workplace with you? Did you learn anything new about how to focus on other ways to complete tasks and increase production?

Sometimes the words *teams, teamwork, groups, workgroups,* and *group work* are overused and loosely applied. As we will use the primary words, a team is a workgroup that relies on collaboration to achieve success and achievement. A group is two or more people (no more than twenty) interacting with one another, face to face. However, while all teams are groups, not all groups are teams.

Did you ever see the 1977 Steven Spielberg-directed movie *Close Encounters of the Third Kind?* The cryptic statement in the movie ads was "We are not alone." I'm not going to deal with intergalactic beings, but the idea behind *Close Encounters* is also true in organizational life. We are not alone. We constantly work with others. If we are successful in relating to others, chances are good we'll succeed on the job as a group or team leader. We'll be able to juggle a number of things in the air in the midst of chaos without dropping any of them. Why? Because we're all in this together.

## GROUPS

Have you ever figured how many groups you belong to? Probably more than you think. There's family, your spouse's family, education, religion, work, hobby, civic, committees, and sports teams. Business is interested in improving the productivity of groups. Educators are interested in studying the classroom as a social group and the pecking order of people within the groups. The government is interested in small-group activity.

If you have now cataloged all the groups you belong to, ask yourself why you are a member of certain groups and not others. Did you join any of these groups because of family, peer pressure, a desire to be known and seen, or a fear of loneliness? Or did you join because of talents, interests, citizenship, or patriotism? Do these groups do anything for you? If so, what behavioral needs do they satisfy?

## GROUP DEVELOPMENT

Groups play a major role in personal lives, business, and society. The most common and popular description of this process was proposed by American psychologist Bruce Tuckman and contains four stages. I have taken the liberty of adding a fifth stage.

1. Forming

2. Storming

3. Norming

4. Performing

5. Assessing

## *Stage 1—Forming*

Individual behavior is driven by a desire to be accepted by others, to avoid controversy, and to avoid conflict. Forming begins with the initial appointment of a group, getting to know each other, and reviewing the purpose of the group. Stage 1 involves both a task- and relationship-orientation. People try to identify the job that is to be done. They are interested in getting to know one another, feeling comfortable with one another, and discovering acceptable interpersonal behaviors. Many of these activities could be labeled task- and relationship-orientation.

## *Stage 2—Storming*

Some conflict occurs regarding personal issues. A person's patience breaks, and minor confrontations arise as members begin to confront the issues. Intragroup conflict arises over leadership, power, and influence. During this time, group members may become hostile toward one another, express their individuality, and resist group structure. Confrontation may occur in part because of inability to decide on a goal. Even though members may desire closeness, there is often considerable goal ambiguity and anxiety during the first two stages. As problems arise, role conflict, projection of blame, and confrontation become evident. At this point, mutual support is often sought. The group is adjusting and shifting. Fortunately, the majority of confrontations are easily handled.

## Stage 3—Norming

Cohesiveness begins to develop. New standards and rules of behavior and interaction evolve. The group has overcome some of the initial issues and personality differences. People begin to take responsibility for the actions and the outcomes expected.

Norms are the informal rules groups adopt for regulating member behaviors. Examples of these norms can be dress code, language expectations, types of jokes accepted, formal/informal behaviors, etc. The social norms tend to be established and maintained through body language and nonverbal communication. Failure to stick to the rules can result in severe punishments, the most feared of which is exclusion from the group.

The norms have been established. Can you live with these norms? What if it involves you always having to be the designated driver at company parties?

## Stage 4—Performing

Group energy is channeled into the work to be done. Group identity, loyalty, and morale are high. All are task and relationship focused. The group has become adept at making decisions and proposing solutions. Cohesion, compromise, and harmony are sought. Task conflicts are avoided. People begin to accept each other and the job. They become close, an entity. An open exchange of information begins. They try to effect compromises between factions to preserve at least the illusion of unity. They begin to work in a personal, intimate, and supportive climate. When cohesion has been attained, the result is often lower absenteeism and turnover and higher group performance.

## Stage 5—Assessing

The reason for adding a fifth stage is because this step is often omitted. The group has reached closure, and their work is at an end. The group members are proud of what has been achieved and are glad to have been part of the experience. It's time to move on to another activity and goal assignment. This establishes the work group as a problem-solving instrument. Solutions to the task begin to emerge. Members gain insight and find new directions for self-growth. A degree of maturity is evident. The dropping of personal defenses encourages people to take responsibility for their own problems and for what happens. The members know whom they'd like to work with again (or not) and in what capacity. Talents are recognized, weaknesses (deficiencies) are exposed, and assessment prepares the group for beginning again.

One of the reasons it is important to understand the above developmental stages of groups is because of the potential relationships between group cohesiveness and productivity and the emergence of a leader. The leader will have a major impact on the outcome of the group. And from the group, teams may be formed. It is important to remember that groups process intragroup relationships since those relationships affect all members. Some groups are more effective than others; some, not as much. Some people prefer large groups (over ten members); others, small groups (two to seven members). Think of how you would work best.

## GROUP FUNCTIONS

So what do groups really do? Try this answer: Groups provide companionship, share information, solve problems, and provide therapy. They may even set norms or acceptable performance standards for the members. Following are four types of groups that can assist people with certain needs.

1. *Self-help*—Alcoholics Anonymous; Weight Watchers; Al-Anon/Alateen; Gamblers Anonymous; Alzheimer's, cancer, grief support groups; Gold's Gym; Curves; Toastmasters; health and body building groups.

2. *Business contacts*—Lions/Lioness Clubs, Kiwanis Club, Rotary International, VFW, Masonic Lodge, American Legion.

3. *Hobbies*—bridge clubs, model train buffs, chess groups, antique car enthusiasts, scrapbooking, coin collection, quilting/needlework, comic book collection, golf, tennis, and photography.

4. *A sense of belonging*—fraternities, sororities, sports teams, workgroups, committees, churches, synagogues, mosques, Facebook, MySpace, Twitter, Boy/Girl Scouts.

A group leader's role is to facilitate the group's development through a series of sequential stages. You may get all the group work you can handle at work or with family, neighbors, and church without seeking extra areas in more formally organized group settings. However, those who dissociate themselves from active group participation often display unhealthy personality traits and become a threat to themselves, their organizations, or society at large.

Fortunately, most teams are made up of people who care, are motivated, and desire achievement. However, should a leader have someone with unhealthy behaviors, the leader needs to take that person aside and work toward orienting him or her with the needs of the team and how this person can contribute to the effectiveness and productivity of the team. Healthy teams are built through teamwork that presents no threat to productivity.

## TEAMS

A group becomes a team when a leader selects certain members of the organization to serve together with others to work toward a clearly defined and common goal. Such a team might be formed to improve communication, cope with change, take advantage of new opportunities, or reach decisions about perplexing problems. Organizational consultant and author Warren Bennis wrote, "The more I look at the history of business, government, the arts, and the sciences, the clearer it is that few great accomplishments are ever the work of a single individual."

When a team is formed, intergroup dynamics should be understood. Interpersonal communication and decision-making skills will need to be developed. Team members' roles will need to be clarified, and a set of rules will have to be agreed upon. An atmosphere of honesty and openness will need to be established from the beginning.

As the team works together, several things will become paramount: goal consensus, effective communication, identity of outside sources that may influence the team's work, responsibility assignments, how to overcome difficulties, and ultimate result recognition. These components of successful teamwork will occur through focused discussion, brainstorming, and goal setting. New

ideas will emerge, and team members will develop mutual accountability for goal accomplishment.

Thus, teams differ from groups in several ways. For example,
team members have a stronger identification with their team than
group members have with their group. Think of a baseball or
football team with each player having a name—right fielder, second baseman, catcher, pitcher, center, quarterback, defensive end,
guard, etc. Task interdependence is also greater with teams than
groups. Team members have a more differentiated and specialized
role than group members. The Center for Creative Leadership
has identified eight key characteristics of effective teams and their
leaders:

- *Effective teams have a clear mission.* All team members know what they are trying to achieve. There
  is a compelling direction for the team. The leader
  establishes a climate for a flexible rather than rigid
  authority.

- *Effective teams have high performance standards.* All
  team members know how well they have to perform
  to achieve the mission. The task set before the team
  is unambiguous, consistent with the mission, and
  meaningful.

- *Effective teams take stock of their in-house and outside
  resources available to help them.* There is an enabling
  structure for goal accomplishment. The leader has
  established a climate where team members feel
  empowered to work together. They are comfortable
  questioning the leader when issues need clarification.

- *Effective teams spend time assessing the technical skills of the team members.* In addition, they explore whether the team has sufficient maturity and interpersonal skills to be able to work together and solve conflicts.

- *Effective teams work to secure those resources necessary for team effectiveness.* There is a supportive organizational context that helps align everything that the team needs for success.

- *Effective teams spend a considerable amount of time planning and organizing to make optimal use of available resources.* They select new members with needed technical skills or improve needed technical skills of existing members.

- *Effective teams have a high level of communication that helps the team stay focused on the mission and take better advantage of the skills, knowledge, and resources available to them.* There is expert coaching available when assistance and guidance are needed.

- *Effective teams minimize interpersonal conflicts on the team so that energy is not drained that is needed for success.* Conflicting norms must not confuse team members if the mission is to be met within the appropriate time frame.

Mike Krzyzewski, head basketball coach at Duke University, says that the members of a team are like the five fingers of a hand. Some fingers are shorter than the others, but they can all come together to make a fist. If all the fingers were the same size, they might never come together as a fist and be as powerful as the hand with the mixture of finger sizes. Thus, if five talented individuals don't perform as a team, they may not be as strong as the five less-talented players who do perform as a team. A leader's goal is to create a dominant team with five fingers that fit together into a powerful fist.

## TYPES OF TEAMS

Several different types of teams exist within organizations. Four important teams are functional teams, cross-functional teams, self-managed teams, and virtual teams.

### *Functional Teams*

A *functional team* is normally associated with the traditional vertical hierarchy of an organization. Functional teams are usually structured along function lines (accounting, marketing, human resource management). In most cases, functional teams are thought of as departments. However, the leader of a functional team may choose to use an autocratic, consultative, or group-oriented style. Or the leader may employ a centralized or decentralized leadership role.

### *Cross-Functional Teams*

A *cross-functional team* is composed of members from different units or departments in the organization. Occasionally, they also include individuals from outside the organization. The team is tasked with a responsibility that requires considerable input from other cooperating groups or individuals. Such teams may be temporary or permanent. Because such teams include "outsiders," the leader must ensure that everyone understands the mission and timeline for the continuing process and progress. This may be seen with public relations and marketing, public relations and advertising, promotion, marketing and advertising, etc.

## Self-Managed Teams

A *self-managed team* also involves individuals from different departments or units within the organization. The difference is that the team has the authority and responsibility for the decisions made in achieving the team's goals. Thus, a group-centered leadership style prevails. The team shares the responsibility for leadership functions. For self-managed teams to work, the people making up the team must be goal-directed, loyal to one another, and enjoy achieving goals with others.

## Virtual Teams

A *virtual team* is not in a single location. Since the marketplace is global, team members may be in various cities nationally or internationally. The impact of the distances between team members may mean that work distribution may not be directly proportional. Because of the nature of virtual teams, there is some evidence to suggest that they thrive when the membership is made up of volunteers with valuable skills. This may mean the members know each other and camaraderie already exists. Many organizations have special rooms set up for conference calls and video conferencing to enhance the work of virtual teams. It also enhances the travel budget.

## TEAM FUNCTIONS

The most basic team functions seem to center around four items: achieving goals, satisfying psychological needs, encouraging meaningful interactions, and maintaining or strengthening the team.

## Goal Achievement

Effective teams provide assistance to their members in accomplishing tasks, solving problems, and achieving goals. Also, they assist one another in the learning of problem-solving procedures.

## Satisfaction of Psychological Needs

Teams also satisfy many psychological needs. For example, a team can provide their members friendship, support, and even love. Team members offer verbal encouragement for ideas, technical assistance on some problem, or reinforcement of self-image, value systems, and beliefs. They provide a means of coping with opposing viewpoints. This is why some teams seek to work on projects together or look for other activities to keep the fires burning.

## Meaningful Interactions Encouraged

Meaningful interaction occurs through face-to-face communication as team members initially learn of their effect on others. All ideas and contributions are valued. Differences are recognized and respected. Questions are asked and clarification attained. Team members participate freely in discussions and make comments when appropriate.

## Team Maintenance and Strengthening

Effective teams like to keep their membership intact. Members enjoy one another and find strength in unity. In fact, many teams attempt to preserve themselves when they encounter a threat to their existence. Behaviors that symbolize this maintenance tendency are keeping interpersonal relations pleasant, arbitrating disagreements, providing encouragement, stimulating self-direction, and increasing interdependence.

To be effective, team members must understand how to work together. They must know what behaviors will lead to a high level of collaboration. The team leader is responsible for setting the ground rules for team activities and for encouraging team members to share their values and concerns.

# CHARACTERISTICS OF EFFECTIVE TEAMS

The most productive teams are usually those that can best carry out the steps of the problem-solving process. Some of the characteristics of a well-functioning, effective, creative group were modeled after the work of management expert and author Douglas McGregor. See Table 9.1.

Table 9.1:

1. The atmosphere tends to be informal, comfortable, and relaxed. There are no obvious tensions. People are involved and interested with no signs of boredom.

2. The team's objective is well understood and accepted by the members. There will have been free discussion of the objective at some point until it was formulated in such a way that the team members could commit themselves to it.

3. Team members listen to each other. Every idea is given a hearing. People do not appear to be afraid of putting forth a creative thought, even if it seems extreme.

4. Criticism is frequent, frank, and relatively comfortable. There is little evidence of personal attack, either open or hidden. The criticism has a constructive flavor.

5. The leader does not dominate the team, nor does the team defer unduly to the leader. Leadership shifts from time to time, depending on the circumstance.

6. When action is taken, clear assignments are made and accepted.

7. There is a lot of discussion in which almost everyone participates, but it remains pertinent to the team's task. If the discussion gets off subject, the leader brings it back quickly.

8. The team is comfortable with disagreement. It does not suppress or override disagreements by premature action but examines reasons carefully. The team seeks to resolve conflicts rather than to dominate the dissenter.

9. Most decisions are reached by consensus. It is clear that all team members are in agreement and willing to go along with the rest of the team.

10. Members are free to express their feelings as well as their ideas. There are few hidden agendas. Everyone appears to know quite well how everybody else feels about the matter.

11. The team is conscious of its own operation. Frequently, it will stop to examine how well it is doing or what may be interfering with its operation.

If the team is motivated to cooperate, members will work toward the goal. They will show more positive responses to each other, more favorable perceptions of each other and of their roles, more involvement, and greater satisfaction with the task. Similarly, the members of a cooperative team are less likely to work at cross purposes. They are more efficient and productive and better able to recall meaningful contributions as well as their own ideas.

## DISADVANTAGES OF TEAMWORK

Although there are many advantages to teamwork, there are also a few disadvantages. One of those is the pressure sometimes exerted on members to conform to group standards. Another is that if one person is more productive than the others, team members may ostracize this person, or the opposite could happen. One of the disadvantages is that sometimes a member will shirk responsibilities because there are others who will pick up the slack. You might remember working on a team in college where you had a "social loafer" who would not do his or her share of the teamwork. On the other hand, you also worked with people who would show up for meetings prepared and ready to work.

### *Groupthink*

Another of those dysfunctional effects of team behavior that limits and interferes with objective, critical feedback is *groupthink*. Certain team members often have strong, positive feelings toward the team and are highly motivated to remain part of that team. They have a strong sense of solidarity, and they drive for consensus at any cost. In fact, it is estimated that groupthink always occurs in a cohesive group. The outcome is that at times, a team makes a unanimous decision based on the status of a member and that person's verbal strength without confidence that all decision procedures have been followed. A "me-versus-you" or a "we-versus-they" attitude fosters poor decision making and problem solving.

## Symptoms of Groupthink

There are at least eight major symptoms that characterize group-think, according to retired Yale professors Irving Janis and Leon Mann. These symptoms can occur in any team that has a decision-making goal focused on consensus:

1. An illusion of invulnerability, shared by the members, which creates excessive optimism and encourages taking extreme risks. (Might makes right. We shall overcome.)

2. Collective efforts to rationalize warnings to reconsider before they recommit themselves to their past policy decisions.

3. An unquestioned belief in the group's inherent morality, causing members to ignore ethical or moral consequences of their decisions.

4. Stereotyped views of rivals and enemies as evil, weak, or stupid.

5. Direct pressure on any member who expresses strong arguments against the group because such dissent is contrary to what is expected of all loyal members.

6. Self-censorship of derivations from the apparent team consensus.

7. A shared illusion of unanimity, assuming that silence implies consent. (Don't make waves. Let's hurry this along.)

8. The emergence of self-appointed "mindguards" to protect the team from adverse information. (Don't sweat the small stuff. Poo-poo on that. It's not worth our time.)

As you think about groupthink and other disadvantages of teamwork, remember this: Teams function as their members make them function. As any team develops strong cohesiveness, its members tend to share an illusion of invulnerability. It's like the end of *Les Miserables*, an underdog win of the big game in sports, holding on to the American dream, or going to see the "wonderful Wizard of Oz."

As a leader, you must do all possible to ensure the members are not being protected from adverse information. You also must recognize that conflict is often a necessary precondition for creativity in problem solving.

## TEAM LEADERSHIP

Teams will vary in their satisfaction and effectiveness. Some will be more successful than others. When asked what makes one team more successful than another, I frequently answer, "the leader." Why? For the simple reason that the team leader's role in building an effective team is critical to its success. Leaders need to maintain the same intensity with the team that they would with their boss, especially when they are the right person for the job, a good fit with the organization, and respect for that person is there or can be quickly attained.

### FUNCTIONS OF THE TEAM LEADER

As there are primary functions of a team, there are at least three critical functions for team leaders to perform: dream, design, and develop.

## *Visualize*

Leaders must ensure that their team has a clear vision of where they are going. This is sometimes accomplished by metaphorical language that paints a picture of the outcome expected. "We'll be the Harvard of the Southwest." "We'll be the company designed for the stars."

## *Propose*

Leaders have the opportunity to make an impact on their team's decisions and to make system changes necessary to maintain and achieve excellence. Output variables at every level should contribute positively to team effectiveness.

## *Advance*

Leaders must continue to improve their team, even if it is already a well-designed team. This step is an ongoing process to reach the outcome acceptable to stakeholders. It involves knowledge and skills, strategy, and individual satisfaction.

Therefore, as a leader, you are responsible for establishing the basic structure of setting agendas, identifying the roles of specific members, setting the expected outcomes, facilitating meetings, and monitoring progress. You are responsible for developing, maintaining, and transforming the individual members into a team whose decisions are consensus-based and who have a unity of action. You are also responsible for addressing the "who, when, what, where, and how" issues as they develop and for formulating a plan to resolve these issues. Thus, it is important that you ensure open feedback on the issues that do not attack personalities. All differences must be addressed so the mission and responsibilities stay within focus.

## KEY ROLES OF THE LEADER

The leader's role is paramount in any team-based organization. Key roles of the leader, according to self-employed writer Shari Caudron, include the following:

1. Building trust and inspiring teamwork

2. Coaching team members and group members toward higher levels of performance

3. Facilitating and supporting the team's decisions

4. Expanding the team's capabilities

5. Creating a team identity

6. Anticipating and influencing change

7. Inspiring the team toward higher levels of performance

8. Enabling and empowering group members to accomplish their work

9. Encouraging team members to eliminate low-value work

The leader's work is especially important in the early part of team development to ensure the team does not lose sight of its mission or become bogged down with interpersonal conflict. Likewise, the leader must recognize that personal behavior and attitudes can help or hinder teamwork. That's why choosing group members and hiring well are important. Prequalifying applicants, finding interested people, selecting those who have a stake in the outcome, or working with focused people is so important for the leader's success—as well as looking good to superiors.

## TRAINING FUTURE LEADERS

Josiah G. Holland, an American journalist, has written, "There is no royal road to anything. One thing at a time, all things in succession. That which grows fast withers as rapidly; that which grows slowly endures." The same is particularly true about training future leaders. Jack Welch, former chairman and CEO of GE, and noted business journalist Suzy Welch have recommended the following for all future leaders:

1. Leaders relentlessly upgrade their team, using every encounter as an opportunity to evaluate, coach, and build self-confidence.

2. Leaders make sure people not only see the vision; they live and breathe it.

3. Leaders get into everyone's skin, exuding positive energy and optimism.

4. Leaders establish trust with candor, transparency, and credit.

5. Leaders have the courage to make unpopular decisions and gut calls.

6. Leaders probe and push with a curiosity that borders on skepticism, making sure their questions are answered with action.

7. Leaders inspire risk taking and learning by setting the example.

8. Leaders celebrate.

To put it simply, today's leaders must plan for future leaders. To achieve the best succession, for example, you would need to facilitate an assessment of the current workforce, identify the competencies needed, assess those individuals with potential without demoralizing those not chosen, and assist with a leadership development plan. Have you prepared or are you a part of a leadership succession plan?

## CONCLUSION

An understanding of group and team behavior enhances the possibility of desirable consequences. To achieve that goal, you must view the team as an entity dependent on face-to-face interaction. Open and straightforward communication is the best way for team members to share ideas and feelings, thoughts and opinions, and allow decision making to be based on dialogue. Once trust is established, every team member can actively and in good conscience do the work required.

Are you enabling cooperation and discouraging competition? Will you also demonstrate the results of cooperative, successful performance?

# CAN YOU OUTWIT, OUTPLAY, OUTLAST, SURVIVE?

## MOTIVATION AND EMPOWERMENT

The greatest natural resource in the world is not in the Earth's waters or minerals, nor in the forests or grasslands. It is the spirit that resides in every unstoppable person.

—Cynthia Kersey, success coach and author

I will lead blind Israel down a new path, guiding them along an unfamiliar way. I will brighten the darkness before them and smooth out the road ahead of them. Yes, I will indeed do these things; I will not forsake them.

Isaiah 42:16

I have often thought that the problem with home exercise equipment is that it won't pick you up off the couch, place you on the machine, and force you to exercise. It's a daunting challenge for future machines. Until we have kindly robots in the home that will perhaps wake us up, have our coffee ready and our clothes clean and laid out, and lift us from a relaxed pose and get us into a run, walk, bicycle, sweat-generating position, obesity and heart problems will continue to plague our nation.

What is it that we find so difficult about movement parading as exercise? Why do we prefer the sweet couch potato role when, as children, our parents couldn't get us inside for dinner? What is so appealing and diverting about our favorite La-Z-Boy? Why are we so willing instead to throw money at treadmills, elliptical trainers, and let our gym memberships lapse unused? Why are we so content to watch sports but not participate in them (but think we somehow did)?

What form of motivation does it take to move us? Besides expensive personal trainer-enforced exercises, what is an innovative approach that would influence people to think, act, and move forward? If you were an employee at the Wynn Hotel in Las Vegas and you were to receive a "Gotcha" award for superior performance entitling you to an extra day off with pay, or a gift certificate for merchandise, or a free meal at an upscale restaurant, would you be motivated to continue high performance? If you were an employee at the Mirage and were treated to a Hawaiian vacation for superior performance, would you be motivated? Or would it have to be an even bigger prize? If you were a salesperson for Carmax and received $250 for every car sold, would that continue to motivate you to sell more cars?

I wonder if Payton Manning (quarterback of the Indianapolis Colts) or LeBron James (Miami Heat basketball team) ever have problems with motivation?

Vast amounts of information have been written about motivation. However, Dr. Seuss may have summed it up best in *Oh! The Places You Will Go!*

1.   You have brains in your head

2.   You have feet in your shoes.

3.   You can steer yourself in any direction you choose.

4.   You're on your own.

5.   And you know what you know.

6.   YOU are the guy who'll decide where to go.

Are you a fan of the TV show *Survivor?* If so, you've noticed the words on their logo: Outwit, Outplay, Outlast, Survive. Those four words keep people motivated to stay on the island, in the jungle, or wherever they are. Motivation is a set of forces that causes people to engage in one behavior rather than in another. From the leader's viewpoint, the goal is to motivate people to behave in ways that are in the organization's best interests. Thus, the leader uses means to get followers to work hard, come to work regularly, and make positive contributions to the organization.

Basically there are two ways to view motivation, and both are centered on goal achievement. The first, or traditional, way is to define motivation as a process of directing (stimulating or actuating) people to action in order to accomplish a desired goal. That is, motivation is a function leaders perform to get followers to achieve goals and objectives. A second way is to view motivation as representing an unsatisfied need that creates a state of tension (disequilibrium), causing a person to move in a goal-directed pattern toward need satisfaction (equilibrium).

## INTERNAL AND EXTERNAL DRIVERS

Before we look at the traditional way of dealing with motivation, it will help to develop an applicable theory of motivation. The one I prefer is: Motivation is either an internal or an external drive that directs a person toward need satisfaction or a goal.

### INTERNAL DRIVES

An *internal drive* (i.e., intrinsic motivation) provides for expression of skills and talents. Satisfaction comes because work is gratifying in and of itself. Leaders and followers find the mission of their organization so interesting or so much the type of thing they want to do that motivation comes from within.

Consider the unusual motivation of a widow, Sara Winchester, and her unfinished mansion in San Jose, California (that cost $5 million at a time when the workforce earned 50 cents a day). The mansion has 150 rooms, thirteen bathrooms, two thousand doors, forty-seven fireplaces, and ten thousand windows. Enough materials had been purchased at the time of the owner's death to have continued building for another eighty years. What would motivate someone to build such a "house"?

Her grief and longtime interest in fortunetellers led her to seek out a medium to contact her dead husband. The medium told her, "As long as you keep building your house, you will never face death." Winchester believed her and bought an unfinished seventeen-room mansion in 1918 and expanded it until her death at age eighty-five. Today, the house is a tourist attraction and a silent witness to the internal motivation process (and the fear of death) that held her and hundreds of people in bondage.

Jack Welch was able to turn GE into one of the largest and most admired companies in the world. His internal drive was what moved the company toward and through change. His colleagues were encouraged to always be thinking about change and to make whatever changes would improve operations. As a leader you also are driven by some internal motivation. That drive will assist your leadership in strategy, planning, and development.

## EXTERNAL DRIVES

An *external drive* (i.e., extrinsic motivation) also provides for expression of skills and talents but is induced from an outside source. Someone provides an external, tangible reward (e.g., financial incentive) to get something accomplished. Homeland Supermarket and Ace Hardware use loyalty cards for discounts. The airlines use frequent flier programs. Car dealers and sales companies use bonuses and commissions. Barnes and Noble provides a MasterCard that, if used, generates points that can result in $25 gift cards. Extrinsic motivation is everywhere.

Which motivates you the most—extrinsic or intrinsic?

In most situations, more people are motivated by the intrinsic (e.g., recognition, leadership position, appreciation, satisfaction) than by the extrinsic (e.g., money, nice home, corner office, Leader of the Year award). Everyone needs something, but different people need different things. The extrinsic motivators tend not to last long-term. You're going to want a raise again next year, so having given you one last year doesn't last long.

## HUMAN NEEDS

Human needs will serve to satisfy an understanding of the first strand of motivation. Needs are requirements for work or social satisfaction. But it is the unsatisfied needs that motivate a person's actions. Many people have attempted to explain the range of needs, but American psychologist Abraham Maslow's hierarchy is the most representative. He placed all human needs into the following rankings: basic, safety, social, self-esteem, and self-realization.

## Need Hierarchy

The most *basic* needs are physiological—oxygen, water, food, sex, sleep, homeostasis, excretion. A person does not search for much else in life when these elements are not provided. When basic needs are satisfied, *safety* needs emerge: security of body, employment, resources, morality, family, health, property. Such needs are often coupled with the security needs of an organized, orderly, predictable environment.

When the safety/security needs subside, *social* needs (i.e., love/belonging) arise. These belongingness or love needs include friendship, family, sexual intimacy, and encompass both giving and receiving love. One of the strongest desires human beings have is to belong and be accepted by others. Once the social needs have been met, *esteem* needs become important. These include support, confidence, achievement, respect of others, and love. These needs may be met by self-estimations of strength, confidence, and freedom, and by others' recognition of their status, prestige, reputation, importance, or competence.

To illustrate: I know a university professor who uses "door prizes" to motivate students. Is he using social or esteem needs? Even though the prize is only a candy bar or a bag of cookies, it has the appeal of motivating students to attend class because they never know when their name will be selected. It also is another way of giving them self-esteem. They may even be chosen again as the professor uses this technique to learn everyone's name and information about them that he can use during the semester. The self-concept comes from significant others who have loved or respected the person.

When esteem needs are satisfied, the need arises for *self-actualization*—doing what one is fitted for, fulfilling one's potential, and becoming all one is capable of becoming. Included in this category are the needs for morality, creativity, spontaneity, problem solving, lack of prejudice, acceptance of facts, creative expression, and contribution to worthwhile objectives.

I have discovered that many of these five needs, from the most basic to the highest level, can be satisfied through social contact. That is why I allow the work environment to be tailored to the needs of faculty and staff. They can concentrate on achieving personal goals. It's amazing what a coffee pot or a refrigerator with bottled water can do to satisfy needs of individuals. Opportunities are available for the satisfaction of growth opportunities to exercise potential, recognition of accomplishments, and coaching to overcome problems.

People constantly want something "better." Any one need they have probably never will be satisfied. However, they continue to move toward the higher-level needs: esteem, self-respect or the desire for others to think well of them; and self-actualization, desire for self-fulfillment and achievement. So Maslow suggested that, on the average, individuals can be 85 percent satisfied with their physiological needs, 70 percent in their safety and security needs, 50 percent in their love needs, 40 percent in their esteem needs, and 10 percent in their self-actualization needs. (Note: Maslow's theory is far from established, and his suggested percentages of fulfillment at each level are untested.)

## TASK MOTIVATION AND GOAL SETTING

The second strand of motivation theory is based on the premise that a person's conscious goals are the primary determinants of task motivation. Have you noticed, for example, that hard goals result in greater effort than easy goals and specific goals result in higher effort than no goals or more generalized goals? That's why goals should be clear, challenging, and specific.

The relationship between tasks and goals, between people's behavior and their goal attainment/need satisfaction, is called the *path-goal theory of motivation.* The basic postulate implies that leaders must set important goals for those who follow them and clear the paths to those goals. If they do so properly, they can maximize motivation to achieve goals, provide insight as to the relationship between action and goal attainment, and create understanding about the relationship between satisfaction and performance.

## ACTION GUIDES FOR MOTIVATING SELF AND OTHERS

If the preceding theories are not applied to the human relationships, they remain just that—*theories.* Motivation is possible, and an organization's psychological needs can be met if the leader will learn and use the necessary skills. Wherever and whenever human relationships are a problem, it is up to the leader to correct them.

Frankly, it's amazing how many ways you can think of to motivate the people you work with, many that do not include pay raises. For example:

1. People like praise, so give them public recognition for special efforts.

2. Make their work more meaningful by finding ways to help them enjoy what they do.

3. Delegate additional responsibility (not more work).

4. Involve people in analyzing and designing solutions to various problems.

5. Ask questions, and listen to what they think—their aspirations and passions.

6. Build on their strengths, and help them eliminate their weaknesses.

7. Provide one-on-one coaching for professional development.

Different people will have quite different motivators, but leaders must remember that ultimately, motivation comes from people motivating themselves.

## PERSONAL NEEDS

I asked 251 people in various organizational settings to describe an incident of what they believed to be a time when another person motivated them. Their answers suggest a surprising level of consistency in motivational practices. The results revealed that a majority (61 percent) of motivators came from an external source. These motivators include:

1. Example/role model

2. Coworkers' and friends' encouragement

3. Superiors' encouragement

4. Confidence and trust from others

5. Praise and verbal encouragement from others

6. Approval and recognition by others

Did you notice that money and promotions did not make the list? That's why it's important to identify what motivates them.

Females seem to be motivated more by interpersonal exchanges than are men. Likewise, females are usually motivated by intangible motivators (e.g., a friend's smile and encouragement or love and acceptance from peers). Males also look for tangible motivators (e.g., a well-spent 8:00 a.m.–5:00 p.m. day, a raise in pay, or a title that attributes positional power). Of course, in due course, women like pay raises, good working conditions, and good assignments. Thus, as a leader, you cannot assume that a particular motivational attempt will work equally well for both males and females. More research is needed in this area.

When I don't know what people want and need, motivational attempts are likely to fail. So I've had to learn how to discover what people like or need. I've had to seek techniques to bring people out, get them to discuss their dreams, whether they enjoy traveling for business, what they find fulfilling about their job, or how their personal values align with the organizational values. Practice helps!

## FOLLOWER NEEDS

There are at least five needs of people who align themselves with an organization, a group, or team:

1. Followers have a right to know precisely and accurately what is expected of them—clear descriptions, delineations of authority, and responsibility.

2. Followers like to be involved in a task, whether designing it or establishing goals and objectives. Followers are not just numbers, not just cogs in a machine. They have ideas about how things should be done and questions about why certain things are

done the way they are. They want to be involved. So
you should ask them for help in setting goals.

3. Followers want feedback on how they are doing.
   Unfortunately, many followers do not feel they
   receive the recognition they deserve. As a result,
   their commitment is marginal, and their alienation
   increases. Then, when the commitment and recognition level is low, followers will seek recognition
   elsewhere—often from inappropriate behavior or
   leaving for another job. Therefore, you need to provide recognition of achievements or progress toward
   goals. When necessary, you should revamp the communication system when necessary to provide more
   feedback.

4. Followers have a need to receive help and guidance
   in improving their skills. Most of the time that you
   spend interacting with members is in the form of
   advising, guiding, coaching, counseling, or training.
   On any given day, you are a teacher, judge, specialist,
   generalist, planner, coordinator, organizer, motivator, and/or evaluator.

5. Followers have a need for rewards when they do
   something well. They want to know what is expected,
   to be involved in designing and directing goals, to
   get feedback, to receive help in skill improvement,
   and to be rewarded for a job well done. You need to
   discover how to satisfy those needs.

Leaders cannot ignore the needs of followers. At the same time, leaders must also recognize that they have needs as well.

## LEADER NEEDS

Let me illustrate leader needs by talking about myself. First, I view myself as a highly achievement-motivated leader who is more concerned with achieving success than avoiding failure. So I concentrate my energies on maximizing strengths and taking advantage of opportunities rather than minimizing weaknesses and warding off threats. I give close attention to the realistic probabilities for success and prefer situations where there are clear criteria for success.

Second, I prefer situations where I can influence and control rather than be dependent on chance. Thus, I have a dislike for seeing anything wasted and a tendency to become frustrated over inefficiency. I have a high regard for self-discipline and am often intolerant toward those I perceive as undisciplined. I prefer clear-cut individual responsibility so that if I do succeed, that fact can be attributed to my own efforts. That is why I prefer a competent but difficult work partner over a congenial but incompetent one.

Third, I am future-oriented and can wait on outcomes expected to yield positive results. (However, with this seeming strength of character, I also demonstrate tendencies of being unable to relax on holidays and vacations, of becoming annoyed when others are late for appointments, and of thinking about work-related matters outside the office.) How's your patience concerning the future?

Fourth, I have a longstanding pattern of working hard. I am able to stay on course, regardless of the obstacles encountered. So I try to create structures that harness the energies of others to achieve desired results, monitor the activities of the group, learn from mistakes, and improve performance.

Finally, as a leader, I am willing to take calculated risks. That means I need clear-cut goals and good information available.

However, future events and alternatives are subject to change. Therefore, enough information must be available to estimate the probabilities of a successful outcome or a failure, determine which likelihood is more desirable, and empower people to move forward.

What do you learn from this? As a leader you must recognize the strengths you have even though you do not currently see them in yourself. Realize you will need to embrace your opposites in the workplace. Don't fear letting your vulnerabilities be known, because they might strengthen your relationships. Balance your self-confidence with humility as you seek to meet the needs of others. Define what success means to you and then pursue it.

## EMPOWERMENT

John Throop, management consultant, has written, "In the shift from an industrial to an information economy (and now to an experience economy), businesses rely much more on brains than brawn, and on initiative than following directions 'they' give you." Thus, one of the principles I have always tried to keep before me is that of empowerment. The term *empowerment* is a popular buzzword used a lot by people who probably don't truly understand it. I believe in it because people can't be successfully empowered unless they know where I'm going. But let me ask you: What does empowerment mean to you? How can you recognize it? How can it be evaluated?

In my leadership thought world, empowerment is the process of enabling followers to set their work goals, make decisions, and solve problems. Such empowerment promotes participation in a number of areas and is powerful for motivating others. As Theodore Roosevelt, the twenty-sixth president of the United States, said, "The best executive is the one who has sense enough to pick good men to do what he wants done, and self-restraint enough to keep from meddling with them while they do it."

At the core of empowerment is the idea of power. As previously discussed, power is the ability to get others to do what we want. It conjures up ideas of domination, authority, and influence. However, power is seen and understood differently by those who have it and those who do not. Another view of power is that of collaboration and sharing. Researchers have dealt with power from the standpoint of relational power, generative power, shared power, and integrative power. So don't forget: Empowerment without direction equals chaos.

In an attempt to make sense of empowerment in a broad sense, authors Nanette Page and Cheryl Czuba defined empowerment as "a multi-dimensional social process that helps people gain control over their own lives." Based on that definition, empowerment lets people use their power in their own lives, communities, and society. They can act on issues deemed important. As a social process, empowerment depends upon relationships with others.

In a more basic definition for organizational life, scholar and researcher Andrew Dubrin defines empowerment as "passing decision-making authority and responsibility from managers to group members." Leaders and followers can empower one another to act on those daily work items that need attention or solution. In such instances, empowerment leads to higher motivation and productivity.

There are several effective empowering practices, according to Dubrin, that a leader can use. All are based on a participative leadership style.

1. *Foster initiative and responsibility.* Followers are empowered when the leader gives them greater initiative and responsibility in their assignments.

2. *Link work activities to organizational goals.* For empowerment to work, the empowered activities must be aligned with the strategic goals of the organization.

3. *Provide ample information.* Followers should be given ample information about everything that affects their work.

4. *Allow followers to choose methods.* Allowing people to determine the most efficient work techniques is the essence of empowerment.

5. *Encourage self-leadership.* Encouraging team members to lead themselves is the heart of empowerment.

6. *Establish limits to empowerment.* It is the leader's responsibility to guide follower activities that support the organization.

7. *Continue to lead.* Leaders will still need to provide guidance, emotional support, and recognition.

8. *Take into account cultural differences.* Diversity and cultural values might lead to either an easy acceptance of empowerment or reluctance to be empowered.

Over the years, I have tried to make organizational empowerment a part of my leadership practices because of the power it contributes to a particular follower and to organizational excellence. Thus, in addition to the eight items above, I have discovered that a contributor to empowerment is delegation—the formal assignment of authority and responsibility.

Not all leaders, however, delegate easily or successfully. Perhaps they are insecure, lack confidence in others, are reluctant because of past failures, or they just simply believe they can do the job better than anyone else. In the words of researcher and author Alfred Kingston, "Nothing more impairs authority than a too frequent or indiscreet use of it. If thunder itself was to be continual, it would excite no more terror than the noise of a mill."

Delegation can be motivational. It offers followers the opportunity to expand their skills and demonstrate their competence. It transfers authority to them to make decisions and use organizational resources.

## CONCLUSION

Motivation directs followers' behavior. It is able to energize them to act. Motivation has a dynamic quality. However, followers can be motivated only if they desire to be motivated, which is why much motivation is based on an intrinsic quality rather than extrinsic one. The best motivation is self-motivation. That is why many interviewers learn to discern how self-motivated a person is from their résumé and how the candidate demonstrates such in an interview.

The emphasis in motivation is on understanding follower's internal drives, interests, and values. You must understand what your followers want and realize that fear is seldom an effective tool for continuing self-motivation. Italian racing champion Mario Andretti said, "Desire is the key to motivation, but it is determination and commitment to an unrelenting pursuit of your goal—a commitment to excellence—that will enable you to attain the success you seek."

You have seen that motivation is any influence that causes behavior. No doubt you have ideas of your own that parallel or surpass what you've just finished reading. But one day soon, I think you'll come to believe (as I do) that tenderness, likeability, and empowerment are the real answers to all motivation! Is that what *you* believe?

# III. LEADERSHIP STRATEGY

If you want to build a ship, don't drum up people together to collect wood and don't assign them tasks and work, but rather teach them to long for the endless immensity of the sea.

—Antoine de Saint-Exupéry,
French pilot, writer, and author of *The Little Prince*

12. What's the Heart of the Matter? Analysis and Strategy Formulation

13. Is It Choice, Fate, or Destiny? Vision, Core Ideology, and Mission

14. Can You Survive Turbulent Times? Change and Change Agents

15. Will You Win, Place, or Draw? Conflict and Conflict Resolution

16. What's Our Game Plan? Strategy Implementation and Evaluation

# WHAT'S THE HEART OF THE MATTER?

## ANALYSIS AND STRATEGY FORMULATION

Organizations should take a proactive rather than a reactive approach in their industry, and they should strive to influence, anticipate, and initiate rather than just respond to events ... The stakes are generally too high for strategists to use intuition alone in choosing among alternative courses of action.

—Fred R. David,
educator, author, and strategic planning facilitator

Woe to the rebellious children, says the Lord, Who take counsel, but not of Me, And who devise plans, but not of My Spirit, That they may add sin to sin; Who walk to go down to Egypt, And have not asked My advice, To strengthen themselves in the strength of Pharaoh, And to trust in the shadow of Egypt!

Isaiah 30:1–2 (NKJV)

On one particular consulting assignment, I encountered an organization that, from all appearances, was in a precarious position. It had begun to fight for its survival—cutting spending, downsizing, and liquidizing certain assets. The situation was not unlike any startup company that starts fast, grows fast, and then suddenly finds itself in the predicament of being able to continue growth but with no cash to do so, like a plant that springs up quickly and then wilts. Their internal weaknesses were too evident, and their external threats were gathering momentum.

Their question: What should we do at this point?

Their request: Please help us.

What do you think you would do in such a situation?

They had some options available in which they held no interest. They could borrow money, seek investors, sell the company, merge with a more cash-solvent company, liquidate, or ignore the problems. They had chosen to continue to fight for survival. So we began to look for things that might be contributing to their possible demise. What was the internal fungus that, if it continued to stay where it was, would spread and destroy the company? Did they *truly* believe the organization could be revived? Were they willing to do whatever it took to remove the disease that had them headed down the out-of-existence corridor?

If you had been the founder of this company, could you have let go?

---

There are more than a few organizational leaders who need to move from a theoretical phase to a strategic planning mode—leaders who need to get real, get practical. The first step is to recognize the importance of diagnosis and begin a scanning analysis of the organization and the world around it. In other words, environmental scanners and market analysts are critical. Thus, leaders need to keep up with the megatrends the world is encountering. To survive today's competition, leaders must adapt to change. This requires research, analysis, decision making, commitment, and discipline.

To illustrate: If you were filming a surfing documentary, you would want to survey the shoreline and check on weather worldwide as well as locally. You would want to know the habits and skills of the entrants, the way the waves break, where the rocks and danger points are, and the best angles and lighting for photography and filming. You would also want to capture the best sounds of the ocean and crashing waves. All of this would be done before starting the film.

Old-time surfers always surveyed the shore before surfing and never turned their back on the sea. Rogue waves were always respected. Scanning was expected by wise leaders and planned by those who lived long and prospered. Or they didn't get restaurants named after them, like Duke's Restaurant and Barefoot Bar in Hawaii (founded by Duke Kahanamoku). To survive, surfers kept up with the changing tides and currents as well as weather patterns. They learned to read signs quickly. All leaders of organizations and people must learn to navigate the waters they are in to keep ahead of the waves of change.

After analysis, the next step is to decide what to do and start formulating the strategies (i.e., the game plan) for taking them from where they are to where they could be, should be, or want to be. These strategies will help the organization capitalize on their strengths, overcome their weaknesses, take advantage of key external opportunities, and avoid external threats. Afterwards, there is the implementation of strategies to effect the change decided upon. Strategies will be put to work. Action that mobilizes followers and leaders will begin. An unimplemented strategy serves no purpose. After implementation, there must be evaluations devised to check and make sure all is working well. So let's get to the heart of the matter.

## STRATEGIC ANALYSIS

Determining the exact impact of social forces is difficult. However, assessing the changing values, attitudes, and demographic characteristics of an organization is an important factor in strategy formulation. There are three primary considerations for leaders who desire to establish an environmental analysis program:

1.  *What sources of information should be scanned?* All environments—political, economic, social, religious/cult demographics, competition, cost, budget, money available, and all stakeholders.

2.  *Who should do the scanning and analysis?* Older, wiser men and women—those who have traveled other "oceans," who have actually been on the "waves" themselves, or who have survived similar circumstances.

3.  *What system should be used to implement a scanning program?* The answers to number two will mostly determine the answer. Experts and instincts can guide the decision.

This systematic three-step approach enables leaders to scan outside forces and evaluate how they will affect internal mechanisms. The focus should be on trends that have organizational-wide relevance. The effective organization is the one that can take advantage of its internal capabilities to satisfy its external demands.

To illustrate: DaySpring Cards begins its strategic planning process each year by taking a look at ten key questions. The answers to those questions help drive their planning process.

1. What is the single most important desire for DaySpring? How are we doing now?

2. What is the most important thing we can do today to lead DaySpring to the future?

3. What three words or phrases would you use to describe DaySpring?

4. Is our product and channel scope too big? Too small? About right? Why or why not?

5. What ideas do we need to put the brakes on that are too small to merit the resources required?

6. What position do we want to own in the consumer's mind? What do we own now?

7. How do we grow our core business?

8. What do we think DaySpring will be like in ten years based on industry, market, and technology changes? In product types? In customers? In services?

9. How do we better serve our customer? Who is our target market? When do we want to branch out with other products?

10. How do we better communicate to our people?

A Chinese proverb says, "Every change brings an opportunity." However, change also can bring a threat. Like DaySpring, all organizations are confronted by change. How well they negotiate the hurdles of change is key to survival and success. Some change is external. It occurs "outside" in the environment and is beyond immediate control. Other change is internal. It occurs "inside" and is directly within the sphere of decision-making capability. In spite of the differences between external and internal change, there is one important similarity: Both require that strategic questions— who, what, where, when, why, and how—be posed before action is taken.

## DIAGNOSING THE ENVIRONMENT

Because so much research and analysis are required to formulate strategy, leaders should know how to adeptly analyze their environment. An easy-to-use technique I employ to capitalize on strengths, overcome weaknesses, take advantage of opportunities, and avoid threats is the SWOT analysis.

SWOT refers to internal *strengths* and *weaknesses* and external *opportunities* and *threats*. It is a systematic identification of those factors and the strategy best suited to them. Its logic is that an effective strategy can make the most of strengths and opportunities but at the same time minimize weaknesses and threats. If accurately applied, SWOT analysis has powerful implications for successfully choosing, designing, and selecting a winning strategy.

## SWOT ANALYSIS

SWOT analysis assists leaders in finding the best match between environmental trends and internal capabilities. Three tasks are involved.

1. *Identify distinctive competencies.* What can the organization do very well? What are its unique resources and capabilities? What are the strengths of the followers? What is their ability to overcome any weaknesses?

2. *Find a niche for which the organization is well suited.* For example, there are a number of social and/or economic situations (i.e., niches) in which an organization interacts. Leaders position their organizations in such a way that they take advantage of the opportunities that present themselves and avert threats from the environment.

3. *Match an organization's distinctive competence with its available niches.* Leaders understand their opportunities and threats. They are able to identify where they can be most effective. They understand their strengths and weaknesses. They identify their distinctive competencies.

In general, an effective strategy is one that takes advantage of opportunities by employing strengths and wards off threats by minimizing weaknesses. And in some cases, threats can become opportunities, depending on the leaders and followers outlook and/or resources. See Table 12.1 for an example of a SWOT analysis conducted by the faculty and me in 1999 at my current B-school, when I started as dean.

Table 12.1:

| Strengths | Weaknesses |
|---|---|
| What makes your organization strong? | What weakens your mission? |

| Strengths | Weaknesses |
|---|---|
| Experienced faculty | Unfilled faculty slots |
| College is in one building | Lack of faculty in key areas |
| Rigorous program/curriculum | Lack of sufficient doctorates |
| Christian commitment/values | Unsettling effect of dean search |
| Administrative support | Outdated facility |
| Closeness of faculty | Inadequate lab and classroom support |
| Closeness of student body | Lack of release time for research |
| Ties to the business community | Number of part-time faculty in the college |
| Reputation | Lack of a dedicated computer lab |
| Business Advisory Council | Lack of scholarship funds |
| Good technical support | Inadequate endowment |
| Professional accreditation | Missing key programs (e.g., finance) |
| | Inadequate response to accounting's 150 hours |
| | Faculty salaries |
| | Lack of relationship with Enterprise Square |

| Opportunities | Threats |
|---|---|
| What opportunities exist? | What are the potential threats? |

| Opportunities | Threats |
|---|---|
| Number of available internships | Cascade College threat to accreditation |
| Number of people in area with bachelor degree | PACE threat to accreditation |
| Business community attitudes | 150-hour requirement in accounting |
| Technological advances | Small Church of Christ faculty pool |
| Excellent job market | Small Church of Christ student pool |
| Improving attitude about business education | Competition |
| Global joint venture possibilities | Rapid technological changes |
| Engineering program on campus | Declining morality of the nation |
| Proximity to Enterprise Square | Threat of downturn in economy |
| Proximity to Oklahoma City | |
| University is accepting of change | |
| Business alumni "coming of age" | |
| Society's return to integrity | |

My sense was that the faculty felt good about sharing the information—getting all the cards the table, all the elephants in the room. Now I had an understanding of how they viewed the challenge before us. I knew a new vision needed to be set before them. They needed a better self-image, recognition of accomplishable goals, and the development of an uplifting mission.

## THE SWOT MATRIX

As a follow-up to a SWOT analysis, I have found the SWOT matrix to be an important tool for developing four types of strategies: SO strategies, WO strategies, ST strategies, and WT strategies. Successful organizations pursue WO, ST, or WT strategies so that they can then apply an SO strategy. When an organization like the one at the beginning of the chapter has major weaknesses, it will strive to overcome them, making them strengths (e.g., a building is paid for but it needs modernization or an addition). Note, however, overcoming a weakness does not necessarily mean a strength will be created or found. When leaders face major threats, they will either confront them or avoid them in order to concentrate more on opportunities.

Matching key internal and external factors is the most difficult part of developing a SWOT matrix. The matching process requires good judgment, but no one answer is best. To illustrate:

1. *SO strategies are based on using internal strengths to take advantage of external opportunities.* Any organization should be able to use its strengths to exploit external opportunities.

2. *WO strategies are aimed at improving internal weaknesses by taking advantage of external opportunities.* Sometimes key external opportunities exist, but an organization has internal weaknesses that prevent those opportunities from being seized.

3. *ST strategies are based on using internal strengths to avoid or reduce the impact of external threats.* An organization faced with many threats must muster all its strengths to avoid failure.

4. *WT strategies are directed at overcoming internal weaknesses and avoiding environmental threats.* The attempt is to minimize both weaknesses and threats. WT strategies must be defensive in nature.

The purpose of the SWOT matrix is to generate plausible alternative strategies, *not* to select or determine which strategies are best. Therefore, not all of the strategies developed in the SWOT matrix will be selected for implementation. Sometimes, several internal factors will be matched with several external factors to generate an appropriate strategy. See Exhibit 12.1 as an example of a church I once consulted with about strategic planning.

Strategies do not necessarily have to be developed for all four strategy cells. But they should be tailored specifically for your organization. Leaders need to implement strategy with caution. When change is involved, it is necessary to move people from step three to four on a scale of one to ten rather than quantum leaping from step three to nine.

Exhibit 12.1:

| | Strengths<br>List strengths. | Weaknesses<br>List weaknesses. |
|---|---|---|
| Opportunities<br>List<br>opportunities. | Flexibility in worship styles should lead to a variety of worship services that would appeal to many different ethnic or age groups.<br><br>Availability of talented people could result in several smaller groups or congregations, meeting together only on special occasions.<br><br>Commitment to "restoration principle" could mean meeting in homes for weekly Lord's Supper and fellowship.<br><br>Meeting separately in small groups would allow groups worshipping in many different languages.<br><br>Meeting separately in small groups could open the door for evangelism on the eleven college campuses in the area.<br><br>Meeting separately in small groups would make it easier to evangelize the whole "diocese." | Meeting in small groups separately would eliminate the impression of too much emphasis on one group to the neglect of others.<br><br>Spirituality could be heightened in small group meetings if leaders are properly trained.<br><br>Women in small groups could be as active as the individual groups would allow.<br><br>Small individual groups could be as exuberant or staid as felt best by the group.<br><br>Small groups could make use of the talents of all leaders instead of singling out one.<br><br>In small groups, members of each group would know who of their number was hurting and be able to offer assistance immediately. |
| Threats<br>List threats. | Small groups meeting separately could meet where the people are and avoid the "seedy" environment for the rented building.<br><br>Beaches, mountains, etc., could be used by the small groups to meet wherever they wish (e.g., the lake).<br><br>The intimacy of the small group can counterbalance the pull of the media and government anti-Christian bias.<br><br>The wealth of talented, educated, strong leaders can work together to counterbalance the threat of disunity or loss of identity. | Continual emphasis from elders on need to make services relevant and remain flexible and open to change will help overcome the threat posed by traditions.<br><br>Continual insistence from elders on the need to keep the groups small will keep groups growing and resist stagnation and complacency.<br><br>Intimacy created by small groups meeting separately will appeal to those feeling isolated and disconnected. |

## STRATEGIC FORMULATION

In the sports world, coaches study their opponents before the next game to learn their weaknesses. They then formulate a game plan, using those plays best suited for beating the competition. They also plan how to overcome their opponent's strengths and maximize their own. The week is spent in training, practicing for game day, and attempting to simulate the future real-life events. The question both coaches and team members wrestle with during the week is, "When the heat is on, how will we perform?"

In our organizational world, leaders conduct environmental analyses to learn their strengths and weaknesses. They then formulate plans to capitalize on their competition's weaknesses and minimize their own. They attempt to take advantage of opportunities and to avoid and overcome threats. They prepare to meet challenges and changing conditions in order to continue growing and profiting.

C. K. (Coimbatore Krishnarao) Prahalad, former strategy expert (deceased), has written that strategy has three areas of focus:

1. *Strategic Architecture:* Develop a framework for establishing and communicating your point of view about the future.

2. *A Migration Path:* Determine the basic milestones for getting there as well as what new core competencies you need.

3. *Empower Employees:* Enable associates by giving them the resources and knowledge to move toward that future and encouraging them to invent new approaches for accomplishing difficult tasks.

To effect change, strategies must be formulated and then implemented. A growth strategy is based on research and analysis to determine internal strengths/weaknesses and external opportunities/threats. Strategies chosen for implementation capitalize on an organization's strengths, overcome its weaknesses, take advantage of key external opportunities, and avoid external threats. Forming an effective strategy is the product of a wide range of factors. That is why effective leaders plan for the future.

## DECIDING WHAT TO DO

The formulation of strategy is essentially deciding what to do. To accomplish this, leaders answer five questions:

1. Where has the organization been (i.e., what has been accomplished)?

2. What are the organization's specific purposes? Target market? Talents and interests? Innovation possibilities/opportunities?

3. Where is the organization presently heading? (What are its growth strategies?)

4. What critical environmental factors (i.e., economic, political, demographic, legal/ethical forces) does the organization face?

5. What can be done to achieve goals more effectively in the future?

Leaders must not shy away from answering these questions. It is perfectly permissible to start thinking about implementation when you begin forming a strategy. Each step in strategy development, evaluation, and decision making is undertaken with implementation clearly in mind.

If all the key issues are not dealt with and handled properly, the leaders may find themselves looking for new strategies. Some of those new strategies might include concentration (vertical or horizontal growth strategies), diversification (concentrated—related or conglomerate—unrelated diversification strategies), stability (pause/proceed-with-caution, no-change, and profit strategies); or retrenchment (turnaround, selling out, bankruptcy, or liquidation strategies).

## IDENTIFYING VALUES AND ASPIRATIONS

A leader's values, aspirations, and ideals influence the future of any organization. For example, George Washington is well named the father of our country for these attributes. Every historical reference of his life exemplifies him as an example of his faithfulness to his wife, farm, his men, and his country. He would retire upstairs each evening precisely at nine o'clock with his dear wife and write notes of appreciation to friends for things they had accomplished. During the war of independence, he could tenaciously cheer his cold, poxed, stinky, exhausted men, as well as elegant, wigged dandies with shiny shoes in dazzling drawing rooms of Philadelphia. Everyone's values and ideals were shaped and raised by Washington's influence and instinct about what needed to be done.

What leaders know about *what needs to be done* is critical to deciding *what to do* (i.e., formulating strategy). There is no way to divorce a strategic decision from the personal values of those who decide. Management researcher Kenneth R. Andrews suggests that awareness about the possibility for an alternative opposed by a follower stems from values and has important consequences. It may make leaders more tolerant and less indignant when they perceive this relationship between recommendations and values in the formulations of others. It certainly will force leaders to consider how important it really is to them to maintain a particular value in making a particular decision. It may give leaders insight with which to identify their biases and pave the way for a more objective assessment of all the strategic alternatives that are available.

It should be noted, however, that some people won't follow the leader if they don't value that leader's perceived values or aspirations because they don't value that person as a leader. That is why there is often disagreement as to which direction an organization ought to be headed. To diagnose potential conflict, leaders deal with the values implicit in how people choose paths. These values ultimately influence motivation and commitment.

One way to deal with individual values and aspirations is to ask followers to write what they think should be the *tenets* and *mission statement* of the organization. (Tenets are the fundamental principles or doctrines held by a person or an organization, the values that underlie all actions.) Compiling such a list is a time-consuming process. It may take a year, but it is an exercise that will yield results and bond leaders and followers in a way that may have been impossible before. Hold a retreat to accomplish this activity and witness the positive response.

## DETERMINING ALTERNATIVES

Matching an organization's internal strengths and weaknesses with external opportunities and threats is central to strategy formulation. "Matching" means lining up internal factors with external factors to formulate feasible strategies. For example, leaders try to match a prospective follower's skills and qualifications with the job description, corporate philosophy, dynamics of the corporation, etc. Before matching strengths and weaknesses with opportunities and threats, however, strengths and weaknesses must be identified objectively, realistically, and critically. Once the factors are analyzed and the match is made, the next step is decision making.

Decisions must be made regarding what objectives to establish and which strategies to pursue. Few organizations have unlimited resources, so leaders must select from a number of potentially beneficial goals and strategies. And then these goals must be prioritized. The way a leader solves problems affects what happens not only to them but also to those people with whom they live, work, worship, and socialize. If they are able to generate interest in a program, so will the followers.

## ESTABLISHING GOALS

Strategy is a set of goals and policies. At face value, this description seems simple. People have been setting goals, mapping out strategies, and achieving them since childhood. However, getting an A in biology class, making a touchdown, hitting a home run, learning to drive a car, or graduating from college can be problematic without a plan. Strategic goals are always set for the future and involve multi-year plans (two to five to ten years). They involve deciding where you are now, where you could or should be at some point in the future, and what resources will be necessary to get you there.

Dreams should not be underestimated. On one occasion, a friend complained to American author Henry David Thoreau, "I'll never be a success ... apparently my values are all mixed up. I'm just a dreamer."

Thoreau told his friend to not worry about it. "You've already mentioned one important value: the ability to dream. If you dream of a castle in the air, the effort you've expended need not be in vain, that's where a castle should be. Now, put a foundation under it."

The foundation of every dream of accomplishment, of every vision, is a well-defined, measurable program of goals. However, goals should not be confused with wishes. A *wish* is a vague idea of something hoped for—to be an oil baron someday. It may even be something one is not working to obtain. A *goal* is a practical and effective way of changing dreams into, reality. Thus, goals are an indication of what an organization is trying to achieve and become.

In *Winnie the Pooh,* the following story is told: One morning, Winnie and Piglet are out walking. Piglet turns to Winnie and says, "Winnie, what's the first thing that you think of every morning when you wake up?"

Winnie replies, "I always think, 'What's for breakfast?' What do you think of, Piglet?"

Piglet answers, "I always wonder what exciting things will happen today."

These are the basic dreams of most people: a *breakfast dream* or an *excitement dream.* The former dream is maintenance, and the latter is vision.

Remember the 1992 basketball dream team who won the gold medal at the Barcelona Olympics? Michael Jordan, Magic Johnson, Larry Bird, Charles Barkley, David Robinson, Patrick Ewing, Karl Malone, Scottie Pippen, Chris Mullin, Clyde Drexler, John Stockton, and Christian Laettner. Their opponents didn't have a chance, but the competition didn't seem to care. They just wanted to marvel at the ways these guys played together. No "Dream Team" since has captured the imagination of the world in quite the same way. Leaders know they have to have a dream of what exciting things can be if they expect to accomplish anything.

## CLEARING THE PATH TO THE GOALS

A person's goals determine his or her task motivation. Like time management, the more that is on a person's plate, the better organized he or she is and the more that person can actually accomplish. Consider the collegiate athlete who excels on the football field and in the classroom during the fall season but slacks off a bit in the off-season. Difficult and specific goals result in greater effort than easy goals and in higher effort than no goals or more generalized goals. Thus, leaders are concerned with establishing a well-defined mission and setting clear, challenging, and specific goals for their followers.

## CONCLUSION

Effective leaders assess their own strengths and weaknesses and their followers' strengths and weaknesses. An idea will seldom be launched unless you endorse it—not even an idea backed by a "product champion." You must sanction the idea because you decide where the organization is going.

Introspection would allow you to get in touch with reality and make it clear that you have goals and objectives for your followers. Goals must result from your thoughtful introspection and openness to the followers and your plan for them and the organization. Once you and your followers know what is desired for them, they will recognize you as their power source for accomplishing goals and objectives. Once strategies are formulated and implemented, everyone can plug into your power source, and the results sought should be produced. Is *your* power source charged up and ready to go?

# IS IT CHOICE, FATE, OR DESTINY?
## VISION, CORE IDEOLOGY, AND MISSION

Vision is a picture of the future that you really care about. It is an expression of your core values, your sense of purpose ... Vision brings something from within and says "I really want to put my life energy into creating this."

—Peter Senge,
educator, author, consultant, idealistic pragmatist

Write the vision and make it plain on tablets, that he may run who reads it. For the vision is yet for an appointed time; but at the end it will speak, and it will not lie. Though it tarries, wait for it; because it will surely come. It will not tarry.

Habakkuk 2:2–4 (NKJV)

There's a story that Lynn Anderson, author and minister, tells about the first few years after the pilgrims had sailed to, landed on, and taken up residence in America. See what you think about their vision.

A group of pilgrims landed on the shores of America. With great vision and courage, they had come to settle in the new land. In the first year, they established a town. In the second, they elected a town council. In the third, the government proposed building a road five miles westward into the wilderness. But in the fourth year, the people tried to impeach the town council because the people thought such a road into the forest was a waste of public funds.

Somehow, these forward-looking people had lost their vision. Once able to see across oceans, they now could not look five miles into the wilderness.

How about you? Are you able to look into the wilderness of the future and dream? Is your dream for the future going to make any difference in anyone's life or the world in which you live? What is your dream? Is it an "impossible" dream?

---

"We all live under the same sky," says German statesman Konrad Adenauer, "but we don't all have the same horizon." How true that statement was in the lives of those early pilgrims and is in the hearts and minds of many today. In my consulting with other groups and organizations, I've often been shocked at how few leaders and followers have no vision. They have totally missed the sentiment of what James Allen, self-help author, wrote: "The oak sleeps in the acorn, the bird waits in the egg, and in the highest vision of the soul a waking angel stirs. Dreams are the seedlings of realities."

I once held an all-day workshop for the president and all the vice presidents of an Oklahoma bank to get them to think about what it was they were trying to accomplish. The questions the president had asked me to deal with were: "What is the purpose of this bank? What makes it different from all the other banks in town?" Can you imagine a bank that didn't have a vision of who it was and what it was trying to accomplish—besides making a profit? Actually, the president did have a vision, but he wanted to see what his vice presidents thought.

American psychologist and philosopher William James once stated that after age thirty, one becomes set like plaster and does not change. I realize there are individuals who seem fixed and immovable. However, I think James was wrong. People *can* and *do* change. That is why there is always hope for others. To illustrate: American oil magnate John D. Rockefeller, at age fifty-three, was a miserable billionaire who could not sleep, was unloved, needed bodyguards, and had a rare disease. He lost too much weight, and all his hair fell out. The medical doctors gave him a year to live. As he began to think about eternal issues, he decided to change his ways of thinking about money. He established the Rockefeller Foundation and began to give away his money to help hospitals and health research, schools, and churches. His health improved, and he lived to be ninety-eight. His life changed because of a new-found vision in philanthropy.

I wonder how long Warren Buffett, chairman of Berkshire Hathaway, Bill Gates, former chairman of Microsoft, and Melinda Gates, American philanthropist, will live because of the $33.5 billion endowment they have committed to charities? How will their philanthropic vision change the world? Will they be the Rockefellers of the twenty-first century? Normally we think in terms of organizational vision, but this vision is personal. It is a preferred future, an ideal state. It is what they want to become.

What twenty-first-century vision of our organizational world will rally leaders to transform their dreams and respond to the needs of present and potential followers? I ask because leadership needs to be advanced beyond the current framework of the lack of strategic planning taking place today. And even those who do strategic planning sometimes put the final results in a notebook and shelve it and go on and do what they were doing before. Leaders must move beyond theory to application. Until that happens, leaders will find themselves surrounded by the discouraged and despondent. A new vision and mission for organizations requires new ways of dealing with the challenges of leadership.

Like the cowboy who spurs his horse to gain speed, leaders need to spur themselves toward renewed energy and higher ground. They need a vision better than themselves and the means by which to meet the challenge. They need to rise up, do it, and move forward. Strategy is a choice and is neither fate nor destiny.

## VISION

Political activist and lecturer Helen Keller was once asked, "What would be worse than being born blind?"

She replied, "To have sight without vision."

When *you* think of the word *vision,* what comes to mind? How is vision important to an organization?

Vision is a look into the future, seeing the organization as it should be, and engaging the minds of all those with whom the vision is shared. Think of it in the words of Napoleon Hill, American author and advisor to two presidents: "Desire is the starting point of all achievement, not a hope, not a wish, but a keen pulsating desire which transcends everything."

A vision statement is a future-oriented description of what an organization should look like and how it will successfully fulfill its tenets. It is a clear and compelling reason for the organization to be in business. It is the glue that holds everything together and keeps everyone focused. In the words of David E. Morton, FACHE, a leader must:

1. Create vision and be the keeper of it.

2. Set high standards and be the conscience of the organization.

3. Create an environment conducive to change and innovation.

4. Train or mentor future leaders.

5. Interface with the external environment.

Vision addresses possibilities. As a vision statement is crafted, leaders should keep in mind the words of Max DePree, former chairman of Herman Miller Furniture: "In the end, it is important to remember that we cannot become what we need to be by remaining what we are." Effective leaders know where they are going, and they know how to convince people to follow them.

An unknown author penned the following poem:

Ah, great it is to believe the dream,
As we stand in youth by the starry stream.
But a greater thing is to live life through,
And say at the end, the dream came true.

Not everyone can see that clearly. Leadership expert John Maxwell describes these unseeing people accordingly: "Some people never see it—they are wanderers." Those who can see the dream or vision from the beginning, pursue it, and see it finally come to fruition are true leaders. The specific ingredients of such a vision include a positive appraisal of reality, specific and attainable objectives, and worthwhile and possible forward movement.

Leaders who work with those ingredients also communicate faith, hope, and optimism. Their statements show commitment and conviction. Their verbal statements match their nonverbal behavior. These optimistic and committed communicators have at least two benefits:

1. *The more they talk about a vision, the more followers will come to believe in and become committed to the vision.* Consider the campaign battles waged by rival politicians who are vying for votes. In doing so, they appeal to their constituents and garner support by helping them to capture a positive vision. For example, one sign for a district attorney in our community has a pre-election sign touting, "You can trust a cop."

2. *The more followers hear leaders talk about a vision, the more the followers will come to believe in that vision and be supportive of that vision.* Think of the coaches able to give pep talks that fire up their players to go out on the field or the court and win. Or remember American clergyman and activist Martin Luther King Jr.'s "I have a dream" speech. (Be aware, however, this ability can also work in reverse. The National Socialist German Workers Party leader, Adolf Hitler, had an evil vision for the Jews that nearly eradicated an entire people.)

An inward journey into the core being of yourself and your soul is not always easy. That's why we all need mentors to keep us on track, to keep the fires of success burning. In the words of Maitreya Ishwara, spiritual teacher and visionary author, "Transcending the limitations of mind is not possible for dreamers who are addicted to concepts and intellectual abstractions—only to warriors and lovers of truth who are ready to merge with the ecstatic fire of Now."

Similarly, Ken Hemphill, author, speaker, and entrepreneur, has said, "Vision does not ignite growth; passion does. Passion fuels vision, and vision is the focus of the power of passion. Leaders who are passionate about their calling create vision." In addition, Theodore M. Hesburgh, president emeritus of the University of Notre Dame, said, "The very essence of leadership is you have a vision. It's got to be a vision you articulate clearly and forcefully on every occasion. You can't blow an uncertain trumpet." If followers do not understand the vision, they will feel disenfranchised, anger, fear, and helplessness.

A word of caution: Vision doesn't stick; it leaks. Why? Success, failure, and everything in between. That means the vision will have to be recast repeatedly. You may have repeated it a thousand times, but it will still need to be repeated. Followers will still need to be reminded.

## CORE IDEOLOGY

The framework that makes a vision effective and organizations successful embodies the core ideology of an organization. The core ideology is a set of ideas that sets forth the goals, expectations, and actions necessary for a comprehensive vision. The main purposes behind an ideology are to propose change when necessary and to build commitment to a set of ideals.

The core ideology is composed of two parts: core values and core purpose. American business consultant James Collins and Stanford University professor Jerry Porras emphasized the ideology framework as follows:

> … the fundamental distinguishing characteristic of the most enduring and successful corporations is that they preserve a cherished core ideology while simultaneously stimulating progress and change in everything that is not part of their core ideology.

Isn't that a great description not only of the world's businesses that have lasted years and moved from good to great but also the world's churches?

## CORE VALUES

Core values are the indispensable and durable system of belief within an organization. This system is made up of timeless principles important to leaders and followers. Therefore, whatever these principles or values are, they must stand the test of time. Any principle that changes when the situation changes is not a core principle. Collins and Porras recommended that leaders involved in articulating core values should grapple with six questions:

1. What core values do you personally bring to your work—core values you hold to be so fundamental that you would keep them regardless of whether they are rewarded?

2. What would you say if you were asked to describe to your children and/or other loved ones the core values you stand for in your work, values that you hope they would stand for when they become working adults?

3. If you awoke tomorrow morning with enough money to retire for the rest of your life, would you continue to live and work according to these core values?

4. Can you envision these core values being equally valid for you a hundred years from now as they are today?

5. Would you want to hold these core values, even if at some point one or more of them became a competitive *dis*advantage?

6. If you were to start a new organization tomorrow in a different line of work, what core values would you build into the organization *regardless* of its industry?

The last three questions are acutely significant, since the answers may distinguish what are indeed core values and those values that should change. Do you know the core values of your organization? Google publicizes ten core principles that guide their actions.

1. Focus on the user and all else will follow.

2. It's best to do one thing really, really well.

3. Fast is better than slow.

4. Democracy on the web works.

5. You don't need to be at your desk to need an answer.

6. You can make money without doing evil.

7. There's always more information out there.

8. The need for information crosses all borders.

9. You can be serious without a suit.

10. Great just isn't good enough.

Yahoo values excellence, innovation, customer fixation, teamwork, community, and fun. Microsoft values integrity, honesty, openness, personal excellence, constructive self-criticism, continual self-improvement, and mutual respect. The core values of Amazon are customer obsession, innovation, bias for action, ownership, high hiring bar, and frugality. Every organization has a set of core values, things they would not change, even though they might not be in writing or published on a website.

## CORE PURPOSE

Core purpose is the reason for an organization's existence. A core purpose encapsulates the motivations of leaders and followers. It depicts the DNA of an organization. Collins and Porras recommend a powerful method for getting at an organization's core purpose—the five whys. "Start with descriptive statement, 'We make X products' or 'we deliver X services,' and then ask 'why is that important?' five times." By asking the whys, a leader can begin to zone in on what is the core purpose of an organization. As Pope and Saint Gregory the Great said, "He who is required by the necessity of his position to speak the highest things is compelled by the same necessity to exemplify the highest things."

Once the core values and core purpose have been determined, the organization is well on its way to becoming a skillful, visionary organization. The leaders' values of passion, accountability, efficiency, balance, commitment, empowerment, innovation, risk taking, integrity, or quality will successfully propel the organization into the future.

## MISSION

A mission statement is a formal statement of the purpose of an organization. The mission statement guides an organization, denotes the overall goals, provides direction, and directs the path to decision making. It provides the context within which an organization's strategies are formulated, and it contains the follow components: the purpose of an organization, its stakeholders, and products or services offered. The mission statement spells out an organization's core ideology and visionary goals. It is an enduring statement of core purpose and identifies the scope of operation. Often, companies have their mission statement on their website, framed and hung near the front door or reception desk, or have it positioned with their vision statement so anyone can access it easily.

The mission statement should be simple enough that everyone can state it. After all, someone made famous the two general statements of "Simplify, simplify, simplify," and "K.I.S.S. (keep it simple, stupid)." For example: Coca-Cola is more than teaching the world to sing. "Our mission is to create a growth strategy that allows us to bring good to the world—by refreshing people every day and inspiring them with optimism through our brands and our actions." Apple is more than the iPhone, iPod, or iPad. "Apple is committed to bringing the best personal computing experience to students, educators, creative professionals and consumers around the world through its innovative hardware, software, and Internet offerings."

"The mission of the Navy is to maintain, train and equip combat-ready naval forces capable of winning wars, deterring aggression and maintaining freedom of the seas." "The Army's mission is to fight and win our Nation's wars by providing prompt, sustained land dominance across the full range of military operations and spectrum of conflict in support of combatant commanders." "Making Marines and Winning Battles. These five words make up the Marine Corps Mission Statement."

What's your organization's mission statement? I once asked the manager of a prominent upscale restaurant in Oklahoma City what their mission statement was, and I was immediately interrogated as to why I wanted it, what I was going to do with it, and why they should share it with me. It was posted in the kitchen. He finally went to the back, made a copy of it, and grudgingly handed it to me. Mission statements should be posted on the wall, not hidden in the back office somewhere. So I asked another manager at a department chain store, and he immediately quoted it for me and gestured toward a brochure on the counter with the mission sentence in a customer handout. A certain manager of a food chain not only handed me a copy of his mission statement when I inquired but also two meal coupons for inquiring about it. I was impressed! Could you quote your mission statement? Are you ready to give an answer to anyone who asks what your company stands for?

## CONCLUSION

A vision, even though it is shared by leaders and followers, will still need to be nurtured. There are four actions that I recommend to maintain the shared vision:

1. *Define the vision specifically.* Allow the followers to see its breadth and boundaries. Focus on what will be done.

2. *Express the vision clearly.* The purpose needs to be straightforward and to the point. It's a purpose statement for why you are here, not a slogan.

3. *Obtain acceptance of the vision.* Seek commitment from all followers. Do your best to make it a shared vision.

4. *Restate the vision over and over.* Repetition keeps the purpose in everyone's mind and reminds them of the importance of the shared vision.

Once the followers have a clear vision, once they view everything in that light, they will view every activity in light of the vision. Soon, they will make decisions more easily and allocate their resources in light of the vision. When both you and your followers share the vision, little can prevent accomplishment.

Are *you* finally ready to produce one? Go, go, go!

# CAN YOU SURVIVE
# TURBULENT TIMES?

## CHANGE AND CHANGE AGENTS

A corporation is a living organism; it has to continue to shed its skin. Methods have to change. Focus has to change. Values have to change. The sum total of those changes is transformation.

—Andrew Grove, senior advisor to Intel Corporation

I don't mean to say that I have already achieved these things or that I have already reached perfection. But I press on to possess that perfection for which Christ Jesus first possessed me. No dear brothers and sisters, I have not achieved it, but I focus on this one thing: Forgetting the past and looking forward to what lies ahead, I press on to reach the end of the race and receive the heavenly prize for which God, through Christ Jesus, is calling us.

Philippians 3:12–14

Eskimo Joe's, once only a bar near Oklahoma State University, Stillwater, Oklahoma, began plans quietly but radically to segue into a more profitable bar, food, and apparel company. The owner decided people eat more often than they drink, so why not expand into a restaurant that still has a bar? Over time, the owner made several decisions that at the moment seemed logical—such as venturing out with a different type of restaurant. Unfortunately, the local population never bought into going to that particular restaurant because neither they nor the staff understood its uniqueness. This decision resulted in the company beginning to bleed red ink.

After hiring a consultant to seek a more enlightened way to save the company, the owner decided to move in a strategic manner to (a) redefine the company credo so it could better fit the tastes, values, and wants of its customers and (b) rebuild not only a staff of people with a new attitude but the company overall. To accomplish these tasks, corporate planning had to be introduced, a new executive vice president had to be hired, and a new staff had to be trained. Thus, the company with the funny name and a logo of Eskimo Joe with smiling teeth and his trusty Husky are seen on tee shirts all over the known world, reminding us of the power of visionary marketing leaders. A redefined image increased sales, caused the company to expand operations, and allowed the company to become very profitable, celebrating its thirty-fifth anniversary in 2010.

Would you have gone in a different direction? What do you think were the dynamics of change that affected the past, are affecting the present, and will affect the future? Would you recommend any other changes? Remember, the times are turbulent. Will you survive?

---

"Ch-ch-ch-ch-changes" are everywhere, as David Bowie reminds us in his song "Changes." Over time, he says, we will be a different person. "Time may change me but I can't trace time."

While these verses are interesting, are they really true? Can you not (to some degree) trace time? If you disagree, look at some of your personal photos from various stages of your life. Trust me, I doubt you look much like you did ten, fifteen, twenty, twenty-five years ago. While there's a resemblance, age, extra weight, hair color, hairstyle, effects of stress, gravity, or a number of other things will alter the way you look and the way you look at others and/or things.

As American culture changes, organizations change. Pre-Socratic, Greek philosopher Heraclitus of Ephesus said, "All is flux; nothing stays still," and, "Nothing endures but change." Perhaps that is why years later, Robert Byrne, a Grandmaster chess player and author, could say, "Everything is in a state of flux, including the status quo." Although leaders may try to isolate their organizations and followers from change, it is impossible. No organization is an island.

Change is an attitude or a state of mind. An organization cannot be changed unless the mind-sets of those involved are altered. Thus, in many respects, the followers are the most critical parts of an organization and the most crucial to the change process. Yet the way of doing things (i.e., the system) often is easier to change than the people. To change either an individual or the system, leaders must alter the human and technical features that hinder the organization from achieving its full potential. Think of it this way: Change is only a theory until it shows up at your doorstep.

## CHANGE

Any kind of organizational analysis that leads to growth or development is *planned change.* It is important to remember that not all change is revolutionary destruction. Sometimes, it is simply a renewal or reinvention of elements within the organization. However, change is nearly always a response to pressure. It is the substitution of one thing for another or an alteration that limits or restricts. It is any modification in the behavior patterns of people within an organization. For example, today women have become flight attendants or managers, but in the 1940s, they had to be nurses or elementary teachers.

In the words of Charlie Munger, vice-chairman of Berkshire Hathaway, "We all are learning, modifying, or destroying ideas all the time. Rapid destruction of your ideas when the time is right is one of the most valuable qualities you can acquire. You must force yourself to consider arguments on the other side." Perhaps that is why restaurants and retail have gotten more generous—larger portions, increased sizes of burgers, more fries, free two ounces more on certain brands of toothpaste, or twenty-five more vitamins in a small jar attached to a larger jar for the same price as the larger jar by itself. And you know all about the promotional options and deals used year-round for department stores.

To survive, organizations must periodically change to meet the challenges of a changing world. A review of research regarding organizational change, according to Brittney Duke, vice president of global operations at Saatchi & Saatchi X, says, "There are at least three main principles of change that do not differ (in concept) during a change initiative, regardless of time, technology or industry."

1. *Outside forces create the need for change and are the initiators for change within an organization.* Technology and globalization drive change.

2. *The people who make up the organization change, not the organization itself.* People drive change and must be communicated with clearly and frequently.

3. *There is a process or method for all change initiatives.* Consistency in getting agreement, creating a team

to lead the change, clearing the path by eliminating obstacles, setting short-term goals, and using small successes to fuel bigger ones is critical.

Leaders and followers within an organization must also change. In essence, they must agree with American theologian Reinhold Niebuhr's *Serenity Prayer* (originally written for a service in the Congregational Church of Heath, Massachusetts). Currently, it is used as a foundational tool in Alcoholics Anonymous and other recovery programs: "God grant us the serenity to accept the things we cannot change, courage to change the things we can, and wisdom to know the difference."

## PRESENT AND PREDICTABLE CHANGES

Societal change cannot be isolated from global change. Yet there seem to be distinctive national changes and trends. These present and predictable changes have tremendous potential for helping or harming an organization, depending on the response of leaders and followers to these changes. Consultants Thomas Addington and Stephen Caldwell have suggested four change points in organizational and societal life:

1. *Life is full of the unexplainable and the unexpected.* Such events are bound to happen sooner or later.

2. *People need information and inspiration during the change process.* People need to know what, why, and how, and it's best to communicate face-to-face.

3. *It is normal to experience emotional turmoil during periods of change.* Transitional upheaval is common and legitimate.

4. *People's reactions to change reveal their true colors.* The handling of change and the transition process reveals the character of those involved.

Whether or not one wishes to deal with changes, the changes exist. They are pervasive, and they are altering the way organizations perform. Of course, one of the outcomes of the pervasiveness of change is stress and burnout. Stress is not a simple phenomenon. It has many different causes—work and personal. And the results can be positive or negative. Stress may be noticeable in a dread to go to work, working later than normal, exhaustion, or absenteeism. Stress is one of those things that often is predictable, but sometimes it sneaks up on a leader and reminds the leader that change is necessary—change in self, workload, assignments, or relationships.

## FORCES OF CHANGE

How does change come about? Consider the following six-step model for change. Leaders change organizations because of a variety of forces. These forces may be analyzed accordingly.

### Step 1: Identify external or internal forces.

Change begins with the emergence of either external or internal forces that create a need in some part of the organization. *External forces* are competition, resource availability, technology, values, environmental opportunities, and constraints (economic, political/legal, and social). *Internal forces* are the knowledge explosion, desire for more leisure time, stress and conflict in organizational activities, interactions, sentiments, performance results, and new technology.

Organizational effectiveness depends on the ability to predict these forces of change to maintain stability. If the environment is constant, organizational structure may remain stable. However, if the environment is chaotic, such as with a company in a war-torn country or a neighborhood in a riot zone, the structure must be more adaptable and flexible. Thus, organizations face an ever-present dilemma: How can they be sufficiently organized to operate efficiently, and how can they be sufficiently adaptable to new forces demanding change?

One of the techniques to better understand the forces of change is German-American psychologist Kurt Lewin's Force Field Analysis. In essence, this theory says that change occurs when the forces pushing in one direction are greater than the forces pushing in the opposite direction. For example, many restaurants are changing to blow dryers in their restrooms because it saves money and time spent cleaning up and restocking. But they are also receiving complaints about outages and cleanliness.

## Step 2: Distinguish between driving forces and restraining forces.

Driving forces encourage change, growth, and development. Restraining forces encourage stability and the status quo. Both driving and restraining forces produce distinct attitudes toward other people and happenings and affect responses to what must be done. Combining external and internal forces with driving and restraining forces provides four kinds of forces to consider:

- *External driving forces*—shorter life cycles, needs for different channels of marketing, status of members, and culture and social values.

- *Internal driving forces*—increased demand for greater satisfaction, desire to have more say in decision making, increased knowledge of how to organize, and higher expectations.

- *External restraining forces*—continuing demand of followers for traditional ways of doing things and the inability of groups promoting change to mobilize.

- *Internal restraining forces*—existing power and social relationships, vested interests and coalitions, fear of the unknown, and lack of strategies and confidence to cope with change.

Driving forces could be market opportunities, technology, globalization, new leadership, and need for change. Restraining forces might include cost of new product development, rising aspirations, fear of the unknown, incongruent organizational systems, and dissimilar team dynamics.

Leaders do everything possible to communicate to followers the need for change and to enable their organizations to change. Therefore, it is often helpful to understand the goals of change.

## Step 3: Consider five types of change goals.

There are five types of change goals that all leaders must recognize:

1. *Strategic change goals* alter the relationship between the organization as a whole and its environment—e.g., revised objectives, expansion, change in competition.

2. *Technological change goals* alter physical parts of the organization—e.g., installing new computer equipment.

3. *Structural change goals* alter internal features of the organization—e.g., relationships or processes of communication and decision making.

4. *Behavioral change goals* alter human interactions— e.g., beliefs, values, attitudes, relationships, and behavior.

5. *Program change goals* alter some aspect of organizational structure—e.g., the technical implementation of plans.

## Step 4: Determine the focus of all change efforts.

Targets might include policies, information, and formal work division and flow. Behavioral targets include people, interpersonal relationships, group and team behavior, and intergroup behavior.

## Step 5: Choose goals, criteria, and targets of change.

Once the type of change goal is identified, then the leader may choose the target of change and how to implement the change. Those leaders responsible for implementing change must be carefully matched to the particular change target and resources available. Also, authority and responsibility of both the "changers" and the "changees" must be explicitly defined to prevent conflict.

## Step 6: Evaluate the change effort.

Indicators of success are productivity, morale, and innovative ability. Change results will depend on member identification with change needs and goals. Although it is usually initiated to improve efficiency and/or effectiveness, change can be either positive or negative. However, since change is inevitable, we might as well accept it and deal with it in a positive spirit. As Max DePree, founder of Herman Miller Furniture, said, "In the end it is important to remember that we cannot become what we need to be by remaining what we are."

The call is to be proactive. Don't sit back. As Gregory Slayton, president, CEO, and director of ClickAction Inc., has said, "If the change is always happening to you—and it's only happening to you—then you're a piece of furniture and you're in trouble ... You've got to be a change maker as well as a change reactor."

## RESISTANCE TO CHANGE

Most people, it seems, cling desperately to the past, even when the past wasn't all that rewarding. The familiar is always more comfortable than the unfamiliar. Change means giving up something. So they drag their feet toward the acceptance of change, preferring to just hunker down and wait out change. Perhaps they know what physicist Franz Kafka knew: "In a fight between you and the world, bet on the world." The reality: Change is here to stay. Ask yourself, "Am I part of the solution or part of the problem?"

I have a friend, Vi Morris, a very active senior citizen living in a retirement village. She has hip and back trouble but gets around well. Recently, because of construction, it was necessary to change parking assignments for all those people who had been parking their cars in the east parking shelters to the west side of the parking lot. Three years ago, she had picked the east side for her residence because of the nearness to parking. Now she would have to walk the full length of the building from her apartment to her car. Moving her car was neither an option nor a solution since there were church friends in the retirement village who depended on her driving them around town for appointments or shopping. Needless to say, she's not real happy about this situation. But would you be?

As an education, church, business, and civic leader, anytime I try to change a system of operation, I meet some resistance. Thus, I know about the difficulty in accurately forecasting major problems. I also know something about the enormous amount of time that is needed to iron out problems and get followers to accept change. And I have seen certain followers who hardly commit themselves. They show this lack of commitment by refusing to take initiative and help make the plan work.

The classic case of resistance to change was probably Henry Ford, founder of Ford Motor Co. He assumed the black Model T was the only car anyone needed. So when people started asking for different colors, he responded, "You can have any color you want as long as it's black." I don't know if he said this in a snotty or arrogant way, but people were evidently so glad to get a horseless carriage they took the snide insult and bought Fords. However, that's when his decline started, because the door was opened for General Motors and others to use color and take away market share in the automobile industry.

Consider these ten barriers to change and see how many you recognize in your own organizational life:

1. *A focus on the institution rather than its purpose.* The best organizations are purpose-driven. They know *why* they exist. Those who focus on the institution oppose change because they fear it will threaten their organization. For example, my university contemplated a possible name change, but just the idea resulted in people being scared, appalled, and threatened. The administration had to back off.

2. *Socially self-perpetuating.* Most organizations attract people who are very much like those who are already members. Common denominators may include

race, income, education, loyalty to the founder, or commitment to a specific lifestyle. Such self-perpetuating organizations can be very stable but very slow to change. For this reason, they are very susceptible to groupthink.

3. *Minority rule.* Just because the majority is supposed to rule does not mean things actually work that way. Often, the majority goes along in deference to the minority—a few who do not want change. Those fearful few who resist change immobilize many organizations. I've seen this even in schools and churches. The fearful few may be old timers, the rich, the mean girls, the stars, the cool people, or jocks. But they have enough referent power to stop momentum.

4. *Yesterday's innovator.* Some organizations have been blessed with extraordinarily gifted innovators. They are so good they cannot be matched, and no one wants to try. But even good ideas become obsolete. "All music was new once," as one radio station opines. Yet we have any number of radio stations playing "oldie" music in large cities. If obsolete ideas curtail innovation, the only option left is to perpetuate yesterday's innovations and implement yesterday's dreams. Sounds like a formula for failure.

5. *Not inclined to risks.* All change involves risk. The greater the change, the greater the risk. And to attempt to relate to modern Western culture and maintain integrity can be high risk. So today's standard answer to change is, "Be conservative."

6. *Unwillingness to suffer pain.* Change is always uncomfortable for some people in the organization. Rather than suffer the pain of dealing with a problem and unintentionally inflicting pain on some individuals, most organizations choose to live with the problem. Team members need to be terminated or confronted.

7. *Complacency.* The organization is already successful, and no one feels self-criticism and change are urgent. "Leave well enough alone" is the general attitude. "Stay fat and happy."

8. *Disruption of interpersonal relationships.* Change sometimes means individuals who have been close associates for years are assigned to different task groups. This may interrupt friendships and common social activities. People may even find themselves among new associates they either really like or intensely dislike.

9. *Threat to status.* Realigning duties and activities often threatens the self-image and status of those directly affected by the change. They may feel they will be less highly regarded by their peers as they develop a new persona.

10. *Fear of increased responsibilities.* Some resist change because they fear they will be unable to handle increased responsibilities or don't want the power. Consequently, some refuse to accept certain responsibilities. They fear it will take up more of their precious time without reward, if any.

Some followers resist change more than others because they feel more threatened. As writer George Trusell has said, "People do not basically resist change; they resist 'being changed.'" Thus, those who have the most to lose will resist the most. Cohesive groups are highly resistant to change. Can anything be done about this tendency to resist change?

## GUIDING CHANGE IN AN ORGANIZATION

Resistance to change is a recurring problem. Most leaders know the justification and logic behind their decisions. They expect their followers to accept their judgment without question. Fat chance! I have found that I must follow two communication rules to gain compliance with any new decisions:

### *Rule 1: Provide accurate and detailed information as early as possible about any change.*

Advance notice helps curtail disruptive attitudes and forestalls rumors. If followers are forewarned about changes or told that the new direction may present short-term difficulties, they adjust more quickly to change.

### *Rule 2: Allow followers time to accept change.*

Followers normally accept change if they have time to become accustomed to the idea. Sudden changes usually arouse followers' fears. But if you move slowly, that often helps to prepare followers and makes the change less formidable.

A number of other strategies are available to help leaders overcome resistance to change and guide an organization through change. In summary, leaders must be entrepreneurial, champion the vision, put the dream on display, tell the organization's history, link followers together, and shape the environment. It is helpful to remember some sage advice from leadership expert John Maxwell: "Every new idea goes through three phases: It will not work; it will cost too much; and I thought it was a good idea all along." Sound familiar?

## AGENT OF CHANGE

If leaders can understand resistance to change, they can also understand the importance of managing change. For example, as a leader, one of the many hats I wear is the one signaling me as an agent of change. Why? Because I am the difference between having a vitalized organization or a deteriorating organization. Therefore, I have to catalyze insight and clear thinking among my followers. I have to get them to think more deeply and thoroughly about the coming change and the process for change. However, leaders are seen as the change agents when actually middle management may contain some of the strongest change agents.

As an agent of change, I have learned from consultant James R. Lucas that successful organization change has five overarching requirements:

1. The type of change is aligned with the true need.

2. The size of the change initiative is scaled to the size of the needed change.

3. The change process begins at the right place.

4. The approach to change has the potential to overcome resistance and create the necessary momentum to carry the organization through the inevitable pain of change.

5. The change can be anchored to something that isn't changing.

Therefore, both my followers and I have to let go of the way things are or used to be. Transition from then to now is always uncomfortable, however. That's why very few followers like a neutral zone. They would prefer to go back or rush ahead without deep thought. However, if I can't convince them to let go of the old ways, we will fail at moving forward. But move forward we must. We must begin to behave in new ways. American author and historian Washington Irving said, "There is a certain relief in change, even though it be from bad to worse; as I have found in traveling in a stagecoach, that it is often a comfort to shift one's position and be bruised in a new place." Balance is important.

Stephen Caldwell, American journalist and author, has written, "Great things in the corporate setting always are done by great teams." As a leader, therefore, I know it may take me awhile to get everyone to come to terms with the necessity for change. My followers will need some time to process and transition also. Likewise, I understand that not everyone will embrace the change. So I need to discover what is holding them back. Once I understand that, I create plans to bring my followers through the transition process and coach them during the journey.

## A METHOD FOR MANAGING TRANSITION

Each change is different, and the details for each are unique. There are obviously dysfunctional teams. That doesn't necessarily mean they are a bad team. What it may mean is that the team is not executing, working together, or performing up to expectations. It may mean they lack strategic leadership skills. The leader must figure out where the team needs to be headed and how to get them there. Organizational consultant William Bridges and author Susan Mitchell have presented some essential steps for change agents that I recommend to you:

1. *Learn to describe the change and why it must happen, and do so succinctly*—in one minute or less. It is amazing how many leaders cannot do that.

2. *Be sure the details of the change are planned carefully and who is to be responsible for each detail.* Timelines for all changes must be established. A communication plan must be developed to explain the change.

3. *Understand who should or is going to have to let go of what*—what is ending (and what is not) in followers' work lives and careers and what people (including the leader) should let go of.

4. *Help followers respectfully let go of the past.* These may include "boundary" actions, a constant stream of information, and understanding and acceptance of the symptoms of grieving, as well as efforts to protect people's interests while they are giving up the status quo.

5. *Help followers through the neutral zone with communication (rather than with only simple information) that emphasizes connections with and concern for the followers.* Keep reiterating the "four *P's*" of transition communications: purpose—why this has to be done, picture—what it will look and feel like when the goal is reached, plan—how they will get there, and part—what the leader can (and needs to) do to help everyone move forward.

6. *Create temporary solutions to the temporary problems and high levels of uncertainty in the neutral zone.* A

transition-monitoring team can alert the leader to unforeseen problems. The team should be disbanded when the process is done.

7. *Help followers launch the new beginning by articulating the new attitudes and behaviors needed to make the change work*—and the modeling, providing practice in, and rewarding those behaviors and attitudes. Define the necessary training and resources to develop them.

Each year, more and more, you no doubt realize that you have to stay competitive in the face of demographic trends, technological innovations, and globalization. You must continuously be seeking better ways to manage strategy, process, people, and culture. You must assure an alignment of our strategies, structures, and processes on an ongoing basis. And you must lead every change necessary.

As comedian, actor, and movie director Woody Allen said, "More than any time in history mankind faces a crossroads. One path leads to despair and utter hopelessness, the other to total extinction. Let us pray that we have the wisdom to choose correctly." Wisdom is indeed a need of all leaders.

## LEADING CHANGE

Being a change agent involves some simple rules. However, they are too often forgotten. For example, the state of California a few years back completed the California Performance Review. It called for a massive restructuring of state government. If you were one of the leaders in a branch of state government in California, what would you do? How would you begin?

In an attempt to answer those questions, consultants Christopher Worley and Yvonne Vick devised six admonishments to help in any makeover attempt:

1. *Do no harm.* Implementing change poorly is often worse than not implementing change at all. Take a holistic (whole systems) approach that connects all parts of the organization.

2. *Recognize that change involves personal choice.* Explain the "why" of the change, what's in it for the follower, and how it is the follower's best interest to do things differently.

3. *Realize that the relationship between change and performance is not instantaneous.* Change does not turn on a dime. Few, if any, followers can drop a set of behaviors one day and be performing perfectly the next day. Change involves time because learning is often inefficient.

4. *Connect change to business strategy.* There is value in consistency. Change should only be pursued in the context of a clear goal.

5. *Remember that involvement breeds commitment.* Avoid overestimating how fast to move and what needs to be done in the short run. Likewise, avoid underestimating what can be done in the long run.

6. *Understand that any good change effort results in increased capacity to face change in the future.* There is a difference between installing change and imple-

menting change so that the organization is more capable of managing change in the future.

Change is a strategic imperative today. Therefore, as a leader, you must remember those fundamental and sound principles that are prerequisites for successful change. Implementing tried and true principles will help to improve your relationship with followers and also perk up the organization.

## ACHIEVEMENT OF CHANGE

There have been several times in my life when after reaching a goal I have felt lost. The goal I had set was before me for a specified period of time, and when I achieved what I had been aiming for, there was a sigh of relief and a moment of thankfulness and celebration. But then I wondered, *What do I do now?*

Two examples come to mind. The first was the dedication of a building that I had been intimately involved with. Nurturing that project from idea inception, through the architect, contractor, and decorator, to the dedication of the facility had occupied a couple of years. There was a formal opening, a luncheon for the donors, family, and friends, and several tours. By the end of the day, I was beginning to feel exhaustion from the entire project. I was alone in my office, and depression seemed to be setting in as I suddenly realized the project was over. There was now "nothing" to do.

The second was the completion of a five-year set of goals. I had set those personal goals and worked diligently toward their accomplishment. I was three years into the list when I realized all the goals had been accomplished. As I sat staring at the list, I felt great about completing each item and marking it off the list. But just as suddenly, I begin to feel those same types of depression waves coming over me. What was I going to do for the next two years? How was I going to reinvent myself? What should we be doing now?

Have you had similar experiences? The moment of victory arrives—and make no mistake about it, that is a crucial time for everyone—but now you're wondering whether you'll be able to introduce the next change and work toward that new solution. These moments are dangerous. They can lead you into complacency if you don't find another goal to work toward. They also can tempt you to be too satisfied and let your guard down.

Don't forget that you were hired to make a difference, to make an impact. Take ownership of change, and run the race set before you. Fight the good fight, but choose your battles carefully. Practice stress management, and learn to be tolerant of others' mistakes. Be not weary in well doing, and keep your sense of humor. Follow every rainbow, and find your dream. "Dream the impossible dream." Invent your future.

## CONCLUSION

Change is a continuing problem all leaders, followers, and organizations must face. The ability to adapt to change within an organizational structure is basically in the hands of leaders. Robert Quinn, University of Michigan professor, puts it this way:

> When we see the need for deep change, we usually see it as something that needs to take place in someone else. In our roles of authority...we respond to the resistance by increasing our efforts. The power struggle that follows seldom results in change or brings about excellence. One of the most important insights about the need to bring about deep change in others has to do with where deep change actually starts.

Can you communicate change to your followers? Can you direct and hold the followers together by effectively communicating during the change period? Can you effectively bring about the change necessary at this time in the life of the organization?

You know that your followers will resist change. Therefore, you must understand that and help them move positively through the change proposal. Your success as a change agent will be largely determined by your own attitude about change and how you communicate that attitude to your followers. Change allows both you and your followers to exit your comfort zones and enter an improved setting, leading to even better comfort and pride.

Bring it on!

# WILL YOU WIN, PLACE, OR DRAW?

## CONFLICT AND CONFLICT RESOLUTION

Conflict is a lot like water—it spills over; it flows downhill; and, if left unchecked, it erodes whatever it touches. And sometimes it's like red wine—it stains.

—Jason Fried, cofounder and CEO, 37signals

Moreover if your brother sins against you, go and tell him his fault between you and him alone. If he hears you, you have gained your brother. But if he will not hear, take with you one or two more, that 'by the mouth of two or three witnesses every word may be established.' And if he refused to hear them, tell it to the church. But if he refuses even to hear the church, let him be to you like a heathen and a tax collector.

Matthew 18:15–17 (NKJV)

Have you ever wondered if anything could have been done to save the Beatles from breaking up? Can you imagine the number of top ten hits they might have had and how much money they would have made if someone could have saved the Beatles? Conflict between John Lennon and Paul McCartney has been described as a fight over nothing and everything. The pain each one inflicted upon the other has been described as a blood feud. George Harrison and Ringo Starr were bystanders and no doubt would have preferred a solution.

What are your thoughts about what conflicts broke up the Beatles?

There are two schools of thought about the breakup. One is the evil Yoko Ono theory, which alleges that she did all she could to undermine and break up the band. It is hypothesized that she felt threatened by the relationship between Lennon and McCartney and needed to separate the two. Of course, there is the possibility that she was not as nutso as fans have made her out to be. A second theory is the evil Allen Klein theory. Allen Klein became the Beatles' manager after the death of Brian Epstein. Klein is seen as a scoundrel who engineered an alliance of Lennon, Ringo, and Harrison against McCartney. Although, like Ono, it is possible he was only an accessory to the events taking place and was not the triggerman who permanently separated the band members from one another.

Can you think of any other bands that went through something similar but overcame their squabbling through conflict resolution of sorts and were able to stay together?

Two other rock bands went through possible breakup scenarios because of a need for psychological help to quit fighting over misguided feelings. Metallica almost split up before they found the help they needed to recognize their identity and leave behind their celebrity delusions. The Rolling Stones were almost sidelined because of drugs and the realization their manager, Allen Klein, was pocketing their money, along with the rights to their recorded back catalog. (Yep, the same evil Allen Klein of the Beatles.) Mick Jagger and Keith Richards were in need of the help that arrived when Jagger decided to refamiliarize himself with the education he had received at the London School of Economics, especially the numbers, before dropping out. He was able to guide the band back into profitability.

So what do you think? Could the Beatles have been saved? If so, how? If not, who was at fault? Why didn't their managers, producers, wives, or colleagues do something to keep them together? Or was this demise just one of the worst and most wasteful blunders in the history of the entertainment industry?

---

Conflict and a spirit of divisive competition do exist. In horse racing, people place bets on which horse they think will win, place, or show. There are Lennons and McCartneys in organizational life constantly who do the same. In general, their conflicts may range from mild disagreement to a complete breakdown of a relationship. Conflict is beneficial if it contributes to the accomplishment of organizational goals. It is disruptive and destructive if it destroys or eliminates those attempting needed reform. Organizational stress is often a natural outgrowth of change and conflict. Both are ever-present. The potential for stress is inevitable. However, rather than fight one another, leaders and followers should rejoice when others are succeeding. Harmony grows out of union, from win-win relationships.

## SOURCES OF CONFLICT

Like change, most people do not like conflict. Conflict is a disagreement about beliefs or goals, a discord between two or more people usually ending in confrontation. People expect their organization to be a community of reconciliation and wholeness. They think if they do not talk about conflict, they are promoting peace. However, conflict is here to stay. American theoretical physicist Albert Einstein said, "Everything has changed but our ways of thinking, and if these do not change we drift toward unparalleled catastrophe."

Daily, many potential misunderstandings result in stressful conflicts. Some of the most common sources of conflict include the aggressive nature of people, competition for limited resources, clashes of values and interests, role-based conflict, drives for power acquisition, poorly defined responsibilities, introduction of change, and organizational climate. These categories of conflict remind me of *Westside Story*—a story of two rival gangs, the Sharks and the Jets. Their conflict was over misunderstandings due to different socio-ethnic backgrounds, their "territory," and misguided passion. Time to fight, but no time for peace.

It should be noted that what causes fights and quarrels in organizational life are actually desires that battle within people. There's conflict with self, needs or wants not being met, values being tested, perceptions being questioned, and assumptions being made. In addition, knowledge is minimal, expectations are too high or low, and personality, race, or gender differences are present. And that's just the short list. You might as well realize that our own desires and passions are the true sources of all organizational conflict. If leaders and followers keep on biting and devouring each other, they and their organizations will be destroyed.

Three other sources of conflict stand out in any organization: communication, structure, and selfishness.

## COMMUNICATION CONFLICT

Communication often results in misunderstandings and produces stress. Three common sources of misunderstandings are semantics, lack of clarity, and too many links in the communication chain. First, semantics is the study of word meanings and focuses on the relationship between words and their effect on people. Semantics does not refer to dictionary definitions of words. Rather, it supports the idea that meanings are in people. If I want to know what a word means as someone else uses it, I must ask that person for the definition instead of consulting a compendium of meanings. For example, my wife and I had a fifteen-minute lively debate one evening over our definitions of "cute," "pretty," and "beautiful" and never could agree. We grew up in the same state and by that time had known each other for years. I doubt any two people could agree on such judgment calls. It's hard enough to predict which dog should win in a dog show or which cook should take the ribbon at the Pillsbury Bake Off. I don't dare start a definition of "sexy." Probably best not to go there.

In the O. J. Simpson murder trial, Salvadorian Rosa Lopez said, upon cross-examination, that her comments, "If you say so, sir" meant yes, while "I don't know, sir" meant no. Today, we all know what President Bill Clinton meant when he said he did not have sex with Monica Lewinsky, but at the time, we did not really know his meaning.

That's why you must select your words carefully in stating policies or giving instructions, directions, and orders. Followers think, feel, and act according to the images their nervous systems create. They react to the world according to how they symbolize it, much like a formula. Therefore, you must respond sanely to followers' words and with tolerance for differences, thereby reducing stress and improving organizational climate.

Second, a lack of clarity suggests inadequate and unclear communication. Accurate and correct information is especially necessary in the wording of instructions. The less detail given or the more ambiguous instructions are, the more inaccurate detail members will supply, and the more stressful the relationship will become. That is why you must plan communication paths that lead to understanding, encode your words carefully, and not expose your followers to a barrage of words or lose them in a jargon jungle of word confusion. In other words, you need to put things in a layperson's language.

Third, too many links in the communication chain refers to the number of people through whom a message passes. If there are too many links and leaders and followers are too far apart, there is more likelihood for misunderstandings. As the message travels down the chain, it will change, details will drop out, new details will be added, some things will be made more important, and some will become less important. A verbal message will seldom arrive at its destination in the same context it began. If you have ever played the game "Gossip" or "Telephone," you know what happens as communication travels from one person to another. By the time the message reaches the last person, it has been altered significantly or become completely garbled. Sometimes we just give up passing the message because we know there is no way to make sense of it.

People's ideas, attitudes, beliefs, and even volume cause message distortion. The careless use of words or a reliance on wrong words to convey a meaning can result in a loss of understanding. And the more distorted a message becomes, the more stressed people become when they recognize they are dealing with incomplete information. The same holds true when they believe the leader's attitude or beliefs keeps him or her blinded to what is being said and closed to other ways of thinking.

These are three sources of communication conflict that can put followers in an ambiguous position (i.e., not fully understand what is expected). My followers, to illustrate, can create enough stress for themselves and one another without me creating undue tension through inadequate instructions. Thus, there are a few things I can do to reduce communication stress. For example, I can provide recognition for jobs well done, help followers with their problems, provide adequate information on how to perform a task, and explain reasons for changes and how they will benefit the people as well as affect things like stress, materials, efficiency, profitability, safety, etc.

## STRUCTURAL CONFLICT

Structure refers to the organizational factors a leader can control. Structural conflict refers to the organizational factors that seem out of control. These include size, clear lines of authority, responsibility, homogeneity or heterogeneity of staff, participation, goals, and objectives. Any of these factors, and a myriad of others, can create organizational stress. For example, if mission, authority, or responsibility are obscure, followers will not know what is expected. Conflict will arise because of an incompatibility of expectations, and stress will be experienced.

Part of the daily wear-and-tear on organizational health and performance can be traced to dubiousness and conflict. Can anything be done about such pressures? Observe five recommendations. Do not:

1.  *Overreact to crises.* Scale down your emotional reactions, like anger, panic, and frustration. Count to ten. Breathe.

2.  *Take things personally.* Criticism should be related to behavior and not the individual.

3.  *Worry about things that are out of your control.* Do what you can to remedy an unsatisfactory situation. Once it is out of your hands, quit worrying about it.

4. *Drain your emotional reserves.* Know when emotional reserves are being taxed. Is it a certain time of day after a sugar or caffeine low or after personal e-mails?

5. *Over-organize uncommitted time.* Create flexible schedules that foster creativity. Give in to spur-of-the-moment impulses.

You must do all that you can do to reduce both communication and structural stress. You can do things like plan recreational activities with followers—golf, tennis, table games, lunch, or social events where laughter abounds. However, you must recognize that the real culprit of conflict is often selfishness.

## SELFISH CONDUCT

Selfishness probably begins at birth—feed me, change me, hold me, bathe me; now, do it again—and does not seem to end until death. "Me before you, always." "I'm the center of the universe." "I want what I want, because I want it." Such are the attitudes of selfishness. There is a joke on college campuses that circulates among male students that asks, "How many freshman girls does it take to screw in a lightbulb?" Answer: "One. She holds the bulb, and the world revolves around her." Do you know a similar joke about males?

Taken to extremes, the selfish person does what the self wants, when the self wants, and how the self wants, even if it hurts someone else. This selfish philosophy is promulgated through slogans such as: "Watch out for Number One." "I owe it to myself." "It may cost more, but I'm worth it." "The most important person is me." Without exception, when conflict exists, it can usually be traced to a selfish spirit in one person, perhaps in both persons. Someone is unyielding in attitude.

Therefore, you need to pursue those things in life that enable you to be a better servant, not selfishly place yourself at the center of the universe. You must recognize a critical key to avoiding conflict is to get followers involved in productive activities. You must encourage them to see the importance of learning to serve others. That may entail doing activities with them as a group and having an enjoyable time doing it. Let your creative people plan those activities.

## RESULTS OF CONFLICT

Conflict can have a number of effects on followers. Conflict can hamper productivity, lower morale, and cause inappropriate behaviors. On the other hand, it can help address problems, energize work to be done on the most appropriate issue, and help people learn how to recognize their differences. President Abraham Lincoln said, "The dogmas of the quiet past will not work in the turbulent future. As our cause is new, so must we think and act anew." Often, the key is to understand how to look at the same things differently. Three negatives, however, do stand out:

1.  *Conflict magnifies faults and weaknesses in others.* In the midst of conflict, leaders and followers seek to justify their position and win the dispute. In an attempt to "prove" the leader's stand, the leader discredits the follower's views. Focus is placed on the follower's life to illuminate additional faults and weaknesses that add support to the leader's feelings and opinions. These techniques usually result in serious damage to relationships and organizational productivity.

2. *Conflict creates divisions.* Division tears both large organizations and individual relationships apart and can destroy them. At these points, people may start making plans to sever ties, look for new departments, or even new arrangements. This may be passive aggressive, but it avoids further direct conflict at the time.

3. *Conflict causes people to expend energies on nonproductive activities.* Conflict leaves people physically and emotionally drained and consumes a great deal of thinking time. If conflict is related to legal issues like sexual harassment, it could lead to court action, which further takes away from work and brings negative attention.

Conflict does not always have to end in hostility and a fist-in-the-face confrontation. Some disagreements are often needed and can be beneficial. Disagreement can:

1. *Lead to growth.* Disagreement can lead to changes that ultimately produce improvements. Since many leaders are naturally combative, they should welcome debate and a chance to prove their ideas. "Yes men" are not of great value for improvements. An automobile gauge that always points to "full" even when it is "empty" or says the motor is "cool" when it is "hot" will lead you astray.

2. *Reveal the need for change.* Mature leaders welcome disagreement because it forces them to evaluate their own beliefs and make positive changes where needed.

3. *Help people be tolerant of opposing views.* Disagreement can become an excellent teacher of tolerance. Learning to accept differing viewpoints without developing hostile reactions is another mark of the mature leader. The effective leader learns to "agree to disagree" and to "disagree without being disagreeable."

In conflict, leaders can learn to avoid developing a critical attitude, even when followers are critical and exhibit hostility toward them. They can discover a path to positive results.

## CONFLICT RESOLUTION

Ultimately, conflict can lead to confrontation. Sometimes, the only way to resolve disagreement is to approach it head on, face-to-face, and work toward peace. Thus, confrontation is both a difficult and important task for all leaders. Fortunately, there are multiple conflict management strategies to choose from. As American socialist writer and philosopher Eric Hoffer wrote, "The only way to predict the future is to have the power to shape it." The same is true about being ready for conflict with a backup plan for resolution.

### CONFLICT MANAGEMENT STRATEGIES

Research has found that leaders tend to use one or two of several strategies more than others. Here are some familiar ones:

1. *Forcing*—using formal authority or power to satisfy a concern without regard to the concerns of the followers: e.g., "You'll take this shift." "Brook is going to work with you on this." or, "That's the way I have it lined out."

2. *Accommodating*—allowing followers to satisfy their concerns while neglecting leader concerns: e.g., "Okay, if that will make it easier for you, I'll make it happen." or, "Blair, would you mind redrawing this design?"

3. *Avoiding*—not paying attention to the conflict and taking no action to resolve it: e.g., "Oh, they'll work it out." "They always have some little argument over new activities." "Just shut the door."

4. *Compromising*—attempting to resolve a conflict by identifying a solution that is partially satisfactory to both the leader and followers but not completely satisfactory to either: e.g., "Let's just give you this half of the territory and her this part, call it even, and get on with it, okay?" or, "I'm sure you two are unselfish enough to work this our satisfactorily between the two of you." or "Just keep me advised what you decide."

5. *Collaborating*—cooperating with followers to understand their concerns and expressing leader concerns in an effort to find a mutually and completely satisfactory solution (i.e., win-win): e.g., "I can see this is important to you both." or, "What would it take to seem fair to you, Anna Grace? Morgan? Aidan? Okay, great input; here's how it looks to me."

To further illustrate: I predominately use collaboration instead of force, accommodation, avoidance, or compromise when an interpersonal conflict arises. Why? Because collaboration promotes creative problem solving, and it fosters communication and mutual respect. However, collaboration takes time. Therefore, if conflict resolution is urgent or too trivial to take the time to collaborate, I might use benevolent force (power). In other situations, one of the other three strategies might be chosen. These choices would indicate that I understand interpersonal conflict situations and use appropriate conflict management strategy for each situation. However, no one is that perfect!

## MATCHING STRATEGIES TO SITUATIONS

There are a few key variables that define conflict and determine which strategies are most likely to be effective. For example:

1. *Time pressure*—when speed of decision is critical

2. *Issue importance*—extent to which priorities, principles, or values are involved

3. *Relationship importance*—need to maintain a close, supportive relationship

4. *Relative power*—how much power both leaders and followers have

To illustrate, if I am dealing with a moderately important issue, I may use compromise to reach a quick solution. However, compromise will not totally satisfy either a follower or me. If the conflict is over a fairly important issue, I might use accommodation because it also is a quick way to solve the issue. It also will not put unnecessary strain on my relationship with the follower. Finally, if there is no time pressure or a clear advantage to waiting for resolution, I might use avoidance. Of course, if either the issue or the relationship is important, avoidance is a poor strategy.

## REACHING CONSENSUS

Collaboration is often necessary to reach agreement. If you choose to use collaboration, however, you must be able to recognize and respect everyone's ideas, opinions, and recommendations. Everyone must agree on a point being discussed before it can be part of a decision. A few of the guidelines I've learned on reaching consensus are to avoid:

1. *Arguing.* Present a point of view as logically as possible.

2. *Thinking you must win.* Occasionally there is no win-win possibility.

3. *Changing your point of view just to achieve harmony.* Unanimity is not the goal.

4. *Voting.* Keep asking questions.

5. *Thinking that just because agreement seems to have been reached that everyone has willingly agreed to the solution.* Sometimes, there is no convincing some people.

The goal of reaching consensus is to have everyone logically accept a point of view. If you can understand and accept the differing views, you should be able to reach consensus.

## CONCLUSION

Conflict must be accepted as a continuing result of people living and working together. Resolution of conflict via confrontation is a sensible solution for a more productive organizational environment, particularly during periods of change. You, as a leader, must guide any energies being wasted in conflict into productive accomplishment of goals. Deal with it, and performance will start to improve immediately.

If the conflict reaches too high of a comfort level, you now have techniques to use to reduce it. Keep in mind, however, that no one option will always be the right choice. Which one you choose will depend on your desire to be more cooperative and less assertive or less cooperative and more assertive.

How's your confidence level in solving the next conflict situation in which you find yourself? Are *you* ready to navigate around and survive turbulent times?

# WHAT'S OUR GAME PLAN?

## STRATEGY IMPLEMENTATION
## AND EVALUATION

Successful strategists take the time to think about their businesses, where they are with their businesses, and what they want to be as organizations—and then they implement programs and policies to get from where they are to where they want to be in a reasonable period of time.

—Fred R. David,
educator, author, and strategic planning facilitator

So they said, "Let us rise up and build." Then they set their hands to this good work... So I answered them, and said to them, "The god of heaven himself will prosper us; therefore we His servants will arise and build ... So the wall was finished on the twenty-fifth day of Elul, in fifty-two days. And it happened when all our enemies heard of it, and all the nations around us saw these things, that they were very disheartened in their own eyes; for they perceived that this work was done by our God.

Nehemiah 2:18, 20; 6:14 (NKJV)

Every leader I've ever known or worked with, whether in business, education, nonprofits, or civic and church organizations, had a preference for their goals and how they were to be met. These leaders would spend endless hours drawing up the plans that were to be carried out, often with varying degrees of effectiveness. For most of them, the plans were just the starting point. All the essentials that should come afterwards were sometimes followed up on and sometimes (most times) not.

There is one leader who not only wrote out plans but also followed through to build a winning organization. His followers helped create a successful organization because of the way they executed their strategic plan at a level of competitive greatness. This leader I never met, and he is now deceased, but I watched and admired him for years: Coach John Wooden.

Coach Wooden was a genius at leadership. One of the reasons was because he mastered the art of keeping his plans simple. Another was that he taught his followers good habits. He not only possessed great qualities and characteristics of a leader, but he taught those same qualities and characteristics to his teams via a simple formula: conditioning plus fundamentals plus unity equals winning, a simple formula that when worked properly brought winning records.

Have you ever known such a person? Who was he or she?

Wooden was the head basketball coach for the UCLA Bruins for twenty-seven years. During that time he won 620 games and ten NCAA titles during his last twelve seasons, including seven in a row. His teams also had a record-winning streak of eighty-eight games and four perfect seasons. They also won thirty-eight straight games in NCAA tournaments and a record ninety-eight straight home games. Wooden was named NCAA College Basketball's "Coach of the Year" seven times. He also received *Sports Illustrated* magazine's "Sportsman of the Year" award.

Wooden's leadership and coaching set record after record. How was that possible? Why has no one else been able to match those records? If you were to try to copy his plans and implement them successfully, could you be as successful? Can you explain why or why not? What's *your* game plan?

---

Once all the interactive relationships are in place and strategies have been set, they must be put to work. Strategy implementation implies *action*—mobilizing members and leaders. Motivation is critical since implementation requires personal discipline, commitment, and sacrifice. Strategies formulated but not implemented serve no purpose. They were just mental gymnastics.

Strategy implementation is designed to achieve results. It hinges on four possible relationships between leaders and followers. These relationships may determine whether the strategy can be implemented partially or fully or not at all.

1. Leaders *don't* understand the follower's needs, wants, and abilities.

2. Leaders *do* understand the follower's needs, wants, and abilities.

3. Followers *don't* understand the strategic plan.

4. Followers *do* understand the strategic plan.

These relationships depend on how well the leader understands or does not understand the follower's needs, wants, and abilities and how well the followers understand or do not understand the leader's strategic plan. Both leaders and followers may *choose* to understand or not understand. When either chooses to not understand, they are working at cross-purposes. Of course, there are times everything may just be muddled, too ambitious, or circuitous for anyone to understand.

## STRATEGIC IMPLEMENTATION

To make strategies easier to implement, leaders think in terms of action. They consider the following actions for change, using action verbs at the start:

1. Examine internal and external forces that require a change.

2. Diagnose reasons for change.

3. Examine constraints and limitations that may inhibit change.

4. Identify performance objectives and outcomes.

5. Apply methods to implement change.

Leaders attempt to reach a state of mutual understanding with their followers. They know that for comprehension, followers need openness and effective listening (attention), suspension of judgment, congruence (agreement), and feedback (reaction). In short, they work to improve the two-way flow of information and promote good listening habits. They focus attention on their messages, motivate their listeners, tailor the information to their followers, talk about familiar and understandable things, repeat the important points in their message, and use illustrations to achieve understanding. They are responsive to what is heard, read, and seen. They believe they are responsible for understanding. Therefore, in order to develop confidence, reliance, expectation, and hope, effective leaders develop communication policies of openness, honesty, and trust.

Leaders encourage followers to be credible sources. They are empathetic and recognize that listening is an active process involving meanings, feelings, and cues. They know both how to give and receive constructive criticism. They also place a high priority on understanding. Such measures build bridges and provide answers to communication problems. They realize that strategy implementation impacts everyone.

For our purposes, strategy implementation may be thought of in three phases: structuring for strategy, controlling for success, and focusing organizational efforts.

## STRUCTURING FOR STRATEGY

The successful functioning of an organization requires much more than drawing an organizational chart or describing well-designed jobs. It also is more than deciding who performs what tasks or who works with whom. It is more than identifying the main trends of organizational structure in modern management theory. Leaders must set into motion an organization that works efficiently and effectively toward its desired end. In short, they structure for strategy.

To illustrate the age-old question of whether structure actually does follow strategy (or vice-versa), Alfred Chandler, a former business professor at Harvard Business School, conducted a classic study of DuPont, General Motors, Sears, and Standard Oil. He found that corporations in their early years tended to have a centralized functional organizational structure. As new product lines are added, sources of supplies purchased, and distribution networks created, organizations shift to a decentralized structure. His research generally supported his hypothesis that structure follows strategy. (However, it should be noted also that structure does have an influence on strategy.)

## CONTROLLING FOR SUCCESS

Strategic control determines whether an organization's strategies are successful in reaching its goals. If strategies are failing, then controls are typically modified so goals may be achieved. Although "control" is generally discussed as budgeting, strategic control is much broader than simply controlling budgeted expenditures. In some ways, strategic control is similar to the control exercised at a dam. The engineer controls the water flow needed for the community below. Too much water encourages uncontrolled growth. Too little water withers growth. Thus, leaders will do all they can to control for success. Two factors are pivotal: establishing policies and allocating resources.

## *Establishing Policies*

Policies are broad guidelines and rules that express the limits within which actions occur. These rules may take the form of contingent decisions for resolving conflict between or among goals. For example, GE says it must be number one or two in whatever market it competes. Southwest Airlines will offer no meals or reserved seating on flights. Cisco will only take over companies with fewer than seventy-five employees if 75 percent of the employees are engineers. Nordstrom operates on the policy that the customer is always right. The overall purpose of any policy is to guide the thinking, decision making, and actions of followers.

Policies may be segmented into two categories—strategic policies and implementation policies. *Strategic policies* guide the strategic planning process in an organization. Selecting the best policy must entail defining ground rules to implementing the policy.

*Implementation policies* do the same for the strategy implementation process. For instance, some of the issues involved in setting policies for an organization include: scope of activities, organizational image, fundamental goals/objectives, societal/community responsibility, and organizational orientation. Some of the issues involved in implementing policies include: type of structure, leadership styles, motivation systems, coordination techniques, and evaluation systems.

Whatever the policies, leaders must assume flexibility and not etch operational rules in concrete. They must be consistent with today's environment, internally and externally, recognizing that these might change somewhat in a year or five years. A change in policy should quickly follow a change in strategy.

## Allocating Resources

Strategy implementation also consists of allocating resources according to goal priorities. The process typically involves reviewing budgets, revising program scheduling, initiating strategic planning, planning personnel load, and setting objectives. The ultimate decision is who gets how much and is important, as everybody can make a case for getting a bigger piece of the pie. Thus, two issues stand out: What budgets and programs are needed to carry out the strategic plan? How should energies on achieving organization-wide objectives be focused? How well these two issues are handled determines whether an organization is results-oriented and directed toward strategy accomplishment or is bogged down and wandering off the path.

All leaders must have the resources (followers, monies, rights, and permissions) needed to carry out the various programs. Examples of important resource allocation issues include the following:

1. How much should be allocated to try to rebuild or reposition after a time of decline and weakness?

2. How much should be budgeted for advertising and promotion?

3. What extra resources will be needed to install a newly acquired computer and software system and establish effective reporting measures and financial controls?

4. What resource allocation implications are shifting from a growth strategy to a maintenance position?

5. What will it cost to establish a distinctive competence in the community?

How well leaders resolve such decisions determines success. Effective leaders will shift resources in support of strategic change.

## FOCUSING ORGANIZATIONAL EFFORTS

Critical tasks and key activities are linked directly and clearly to strategy implementation activities. Matching structure to strategy provides a valuable linkage. Scholar and author Rensis Likert wrote a classic work on the characteristics of ineffective and effective organizations. His challenge:

1. Organizations that are *ineffective and unsuccessful* typically have low follower involvement and interest and lack performance results.

2. Organizations that are *effective and successful* have high follower involvement and good results.

Leaders look inward, analyzing whether they promote effective, successful growth or are a hindrance to excellence. It is true that an organization may grow in spite of its leadership, but its growth cannot be sustained and nurtured by either absentee leaders (mentally, physically, or spiritually) or by a structure that does not follow strategy. Ideally, organizational structure flows from decisions about strategic direction. When the organizational structure is out of sync with the followers, it is little wonder they are not loyal to leadership.

Sometimes the organizational structure may seem out of sync because the leaders and followers don't fully understand the skills and abilities available in certain people. To illustrate: A good way to introduce yourself to a new leader is to make an appointment to welcome him or her to the organization. Introduce yourself, tell what you are responsible for, what you love about the job, what you'd like to do more of in the future, and why you're willing to help in any way you can. If you're the new leader, listen to what the follower is saying, what his motivators are, what her talents are, what her obvious interests are, and what his frustrations with organizational policies are. Think how you can use this person for strategy implementation. (I know of a marketing director for Integris Hospital who introduced herself to a new CEO and got acquainted early with him. She reported that she moved up the ladder quickly because the CEO remembered her and what he had learned at that let's-get-acquainted session.)

## STRATEGIC EVALUATION

The final stage in the strategic leadership process, after formulation and implementation, is *evaluation*. Kenneth Iverson, Chairman of the Board at Nucor Corporation, says they attempt to keep the evaluation and control process simple.

We try to keep our focus on what really matters—bottom-line performance and long-term survival. That's what we want our people to be thinking about. Management takes care not to distract the company with a lot of talk about other issues. We don't clutter the picture with lofty vision statements or ask employees to pursue vague, intermediate objectives like "excellence" or burden them with complex business strategies. Our competitive strategy is to build manufacturing facilities economically and to operate them efficiently. Period. Basically we ask our employees to produce more product for less money. Then we reward them for doing that well.

Three fundamental activities must be performed to effectively assess an organization's strategies. An organization must:

1. *Review the internal strengths and weaknesses and the external opportunities and threats that represent the bases for its current strategies.* Key questions to ask: Are internal strengths still strengths (SWOT)? Are internal weaknesses still weaknesses? Are external opportunities still opportunities? Are external threats still threats?

2. *Measure performance.* Examine planned versus actual progress being made toward achieving stated goals and objectives.

3. *Implement corrective actions (or contingency plans) as needed.* Improve the internal and external strategic positions as occasions demand it.

Strategy evaluation is a critical stage in the strategic leadership process because internal and external factors do change. Successful organizations anticipate and adapt to changes quickly and effectively. Major changes in the underlying bases of a strategy may not impact current performance until it is too late to avoid or capitalize upon the event or trend. Therefore, alternative strategies should be considered whenever key internal and external factors change significantly.

Strategy evaluation is needed because success today is no guarantee for success tomorrow. In fact, success generally renders ineffective the behavior that brought it about. Success always creates new and different problems.

## MEASURES OF PERFORMANCE

How well did we do? We all want to know. So the most commonly used measures of strategic performance (i.e., success of implementation) include strategic plans, long-range plans, budgets, performance appraisals, policies and procedures, and statistical reports. Many organizations employ comprehensive measures of performance. One particular technique employed is the *strategic audit*. The general format of a strategic audit generally follows a twofold pattern.

First, determine the organization's current position in terms of its mission, goals, objectives, policies, and hierarchy of strategies. Some measures that could be used for such determination might be return on investment (ROI) and earnings per share (EPS). Other examples might be the ISO (International Standards Association of Geneva, Switzerland) 9000 and 14000 standards.

Second, determine the firm's strengths, weaknesses, opportunities, and threats. Remember how to conduct a SWOT analysis? The goal is to establish, maintain, and continually improve operations.

The general purpose of strategy evaluation is to provide a true picture of what is taking place. An evaluation, therefore, should not be cumbersome and restrictive. It should be simple and useful.

There is no one ideal strategy evaluation system. The larger the organization, the more elaborate will be the system—profitability, market share, cost reduction, etc. The smaller the organization is, the simpler the system—sales quotas, cost reduction targets, profit objectives, surveys of customer satisfaction, etc. Evaluation should not dominate decisions; however, it should foster mutual understanding, trust, and support.

## TESTS FOR STRATEGY

Once strategies have been formulated and implemented, they must be evaluated. The NASA space station being shared by the United States and Russia might be a perfect example. Can you imagine the amount of planning and training that had to be done prior to launch, docking, working together, and returning to earth? Strategy author Seymour Tilles has provided one of the best-known sets of criteria for testing strategy: appropriateness, internal consistency, external consistency, risk acceptability, duration of commitment, and workability.

### *Appropriateness*

The first major test question asks: *Is the strategy appropriate in light of the available resources?* Physical forces include money, competence, facilities, and member loyalty. In conjunction with these factors, leaders must decide two basic issues in relating strategy and resources. What are the critical resources, and is the proposed strategy appropriate for available resources? One of the most difficult issues in formulating strategy is the achievement of balance between strategic goals and available resources. Thus, leaders must decide how much to commit to opportunities currently perceived and how much to keep uncommitted in reserve.

## Internal Consistency

The second question asks: *Is the strategy internally consistent?* Internal consistency refers to the cumulative impact of individual policies on goals. In a well-worked-out strategy, each policy will fit into an integrated pattern. These strategies must reflect not only the current but the evolving elements within the organization. For example, a new project test might be divided into certain aptitudes and expectations. Internal consistency reliability tests will provide a measure that each of these particular aptitudes is measured correctly and reliably. The same could be said about the implementation of new policies. Do they fit into an incorporated whole?

## External Consistency

The third crucial question a strategist asks: *Is the strategy consistent with the external environment?* An important test of strategy is whether it makes sense with respect to what is going on outside the organization. Strategy must reflect not only the current but the evolving elements in the environment because these elements open up opportunities and/or pose threats. Are you thinking of opening a rest home in an area where starter homes are being built for young couples and singles? Wouldn't a Starbucks or Gymboree be better?

## Risk Acceptability

The fourth critical question is: *Does the strategy involve an acceptable degree of risk?* All types of risks are associated with strategic decisions. Each organization must decide its own comfort zone with risk. The risk spectrum ranges from no risk to a situation where survival is at stake. Should you stay on the bunny slope all day or move over to the black diamond slopes and go for the gold? Three qualitative factors assist evaluation of risk inherent in a strategy: the amount of resources appropriated, the time span to which resources are committed, and the proportion of resources committed to a particular course of action.

## Duration of Commitment

The fifth pivotal question a strategist must ask is: *Does the strategy have an appropriate time horizon?* Viable strategy reveals not only what is to be accomplished but also when the goals will be achieved. The longer the time horizon, the greater is the range of alternatives. Thus, goals must be established far enough in advance to allow the organization to adjust to them.

## Workability

The sixth key question for evaluating and choosing strategy alternatives is: *Does the strategy work?* Is it reasonable and doable yet challenging and not boring? Will it keep the excitement level and motivation up? Are there rewards as you move along? If a strategy will not work, there is little reason to implement it.

If the above criteria (i.e., tests for strategy) can be met, an organization has the right strategy for itself. Although these criteria do not guarantee success, they are valuable for giving leaders both the time and room to maneuver. And these key questions also provide many decision-making opportunities. Unacceptable answers may necessitate either a change in strategy or corrective and preventive actions.

## CONTINGENCY PLANNING

Regardless of how carefully strategies are formulated, implemented, and evaluated, unforeseen events can make a strategy obsolete. So a plan B is always in the back of a leader's mind. What if we're cut off at the pass? What if it rains every day of the dedication ceremonies? How will we handle a mechanic strike when a new product launch is just around the corner?

To minimize the impact of newly discovered weaknesses and/or threats, leaders develop contingency plans to support their formal plans. A contingency plan is an alternative plan that can be put into effect if certain events do not occur as expected. It provides a similar function as a safety chute if the main parachute does not open. Such contingency plans, however, should be compatible with current strategy and economically feasible. They also should be subject to evaluation.

## CONCLUSION

Strategic leadership involves the major purposes of an organization, department, or unit. The long- and short-term needs must be balanced to ensure success. You must act, think, and influence in ways that lead to mission accomplishment and high performance. You must provide the direction and inspiration needed to create or sustain an organization. You must remain flexible in your strategic planning, especially given society's rapidly changing conditions.

Here are seven steps I recommend highly for strategic planning:

1. Form a dream team.

2. Clarify the mission and tenets.

3. Gather the appropriate data.

4. Create a strategic vision.

5. Identify strategic needs and issues.

6. Devise an action plan to manage the needs and issues.

7. Monitor and evaluate progress periodically.

Changes of the magnitude taking place globally require you to embrace new ways of thinking and remain flexible. Following these steps will enable you to provide sustained, proactive, initiatory leadership. You will be on the way toward creating a needed revolution within your organizational world.

Are *you* ready to implement the plans you've been dreaming about but sitting on? What's preventing you?

# IV. LEADERSHIP ESSENTIALS

If your actions inspire others to dream more, learn more, do more and become more, you are a leader.

—John Quincy Adams, US sixth president

# CAN YOU TRUST SOMEONE
# WHO SAYS TRUST ME?

## TRUST AND CREDIBILITY

For it is mutual trust, even more than mutual interest that holds human associations together. Our friends seldom profit us but they make us feel safe.

—H. L. Mencken, American journalist, satirist, critic

The Lord is my rock and my fortress and my deliverer; The God of my strength, in whom I will trust; My shield and the horn of my salvation, My stronghold and my refuge; My Savior, You save me from violence. I will call upon the Lord, who is worthy to be praised; So shall I be saved from my enemies.

2 Samuel 22:2–4 (NKJV)

The place is Niagara Falls, New York, and high above Niagara, a man is rolling a wheelbarrow with two hundred pounds of dirt back and forth over the falls on a tightrope. After completing the trip safely several times, he asks the crowd, "How many of you believe I can roll a person across?"

One observer excitedly shouted, "I know you can do it!"

The tightrope walker responded, "All right, sir, you're first." The observer left in haste.

Why? He said he believed it. He thought he believed it. So why did he leave?

If you had been there, would you have gotten in the wheelbarrow? Or would you have run away from the opportunity? Why? How courageous do you think you really are? What would keep you from getting in the wheelbarrow? Money? Insurance? Safety gear?

---

The man who refused to get in the wheelbarrow left because he did not have enough faith to commit himself to the wheelbarrow. He was unwilling to trust in the beliefs of the pusher mainly, wind conditions, rope sway, and other spectators. After all, can you really trust someone who says, "Trust me"? Trust can occur only between persons who trust one another. In fact, mutual trust between leaders and followers is the key to open communication. The more one trusts the situation, the more open one will be with the other.

American cellist and virtuoso Yo-Yo Ma illustrated the importance of trust and communication for the individual members of a string quartet when he said, "…you have to take time, lots of time, to let an idea grow from within…when you sign on to something, there will be issues of trust, deep trust, the way the members of a string quartet have to trust one another." The result? Beautiful music and satisfaction.

We believe that Lao Tzu, the father of Taoism, was correct when he wrote, "He who does not trust enough will not be trusted." In fact, one model for guaranteeing the future of twenty-first-century organizations is creating trust within the organizational community. The same is true of communities, the nation, and the world. That is why the slogans of President Barack Obama—"Change We Can Believe In," "Vote for Change," "Our Time for Change," and others—won the hearts of young people in 2008. Yet by 2010, the trust barometer had started moving downward because of the probable impossibility of fulfilling all the campaign promises. Many had grown cold toward economic stimulus and the spiraling trillion dollars of debt load.

## TRUST

Leaders must create an environment of trust. Unfortunately, trust within organizational life is in short supply in this post-Enron era. In September 2010, Hewlett-Packard Company sued Mark Hurd, the CEO they had ousted in August, to keep him from taking the top job with their rival, Oracle Corporation (a database software maker). Why? They didn't trust him not to tell Oracle secrets about HP operations. Since Oracle had hired him to help lead their efforts to grow their business, Hurd could diminish the value of HP's trade secrets, hurt customer relations, and give Oracle a strategic advantage. Would you trust Hurd?

Trust is pivotal in every organization. Trust is often equated with confidence, reliance, expectation, and hope. Unfortunately, the topic raises the question of how to rebuild trust in an era of rage. In fall 2010, there were 26 million people in the United States unable to find full-time jobs. Is it any wonder that many Americans are outraged by the disparity in pay between executives and average workers as real income steadily declines? How is it possible to rebuild trust in such situations? Will corporate boards be able to develop compensation systems that reward everyone fairly and consistently? If you have any doubts about the possibility of rebuilding a trusting climate, ask your banker friends how they feel about the Dodd-Frank Wall Street Reform and Consumer Protection Act and see how he or she feels. They may agree with you.

About the time the twenty-first century arrived, trust was beginning to be viewed as a new center of strategic power. The reason? Trust held competitive clout. Organizations with high trust cultures seem to become more profitable. That is why Arie de Geuss, former head of Shell's strategic planning group, could say the key to "sustainable competitive advantage" is having a high-trust culture that empowers an organization to learn faster than its competitors.

If it is true that trust is today's new center of power, leaders must know that trust involves an element of blind faith (not unlike Danish philosopher Soren Kierkegaard's "leap of faith"), the firm belief in honesty, truthfulness, justice, or power of another person. In fact, organizational consultant and author Warren Bennis says that the four ingredients leaders have that generate and sustain trust are constancy, congruity, reliability, and integrity. Sustained high performance is only possible if high trust exists. As a result, according to Mike Armour, president of Strategic Leadership Development, trusted leaders and trusted organizations have more influence and power than ever.

Trusted organizations that encourage a policy of openness, honesty, trust, and ongoing communication typically have lower turnover and higher morale than those organizations that have not encouraged the same things. Winning the respect of followers, developing mutual feelings of trust, and opening clogged lines of communication are goals worth striving for. American philosopher and poet Ralph Waldo Emerson wrote, "Trust men and they will be true to you; treat them greatly, and they will show themselves great." However, neither leaders nor followers can really trust one another until both show they are trustworthy.

Winning the respect of employees, developing mutual feelings of trust between leaders and followers, and opening clogged lines of communication are the kinds of accomplishments most leaders hope for but few achieve. That is why leaders create climates conducive to productivity. Healthy, trusting relationships encourage followers to achieve their full potential.

Greek philosopher Aristotle wrote, "Wishing to be friends is quick work, but friendship is a slow ripening fruit." Thus, three points seem especially important in developing trust: First, there are degrees of confidence in a trusted individual. Those levels of trust increase with time and demonstrations of trustworthiness. Second, some minimal amount of risk is involved in trusting another person. Sometimes it appears risky to reach out to others, but the effort usually results in growth. Third, congruence is critical in any trusting relationship. Everyone prefers others with whom they have agreement or harmony.

## CONFIDENCE IN TRUST

Deciding whom to trust is a complicated task based on a variety of cues—talking speed, gestures, body language, physical appearance, similarity of others to yourself, and comfortableness with others. Trust cuts across all social arenas and is the glue that cements good social and working relationships. However, trust is fragile. Followers often withhold trust until they feel safe and are convinced the leader is trustworthy.

At different trust levels, there are three ways to describe attitudes and behaviors, say executive coach Richard Huseman and John Hatfield, Stanford University professor. Notice: (a) no trust, (b) low trust, and (c) high trust. In the first two instances, trust needs development or restoration. One reason for the first two could be that trust was destroyed by a careless action or word. Be aware; trust is closely aligned with truth. As Irish writer Oscar

Wilde said, "The pure and simple truth is rarely pure and never simple." Trust may have the same qualities, which may have led author Aldous Huxley to write, "Ye shall know the truth, and the truth shall make you mad."

Trust is destroyed easily and rebuilt slowly. Television personality and author Dr. Phil McGraw says the best predictor of future behavior is past behavior. For instance, in a marriage, a betrayal sometimes takes a lifetime to rebuild a trusting relationship. Rebuilding trust is difficult and very time-consuming, if it ever can be rebuilt. Rebuilding trust may require both parties meeting and forgiving each other. It may require a promise to not repeat the problem, sometimes even to the extent of entering into a verbal and written contract. The one who damaged or broke trust must accept accountability for his or her actions, which could require a change in behavior or attitude.

There are a number of ways by which a leader can develop trust and confidence in followers. For example, you might share credit generously, seek advice and feedback, make promises only when they can be kept, be explicit and direct, or be timely. Since building relationships is rooted in building trust, you also will want to demonstrate trust.

## RISK IN TRUST

Trusting is risking. If people lived in a risk-free environment, there would be little need for trust. When professors take students for a semester abroad and each knows they have to live with one another a few months, lots of interviewing takes place to settle on whether each person can take the others' values and rules and personalities before the dotted line is signed. Good decisions help avoid risk and often make good friends for years or for life.

Trust is analogous to "going out on a limb." If you had worked for movie mogul Samuel Goldwyn, who was known for his ambition, bad temper, and genius for publicity, what would you have been willing to risk after you became aware of his philosophy for operations? "I don't want any yes-men around me. I want everybody to tell me the truth even if it costs them their job." If you told him the truth, could you trust him to let you keep your job?

Once the limb of trust is cut, mistrust develops. For example, followers trust leaders to guide, guard, and direct them, and if that trust is betrayed, it will be very difficult to regain their trust or use any motivation technique to move them to higher ground. Neither leaders nor followers can really trust each other until the other demonstrates their trustworthiness.

To illustrate: Leader *A* lacks trust in Follower *B* because of loose talk regarding a confidential matter by *B* several weeks ago. Thus, *A* tends to conceal his attitudes about a certain related issue, *X*, when communicating with *B*. Leader *A*'s concealment is accomplished by evasive, compliant, or aggressive communication. The short-term result is that Follower *B* assumes disagreement in some cases regarding *X*. The long-term result is that *B* disregards the majority of what *A* says. The risk is too high to trust *A*.

Trust cannot be achieved overnight. Trust is built slowly and reinforced over time. It requires patience. And it is always a two-way street! If leaders want followers to trust and respect them, they, in turn, must trust and respect their followers. The initiative begins at the top, which requires character and strength.

Patience is critical in all relationships but especially in an organizational environment. In a society seeking instant answers (instant trust), patience is needed more than ever. Any betrayal of trust is considered by most people as an egregious violation. When trust is damaged, it is very difficult to repair. In fact, it often takes longer to rebuild trust than it did to establish it. (For example, couples who go through counseling due to one partner's infidelity often talk of the time it takes to restore trust in the unfaithful partner.) Instant trust reestablishment is a risk on the part of the one offended. Some will conclude the risk is not worth the cost or effort.

## CONGRUENCE AND BALANCE

Research into patient, credible, trusting climates suggests that leaders trust followers who provide them with congruent (balanced, in agreement) information. That is, most leaders prefer followers with whom they have agreement, harmony, or similar experiences. They seek reinforcement from situations that substantiate their attitudes, beliefs, and values. When confronted with opposing viewpoints, the leader often does not trust either the follower or the information.

When inconsistency is present, many leaders typically avoid and distrust those situations, followers, or information. Cognitive dissonance theory (i.e., the absence of consistency, uncomfortableness) suggests that leaders would avoid followers who hold attitudes, beliefs, or values dissimilar to their own. They are uncomfortable with them. Furthermore, these dissimilar individuals are frequently viewed as untrustworthy. If this situation exists in the organization between leaders and followers, however, there is little hope.

The same theory of cognitive dissonance asserts that the existence of inconsistency motivates leaders to reduce it so that consistency can be restored. If there is tension between leaders and followers because of distrust and inconsistency, either could try to reduce the tension to restore trust and consistency.

In other words, the search for congruence (or balance)—the "process"—enables one to grow in character and trust. The tension, however, will always remain because "balance" is an ideal state (like being "perfect") that can never be realistically achieved. Achieving this equilibrium, this euphoric state, is not as important as the process itself—the steps a leader takes and what happens along the way.

Congruence can be illustrated via balance theory. Balance theory assumes that people tend to organize their perceptions in consistent, comfortable ways. That is, people prefer balance (congruence) to imbalance. As an example, consider the following situation: Leaders tell their followers that the organization will be introducing a change in structure and operations. According to balance theory, there are three relationships: the attitude of the followers toward the leaders, the attitude of the followers toward the change, and the followers' perception of the leaders' attitude toward the change. If the followers have a positive attitude toward the change and toward the leaders, and if the followers believe the leaders favor the change, there is a balanced system (or balanced triad).

However, this comfortable system can become unbalanced if the followers feel negatively (untrustingly) toward any of the three possible relations (i.e., leaders/followers, leaders/change, or followers/change). If the system becomes unbalanced (i.e., a negative relationship or feeling exists), the challenge is to restore balance (i.e., create a positive relationship or feeling). It is important to note that the triad system (i.e., balance theory) requires that there be all pluses (positives) *or* two minuses (negatives) and a plus for balance to exist. (Accept this rule on faith; the answer to "why" is not critical to understanding.) So leaders have three options to keeping balance: tell the followers that they oppose the change, allow the followers to develop a negative attitude toward the leaders, or persuade the followers to accept the new change.

Although two minuses (negatives) and a plus (positive) create balance, it should be viewed as a short-lived success. This combination is not always a healthy situation because of the possible negative attitudes of the followers toward the leaders, vice versa, or either toward the situation. Neither leaders nor followers want to live or work in such a tension-filled, unhealthy, negative environment for very long.

The three positive relationships is the best type of balance to attain long-range goals, but this system sometimes becomes stagnant. Thus, some leaders may wish to deliberately cause tension by creating unbalance (+, +, -) to reach a higher plateau (new +, +, + relationships). Instead of introducing a new, needed change bit by bit, they figuratively take the bull by the horns and present the entire "change package" to shock the followers into looking with new eyes at a proposed idea.

When an organization has unbalanced triads from whatever the unagreed-upon situation, followers typically react defensively. Defensiveness is an act of protecting one's views and may represent a somewhat hostile, emotional state of mind. There are several causes of defensiveness. One cause is self-image. It is traumatic to have your image challenged, to risk losing the ability to predict, control, and know yourself. In fact, any fear of change is a basis for defensiveness. If followers perceive a threat, both their perception and subsequent behavior will be affected. Second, defensiveness results from an inability to tolerate differences in others. Although defensiveness is greater in some followers than in others, it does affect the behavior of both leaders and followers involved in a communicative encounter. Thus, it can have a very destructive, self-perpetuating cycle.

## SUPPORT

The achievement of balance and congruence does raise an important question: How can leaders reduce defensiveness in followers? Where does trust enter the picture? Why would they want to follow me? Good questions. Much of it may have to do with whether they like you, whether they've seen you make good judgments in the past, or whether you're viewed as a winner. If some things do not seem that favorable, you may have to convince people to follow.

One way to persuade others to follow is to change their ideas and/or behavior. However, know up front that a leader's attempt to change followers may backfire. Remember the adage about leading a horse to water but being unable to make him drink? Often when followers perceive that a definite attempt is being made to make them change (especially if manipulative tactics are involved), they react in a contrary fashion to preserve their freedom to act or think. Therefore, leaders must provide an open, supportive climate in their organizations. Empathizing, understanding, and being genuine go a long way in reducing defensiveness.

One technique for showing supportive behaviors is the helping relationship. The helping relationship is a special form of temporary interaction between:

1.  *a helper*—someone who has achieved an acceptable level of personal adjustment

2.  *a helpee*—someone who is experiencing difficulty because they lack certain personal skills of adaptation, coping, and problem solving

The primary goal is constructive behavioral change. And, although there is no standard helping skills classification system, there are certain abilities that facilitate the helping relationship (e.g., understanding, support, and action). That is, the helper avoids evaluating—judging the relative goodness, appropriateness, effectiveness, or rightness of the helpee's statements. Additionally, the helper refrains from interpreting—teaching, imparting meaning, or implying—what the helpee might or ought to think. Instead, the helper supports—reassures, pacifies, and reduces the helpee's intensity of feeling. The helper probes—gathers further information, provokes further discussion, and queries or understands—and responds in a manner that assists the helper to understand what has been said or felt.

For trusting relationships, for effective communication of ideas, for win-win compromises, and for effective solution of problems, effective leaders provide a supportive climate for their followers.

## CREDIBILITY

Trust and credibility go hand in hand. Both present reasonable grounds for belief in what someone is saying. As Greek Athenian philosopher Socrates said, "The first key to greatness is to be in reality what we appear to be." Unfortunately, there seem to be degrading standards for integrity in business. Sometimes, those standards are violated enough that they are reported on the news, the front page of the newspaper, or even on 60 *Minutes*. Someone is either fired or goes to jail. Violations of the Sarbanes Oxley Act of 2002, as an example, carry stiff penalties—including jail time and fines. As Phillips Brooks, an American clergyman and author, wrote, "Character may be manifested in the great moments, but it is made in the small ones." In any organization, trust must be developed among every member if success is going to be achieved.

Dwight L. Moody, an American evangelist, said, "If I take care of my character, my reputation will take care of me." If you are credible, you are trustworthy. However, credibility should not be equated with acceptance. For example, British Petroleum's credibility sank in 2010 as their oil spill in the Gulf of Mexico grew. From the amount of oil gushing to the abject failures to stop the leak and environmental impact, BP's statements were viewed as wrong. Their president's apologies and promises were viewed as ridiculous and insulting. Thus, the erosion of their credibility was as difficult to stop as the oil flow.

The important thing to remember about factors influencing credibility is that they vary as a function of each specific situation.

Research has identified several dimensions of interpersonal credibility factors—expertise, reliability, intentions, dynamism, respect, competence, and objectivity. These factors are hard earned, and their balance builds slowly over time. Followers are constantly looking for clues, comparing words and actions, making sure the way leaders talk and the way they walk are credible. While leaders forget it occasionally, they are on trial every day.

Credibility has roots in past relationships. It is often based, in the beginning, upon the reputation of either the leader or the follower. Like trust, credibility is earned over time. It does not happen automatically when a person becomes the leader. Both are granted to others over time as each is built brick by brick. This much we know: Credibility matters. It makes a difference. It serves a purpose and sustains hope. It is closely related to integrity, honesty, fairness, honorable, dignity, and respect.

There are, however, several *myths* about credibility that consultant Steve Mills says need clarification. That list includes the following:

1. *Image is more important than character.* Actually, credibility and character are more important than image. Without integrity, credibility crumbles.

2. *A leader can lead by position regardless of example.* It is possible, but a credible leader leads by example, not power.

3. *A leader's personal and public life do not have to be consistent.* This statement is not even a reasonable excuse. Credibility requires congruency and consistency.

4. *Integrity isn't essential to success.* True success requires integrity and credibility. Success cannot be defined only in terms of money, position, or power.

Concerning credibility, researchers conclude that most important is the listener's perception of the speaker as someone of high character. Thus, leaders who find ways to combine the elements of common sense, good moral character, and goodwill will be viewed as credible sources (and vice versa). If they are able to do so, they will be perceived as intelligent, reliable, and interested in their followers.

That is why leaders combine the elements of good sense, good moral character, and goodwill to be viewed as credible sources. How are leaders to do this?

1. *Be consistent in words and behaviors.* A leader cannot be viewed as constantly changing plans, shifting courses, or reversing decisions. (I can tell you about a president that submitted four different sets of goals within three months one year.)

2. *Share the truth.* Be honest and trustworthy to the extent it is reasonably possible to do so. Do not lie. (There are occasionally things that cannot be revealed to everyone.)

3. *Interact face-to-face.* Effective interpersonal communication will inspire loyalty and build credibility. (If you've ever had to work with a disloyal person, you know the difficulty.)

If leaders can accomplish these three items, they will also be perceived as intelligent (i.e., have correct opinions), reliable (i.e., honest), and interested in their followers (i.e., have favorable intentions toward them). Such measures of trust and credibility are built carefully and patiently. Never doubt that credibility is the soul of leadership. Remember this statement from Richard Baxter, a prominent English churchman of the 1600s: "Men will never cast away their dearest pleasures upon the drowsy request of someone who does not even seem to mean what he says."

## CONCLUSION

The preceding ideas of trust and credibility are age-old topics. Yet for most organizations, adherence to these principles would result in a radical shift in the way an organization is managed. Don't forget that followers are your most valuable resource. You must believe that every follower is filled with unlimited creative potential and hungers for fulfillment of that potential. Therefore, you should empower your followers to put their ideas into practice without going through a cumbersome bureaucratic approval system.

If you are seen as credible by followers, they will also see themselves, their responsibilities, and the organization as credible. There are at least three things you can practice to build trust and enhance credibility:

1. *Demonstrate trust in followers.* Begin with an assumption that (you and) your followers are trustworthy.

2. *Be sensitive to the needs and interests of followers.* Demonstrate interest.

3. *Foster a culture of cooperation.* Keep an open mind about the ideas and projects of followers.

When respect and mutual trust are present, there is little that stands in the way of high-performance groups and successful programs of involvement and growth.

The goal is to get followers to view you as part of the group, feel a sense of team spirit, feel committed to the group, demonstrate service to others, and speak well of the organization publicly and privately. This will only be accomplished through a longtime track record of trusting followers, encouraging independence, treating followers in ways they expect to be treated, and sharing in any glories handed the organization. If you will continue to do these things, recognizing that it is your responsibility to build trust, you will be viewed as both credible and trustworthy.

Perhaps John F. Kennedy, the thirty-fifth president of the United States, said it best:

> Of those to whom much is given, much is required. And when at some future date the high court of history sits in judgment on each of us—recording whether in our brief span of service we fulfilled our responsibilities—our success or failure, we will be measured by the answers to four questions—Were we truly men of courage? Were we truly men of judgment? Were we truly men of integrity? Were we truly men of dedication?

How's *your* courage, judgment, integrity, and dedication? How high is *your* trust quotient?

# ARE YOU BURNING DAYLIGHT?

## YOU CAN MAKE A DIFFERENCE

To laugh often and much; to win the respect of intelligent people and the affection of children... to leave the world a better place... to know even one life has breathed easier because you have lived. This is to have succeeded.

—Ralph Waldo Emerson,
American philosopher, essayist, poet

If only you would prepare your heart and lift up your hands to him in prayer! Get rid of your sins, and leave all iniquity behind you. Then your face will brighten with innocence. You will be strong and free of fear.

Job 11:13–15

It was one of those magical evenings. My wife and I were living in Glendora, California, and had invited twenty business students from Azusa Pacific University to our house one evening for dinner and conversation. After dinner, we formed a large circle in the living room to get better acquainted and talk about their needs and desires for the School of Business and Management. We went around the circle, each person telling their name, their major, where they were from, and what dreams they had for the future.

After that round circle of questions and answers, I asked the group to go around the circle one more time and tell me why they had chosen to come to APU. Of all the colleges in Southern California, why this one? Why a private university that cost at least twice what a state university would cost?

The answers varied from one person to another—they had friends or relatives at the school, they wanted a private education with smaller classes where your professors could know you and vice versa, they liked the idea of going to a school whose mission had a Christian base, they didn't want to move very far away from home, and they wanted to attend a small college rather than one of the large state universities. They could get their degree in four years as opposed to California's slow system, where it was hard to get class schedules that would permit graduation in four years. You get the idea. Then one of the students asked me why I came to APU. Why had my wife and I moved from Texas (we had been living in Abilene), our two grown sons, and other relatives?

I gave them several answers—new challenge, Southern California, an adventure, a vacation every weekend, etc. You know, the types of answers that would be expected. Then I paused for a moment and gave them the real answer: I came because I knew I could make a difference. Then I explained what I thought that difference would look like and what impact I anticipated making on their lives and the future of the school. You could have heard a pin drop. They seemed to have never thought about how they might make a difference anywhere.

It was a magical moment.

How about you? Have you given any thought to how you are going to make a difference in the lives of those with whom you work? If you haven't given that question much thought, why not start thinking about that now? How can your authentic self do that?

---

How many leaders and followers respond the same way? The main reason leaders and followers have not answered the how-can-I-make-a-difference question is they have not committed themselves to future goals. Two other reasons seem possible: Leaders don't trust followers to follow through and make the leader look good. Also, followers are not committed to their leaders and supportive of the organization because they do not (cannot?) trust their leaders' vision, communications, and/or motivational attempts. (Or they don't trust their own.)

These statements may seem too bold at first glance. Yet both leaders and followers are looking for their niche in an organization, and that organization is a channeling agency for commitment. As Mario Andretti, world champion racing driver, said, "Desire is the key to motivation, but it is determination and commitment to an unrelenting pursuit of your goal—a commitment to excellence—that will enable you to attain the success you seek."

## COMMITMENT TO ORGANIZATIONAL GOALS

Followers come to an organization with certain needs, desires, skills, and abilities. They expect (and rightly so) to find an environment where they can use their abilities and gifts and satisfy their needs. When you provide the means for followers to satisfy their desires, commitment is enhanced. If you are undependable and fail to provide growth opportunities, the commitment level will wane. Commitment may be the most important single factor in individual and organization success. Effective leadership flows from commitment to do the right things. As a sign in a surgery center in Oklahoma City says, "It is always right to do the right thing."

There's an old saying that if you don't stand for something, you'll fall for anything. Thomas Watson, the founder of IBM, amplified this feeling in his book, *A Business and Its Beliefs.*

> …the basic philosophy, spirit, and drive of an organization have far more to do with its relative achievements than do technological or economic resources, organizational structure, innovation and timing. All these things weigh heavily in success. But they are, I think transcended by how strongly the people in the organization believe in its basic precepts and how faithfully they carry them out.

According to Richard Steers, professor emeritus at the University of Oregon, commitment is the relative strength of an individual's identification with and involvement in a particular organization. Based on that description, commitment is characterized by at least three factors: (a) belief in and acceptance of an organization's goals and values, (b) willingness to work on behalf of the organization, and (c) desire to maintain membership in that organization. Leaders influence followers to become involved. They call them by name and showcase their talents, gifts, and interests.

Educator, theologian, and civil rights activist Howard Thurman describes commitment accordingly: "Commitment means that it is possible for a man to yield the nerve center of his consent to a purpose or cause, a movement or an ideal, which may be more important to him than whether he lives or dies." That's why well-respected and high-performance leaders must have the following as part of their leadership DNA:

1. A passion for continuous improvement

2. A desire to always be learning

3. A belief in and support of change

4. A compelling vision that excites everyone

5. An ability to think and act strategically

6. A willingness to build a culture of open communication

7. An ability to attract, retain, and develop the best people

8. An initiative to commit to the future

High performance is never the result of any specific action or event. It is not necessarily the result of any one item in the above list. Rather, high performance is a relentless pursuit of excellence, the pushing of a flywheel in one direction over time. It is a matter of building momentum until a breakthrough occurs. As the leader of such a group of people, you must train to run a marathon, taking any barriers down one at a time.

## SPIRITUALITY AT THE WORKPLACE

A topic that has been experiencing a new openness and becoming more common in all kinds of workplaces engages a subject I began running a race toward some twenty-five years ago—a better understanding of spirituality and attainment of a higher level of the same. However, even though I may find it a fascinating topic, at the same time I will admit that spirituality is difficult to define. In an effort to capture the essence of spirituality in one's life, the Persian poet Rumi wrote the following.

All day I think about it, then at night I say it
Where did I come from and what am I supposed to be doing?

I have no idea
My soul is elsewhere, I'm sure of that
And I intend to end up there.

From Western civilization's religious standpoint, spirituality includes a personal moral quality encompassed by the indwelling, empowering, and guiding of the Holy Spirit. For Christians, it would involve being confirmed by God and having the mind of Jesus Christ.

## ORGANIZATIONAL SPIRITUALITY

From an organizational standpoint, spirituality has been defined by freelance writer Michael Ray and veteran book publishing insider Alan Rinzler as "that which is traditionally believed to be the vital principle or animating force within living beings; that which constitutes one's unseen intangible being; the real sense or significance of something." Former *Fortune* 500 executive James Autry wrote a poem called "Threads" to get at a comprehensive definition. The following is an excerpt:

> Listen.
> In every office
> You hear the threads
> of love and joy and fear and guilt,
> the cries for celebration and reassurance,
> and somehow you know that connecting those threads
> is what you are supposed to do
> and business takes care of itself.

Thus, spirituality in the workplace is viewing work as a spiritual journey, an opportunity to grow personally and contribute meaningfully to society. It involves caring and compassion, integrity, being true to self, telling the truth, and living your values in the office. It is a personal matter. And it is something that can be done without ever using the word *spirituality*. However, it is a practice that has been transformational for both people and organizations. Chick-Fil-A, Interstate Batteries, Mary Kay Cosmetics, Service Master, Tom's of Maine, Rockport Shoes, Integrated Project Systems, TDIndustries, and Tyson Foods have all encouraged their employees to be engaged in spiritual activities. As John Tyson, president and CEO of Tyson Foods Inc., has said about having a spiritually open environment, "There's no rational, theoretical, theological debate about it. I just know it's what I'm supposed to do."

Are there such meetings in your organization? Are you involved in any? What is your organization's spirituality climate?

## GUIDELINES FOR PERSONAL AND PROFESSIONAL DEVELOPMENT

Relationships in the workplace are critical. Leaders have to take the time to get to know their followers. To be a salt-and-light influence at work, leaders must recognize their spheres of influence and how they impact those spheres. Bill Hybels, the founding and senior pastor of Willow Creek Community Church in South Barrington, Illinois, has written: "By how we work, who we are, and what we say, we can bring a Christian influence to our jobsite that can have far-reaching effects in the lives of men and women who desperately need to hear of God's forgiveness, and we can bring honor and glory to the name of our Lord."

There are five spiritual principles developed by Judith Neal that have been useful to many leaders in their personal and professional development:

1. *Know yourself.* Examine why you respond to situations the way you do. Reflect on the kind of leader you want to be. Assess how well you are leading and aligning your deepest held core values.

2. *Act with authenticity and congruency.* Be yourself. Don't play a role. Be authentic and congruent. Say what you are really thinking. Create a climate so followers are encouraged to behave authentically and congruently and express feelings.

3. *Respect and honor the beliefs of others.* Build a climate of trust and openness and model the acceptance of opinions and ideas that are different from yours. Do not impose your belief system on others.

4. *Be as trusting as you can be.* Trust yourself, your inner voice, or your source of spiritual guidance. Trust in a higher power and believe that when you ask, you will receive guidance on important issues.

5. *Maintain a spiritual practice.* Spend time in nature, meditation, prayer, reading inspirational literature and the Bible, or walking a labyrinth.

Leaders and followers who faithfully practice their spiritual walk are reported by Robert Rabbin to be calmer, more creative, more in tune with others, and more compassionate. They are ready for the next challenge in life. You might consider searching for a mentor who can help you grow spiritually or pick a friend or small group of friends who will hold one another accountable.

## THE WILDERNESS

There is a story in the Old Testament of the Holy Bible about two men—Joshua and Caleb—that has always been of high interest to me. Their story begins in the book of Numbers chapters 13 and 14. Under the leadership of Moses, the Israelites have escaped from captivity in

Egypt and have marched through the Desert of Paran to the edge of the land of Canaan, the promised land of milk and honey.

Before the Israelites move into this new land to conquer it and take possession, Moses sends a reconnaissance team made up of twelve spies to explore the land. The twelve were all leaders, one from each tribe. They were instructed to spend forty days in the new land and see what it was like. They were to record whether the inhabitants were strong or weak, few or many. They were to note the kinds of towns they lived in, walled or fortified. They were to test the soil to determine whether it was fertile or poor. They were to pay attention to the abundance or lack of trees and bring back some fruit of the land.

At the end of forty days, the twelve returned with samples from the new land and gave their report to Moses and the whole assembly of the Israelites. Even though they had discovered that the new land was indeed rich in every way, ten of the twelve were overly concerned about the large and fortified cities. They had seen descendants of Anak (giants) there and became frightened by the number of Amalekites, Hittites, Jebusites, Amorites, and Canaanites living in the land. Their tales resulted in spreading fear among the Israelites. We would seem like "grasshoppers in our own eyes." Convinced by the fear mongers, the Israelites were ready to pack their tents and head back to captivity in Egypt.

However, two of the twelve spies—Joshua and Caleb—were not afraid, saw possibilities, and were convinced the enemy could be overcome. They were optimistic that the land could be possessed. They cautioned the people against rebelling against God and being afraid of the inhabitants in the land. They assured everyone, "We will swallow them up." Don't be afraid. Why did they have such a firm conviction? They knew their coach!

If you are unfamiliar with this story, what do you think was the result of the arguments of Joshua and Caleb? Were they able to convince their listeners? Would you have been more likely to listen to the majority or the minority?

Sadly, the people listened to the fearful ten and their negative report. In fact, the whole assembly of listeners arose to stone the two for their positive report. Moses had to step in and stop the stoning.

Was their fear actually so strong that it shut ears and caused the brain to forget what God had promised upon leaving Egypt and why they had marched across the desert to arrive at the Promised Land?

Unfortunately, yes.

So what happened next?

God forgave their sin of disbelief based on Moses interceding for them. There would be a punishment, however.

If you had total power over such a situation, what would you do? Would you punish them? If so, how would you punish them? How long would the punishment period last?

God punished the ten for their disbelief, disobedience, and testing of patience. They and their families received the same punishment. Everyone who was twenty years old or more who had listened to the wayward ten, grumbled against God, and lost faith in his promise would die in the desert. They would wander through the desert one year for each day the ten fear mongers had been on their spy mission—forty years. Only Joshua and Caleb, the two who had a different spirit and followed God wholeheartedly, would survive and be allowed to enter Canaan after the forty years of punishment. Be careful, leaders, not to lead your people astray. Think of President George W. Bush and the weapons of destruction never found.

At the end of those forty years of wandering and dying in the desert, Moses was allowed to see the land of Canaan from the top of Mount Nebo, but he was unable to lead the people into the new land. Joshua had been selected to succeed Moses as leader and portioned out the land to be conquered and later occupied and lived in by the twelve tribes. Moses died at the age of 120 on Mount Nebo.

Joshua was now the leader.

What about Caleb? What was his reward?

## GIVE ME THIS MOUNTAIN

For Caleb's story, we need to move to the book of Joshua chapter 14. Canaan had been divided among the twelve tribes of the Israelites. Caleb had been promised the land of Hebron, and he had helped the other tribes to conquer their land. Now at the age of eighty-five, we learn that his heart has never melted with fear. He is as strong as he was on the day that Moses sent him out to spy the land, and he is just as vigorous to do battle. He is ready to conquer that which belongs to him. So he approaches Joshua and seeks permission to move forward with his tribe into Hebron.

"Now give me this hill country [this mountain] that the Lord promised me that day" (Joshua 14:12, NIV).

Joshua did so, and Caleb went up to his mountain and conquered it. From that time forward, Hebron belonged to Caleb, the conqueror.

## THE REST OF THE STORY

Okay. So what's the end of the story?

"Then the land had rest from war" (Joshua 14:15b, NIV).

What's keeping you up at night with worry or fear? What's your mountain? What needs to be conquered before you can move on? Are you going to still believe in yourself and a higher power at age eighty-five?

I have come to believe that every leader needs a mountain to conquer—something difficult that will provide direction and purpose. Every leader needs to discover the passion and enthusiasm that will allow them to transcend merely showing up. Passion and purpose served Caleb well for his lifetime. He found a life-consuming direction that gave maximum meaning to everything he did.

What's your passion and purpose? Former prime minister of England Winston Churchill said, "To every man there comes in his lifetime that special moment when he is tapped on the shoulder and offered the chance to do a very special thing. What a tragedy if that moment finds him unprepared or unqualified for the work which would be his finest hour."

What are *you* waiting for?

## CONCLUSION

The type of burning commitment that Caleb possessed is a useful indicator in measuring the effectiveness of any organization's health. As a leader, your followers must be willing, figuratively, to get into that wheelbarrow we talked about earlier and let you carry them beyond what they can physically see because of your superb balancing skills. They must be willing to follow you to the mountain, like Caleb, and help conquer it.

In the first chapter, I asked you five questions to start you thinking about your own leadership characteristics. Now, here at the end, I want to ask you six questions based on what you have been studying through this book. Let me get personal one last time.

1. Who do you look like as a leader?

2. What keeps you awake at night concerning your leadership?

3. Would you call you organization a high-performing one?

4. What do you think your organization will look like in five years?

5. If you got hit by a bus tomorrow, who could take your place as leader?

6. What do you still need to work on as a leader?

The best solutions come from asking the right questions. Your best answers will determine your future success. So one more piece of advice as you consider the future: *Learn to love the difficult!* Leading an organization is easy. It's only difficult if you actually lead. So we might as well face it: Nothing of importance is easy. So why not conquer your mountain?

Are you ready now to accept the challenge of taking the mountain? The call to be a dynamic leader has been issued. You have been mentored through this book. It is time to accept the challenge. In the Introduction you were introduced to the concept of "Enter to Learn" and "Leave to Lead." It's now time for us to end our whiteboard sessions and for you to lead with a renewed eagerness.

Are *you* ready? Well, then: On your mark. Get set. Go make a difference! Lead! You're burning daylight.

# SOURCES

American Library Association (ALA). "Leadership Traits." http:/
www.ala.org/ala/mgrps/ rts/nmrt/initiatives/ladders/traits/
traits.cfm.

Anderson, Linda Ackerman and Dean Anderson. "Ten Questions
that Catalyze Great Change Leadership." www.beingfirst.
com.

Baeyer, Cornelius von. "Making Ethical Decisions in the
Workplace." http://www. ewfinternational.com/index.
phpoption=com_content&view=article&id=176:...

Bandler, James. "Dangerous Liaisons at IBM: How a Star Executive's Love Affair Ensnared Him in the Biggest Hedge Fund
Insider-Trading Ring Ever." *Fortune* (July 26, 2010): 66–80.

Bennis, Warren. *Why Leaders Can't Lead: The Unconscious Conspiracy Continues.* San Francisco: Jossey-Bass Publishers, 1989.

Bork, Robert. *Slouching Toward Gomorrah: Modern Liberalism and American Decline.* New York: Regan Books, 1996.

Boatright, John R. *Ethics and the Conduct of Business.* Upper Saddle River, New Jersey: Prentice Hall, 2009.

Bodnarczuk, Mark. "Four Dimensions of Leadership." http://ezinearticles.com/?Four-Dimensions-of-Leadership&id=1090117.

Bolman, Lee G., and Terrence E. Deal. *Leading with Soul.* San Francisco: Jossey-Bass, 1995.

Boutall, Trevor. "Tips for Managing Change." *The Good Manager's Guide.* Alibris UK: Trevor Boutall, 1994.

Boxx, Rick. "Dealing with Disruptive, Divisive Employees," in Harold D. Armstrong and C. Herman Reece. The Christian Business Men's Connection (CBMC) Fax of Life. July 26, 2010. http://okc.cbmc.com.

Bridges, William and Susan Mitchell Bridges. "Leading Transition: A New Model for Change." *Leader to Leader* 16 (Spring 2000): 30–36.

Brooks, David. "Head Heart Hand" http://headhearthand.posterous.com.

Business Roundtable Institute for Corporate Ethics, Institute Media Releases. http://www.darden.edu/corporate-ethics/Enron_media_roundup_freeman.htm.

Butcher, Jim. "Honesty, Integrity Most Important to Senior Tulsa Businessman," *Senior News & Living* 13 (July 2010): 1.

Buzzell, Sid. *The Leadership Bible: New International Version.* Grand Rapids, Michigan: Zondervan, 1998.

Caldwell, Stephen. "Strategic Implementation." *The Life @ Work Journal* 1 (October 1998): 39–41.

Caldwell, Stephen. "Strategic Planning." *The Life @ Work Journal,* 1 (October 1998): 34–38.

Chamberlain, Ian. "Churchill Leadership Traits." http://www.winston-churchill-leadership.com/leadership-traits.html.

Clark, Don. "Character and Traits in Leadership." http://www.nwlink.com/~donclark /leader/leaderchr.html.

Clark, Don. "Leadership Styles." http://www.nwlink.com/~donclark/leader/leadstl.html.

Coaches@Work, "Leadership Credibility." White Paper, April 2005. www.coacheswork.com.

Collins, Jim. *Good to Great: Why Some Companies Make the Leap—and Others Don't.* New York: HarperBusiness, 2001.

Collins, and Jerry I. Porras. *Built to Last: Successful Habits of Visionary Companies.* New York: HarperBusiness, 1997.

Cueni, R. R. *The Vital Church Leader.* Nashville: Abingdon, 1991, 37–38.

Cuizon, Gwendolyn. "What Is Organizational Revolution?" http://businessmanagement. suite101.com/ article.cfm/ what_is_organizational_revolution.

David, Fred R. *Strategic Management: Concepts and Cases,* 13th ed. Upper Saddle River, New Jersey: Prentice Hall, 2011.

Dubrin, Andrew J. *Leadership: Research Findings, Practice, and Skills,* 6th ed. United States: South-Western, Cengage Learning, 2010.

Dwyer, Kevin. "Seven Steps to Motivating People at Work." http://saleshq.monster.com/training/ articles/574-seven-steps-to-motivating-people-at-work.

Flower, Joe. "The Five Fundamentals of Dealing with Change." http://www.well.com/ ~bbear/change2.html.

Fried, Jason. "I Know You Are, but What Am I?" *Inc.* (July/August 2010): 39–40.

Friedman, Thomas. The World Is Flat: *A Brief History of the Twenty-First Century.* New York: Picador/Farrar, Straus, Giroux, 2007.

Goleman, Daniel. *Emotional Intelligence: Why It Matters More than IQ.* New York: Bantam Bell, 2006.

Goleman, Daniel, Richard Boyatzis, and Annie McKee. "Primal Leadership: The Hidden Driver of Great Performance." *Harvard Business Review* (December) 2001: 41–51.

Griffin, Ricky W. *Fundamentals of Management: Core Concepts and Applications,* 2nd ed. Boston: Houghton Mifflin Co., 2000.

Hass, Nancy. "Earning Her Stripes," *WSJ.* (September 2010): 52–57.

Heath, Susan M. "Rise Above the Fray: Options for Dealing with Difficult People at Work," About.com.

Hitt, Michael A., R. Duane Ireland, and Robert E. Hoskisson. *Strategic Management: Competitiveness & Globalization: Concepts and Cases,* 9th ed. United States: South-Western, Cengage Learning, 2011.

Hughes, Richard L., Robert C. Ginnett, and Gordon J. Curphy. *Leadership: Enhancing the Lessons of Leadership,* 5th ed. New York: McGraw-Hill Irwin, 2006.

Hutton, R. Bruce. "Where Have All the Heroes Gone?" *Daniels Business Review* (Winter 1977): 2–9.

Iverson, F. Kenneth and Tom Varian, "Plain Talk." *Inc.* (October 1997): 81

Janis, Irving L. *Victims of Groupthink*. New York: Houghton Mifflin, 1972.

Janis, Irving L., and Leon Mann. *Decision Making*. New York: Free Press, 1977.

Kellerman, Barbara. *Followership: How Followers Are Creating Change and Changing Leaders*. Boston: Harvard Business School Press, 2008.

Kleiner, Art. "Diary of a Change Agent." http://www.strategy-business.com/article/ 20251?gko=0791c.

Kotter, John P. *A Force for Change: How Leadership Differs from Management*. New York: The Free Press, 1990.

Kotter, John P. *Leading Change*. Boston: Harvard Business School Press, 1996.

Kotter, John P. *The Leadership Factor*. New York: The Free Press, 1988.

Kotter, John P., and Dan S. Cohen. *The Heart of Change: Real-Life Stories of How People Change Their Organizations*. Boston: Harvard Business School Press, 2002.

Kouzes, James M., and Barry Z Posner. *The Leadership Challenge: How to Keep Getting Extraordinary Things Done in Organizations*. San Francisco: Jossey-Bass Publishers, 1995.

Krzyzewski, Mike. *Leading with the Heart: Coach K's Successful Strategies for Basketball, Business, and Life*. New York: Warner Business Books, 2000.

Lewis, Marilyn Hermann. "Listening Factors in Work Environments" (dissertation, Oklahoma State University, 1982.

Lewis, Phillip V. "Defining Business Ethics: Like Nailing Jell-O to a Wall." *Journal of Business Ethics* 4 (1985): 377–83.

Lewis, Phillip V. *Organizational Communication: The Essence of Effective Management* 1ˢᵗ ed., 2ⁿᵈ ed. Columbus, Ohio: Grid Publishing Inc., 1975, 1980; 3ʳᵈ ed. New York: John Wiley & Sons, 1987.

Lewis, Phillip V. "Strategic initiative," in M. Morrison (Ed.) *Sparks that Leap: Essays on Faith and Learning.* Abilene, Texas: Abilene Christian University Press, 1991: 115–28.

Lewis, Phillip V. *Transformational Leadership: A New Model for Total Church Involvement.* Nashville: Broadman & Holman, 1996.

Lewis, Phillip V., and J. E. Timmerman. "Ethical Decision-making Guidelines: Executive/Student Perceptions," *Proceedings of the Academy of Management—Southwest,* 1988: 44–8.

Lewis, Phillip V., William J. Mitchell, and N. L. Reinsch Jr. "Bank Ethics: An Exploratory Study of Ethical Behaviors and Perceptions in Small, Local Banks" 11 *Journal of Business Ethics* (1992): 197–205.

Likert, Rensis. *New Patterns of Management.* New York: McGraw-Hill, 1961.

Lucas, James R. *Broaden the Vision and Narrow the Focus: Managing in a World of Paradox.* Overland Park, Kansas: Luman Consultants International, 2009.

Lussier, Robert N. *Leadership: Theory, Application, Skill Development.* United States: South-Western College Publishing, Cengage Learning, 2001.

McGregor, Douglas. *The Human Side of Enterprise.* New York: McGraw-Hill, 1960.

Maxwell, John C. *Developing the Leader within You.* Nashville: Thomas Nelson Publishers, 1993.

Maxwell, John C. *Developing the Leaders Around You*. Nashville: Thomas Nelson Publishers, 1995.

Maxwell, John C. *The Maxwell Leadership Bible: Lessons in Leadership from the Word of God*. Nashville: Thomas Nelson, 2008.

McNamara, Carter. "Basics of Conflict Management," adapted from the *Field Guide to Leadership and Supervision*.

McNamara, Carter. "Helping People to Motivate Themselves." http://managementhelp.org/ guiding/motivate/motivate. htm.

Maslow, Abraham. *Motivation and Personality*. New York: Harper & Row, 1954.

Maslow, Abraham. *Toward a Psychology of Being*. New York: Van Nostrand Reinhold, 1962.

Mills, Steve. "Credibility." http://webuildpeople.ag.org/ wbp_library/9507_credibility.cfm.

Murray, Alan. "Leadership Styles." *The Wall Street Journal Essential Guide to Management: Lasting Lessons from the Best Leadership Minds of Our Time*. New York: Harper Business, 2010.

Nanus, Burt. *Visionary Leadership: Creating a Compelling Sense of Direction for Your Organization*. San Francisco: Jossey-Bass Publishers, 1992.

Nash, Sylvia. "Living with Integrity in a Chaotic World." A speech presented to the Christian Business Faculty Association, Azusa Pacific University, October 7, 1994.

Neal, Judith A. "Leadership and Spirituality in the Workplace," in Robert N. Lussier. *Leadership: Theory, Application, Skill Development*. United States: South-Western, Cengage Learning, 2001: Appendix A.

Page, Nanette and Cheryl E. Czuba. "Empowerment: What Is It?" http://www.joe.org/joe/ 1999october/comm1.php.

Patterson, James and Peter Kim. *The Day America Told the Truth.* New York: Prentice Hall Press, 1991.

Reese, Charley. "Washington was Nation's Indispensable Man." *San Gabriel Valley Tribune.* February 22, 1998: A17.

Reh, F. John. "Mentors and Mentoring: What Is a Mentor?" About. com.

Rice, Kenneth. "Four Dimensions of Leadership." http://EzineArticles.com/?expert+Kenneth_Rice.

Ricketts, Kristina G. "Behaving Intelligently: Leadership Traits & Characteristics." Community and Leadership Development, Kentucky Cooperative Extension.

Robbins, Stephen P. and Mary Coulter. *Management* 7th ed. Upper Saddle River, New Jersey: Prentice Hall, 2003.

Pollock, Ted. "Three Ways to Motivate People—On the Management Side." http://findarticles. com/p/articles/mi_moKJI/ is_7_114/ai_89157471/.

Roman, Kenneth, and John Emmerling. "What Real 'Mad Men' Did, and Didn't Do," *The Wall Street Journal,* July 23, 2010: W9.

Rosener, Judy and Jan Grant. "Gender and Leadership." http:// www.referenceforbusiness.com/ encyclopedia/For-Gol/Gender-and-Leadership.html.

Seybolt, John. "Managing in Tumultuous Times." 1 *BizEd* (March/April 2004): 38–43.

Sharlow, Bill. "Leadership Style." 2004–2007 Money-Zine.com.

Shinn, Sharon. "The Holistic Leader," IX *BizEd* (May/June 2010: 58–63.)

Sparks, Dennis. "Thirteen Tips for Managing Change." http://www.ncrel.org/sdrs/areas /issues/educatrs/leadrshp/le5spark.htm.

Stanley, Andy. "Vision Leaks." *Leadership* (Winter 2004): 68–72.

Stanley, Andy. *Visioneering: God's Blueprint for Developing and Maintaining Vision.* Sisters, Oregon: Multnomah Publishers Inc., 1999.

Steers, Richard M. "Antecedents and Outcomes of Organizational Commitment." *Administrative Science Quarterly* 22 (1977): 46–56.

Stengel, Richard. "Mandela: His 8 Lessons of Leadership." http://www.time.com/time/ world/article/0,8599,1821467,00.html.

Straker, David. "Head, Heart, and Hands (HHH)," http://creatingminds.org/tools/head_heart_ hands.htm.

Seuss, Dr. *Oh, the Places You Will Go.* New York: Random House, 1990.

Swanson, Beth Hughes. "Seeking Wise Counsel." *The Life @ Work Journal* 1 (September 1998):33–35.

Swindoll, Charles R. *Strengthening Your Grip.* Waco, Texas: Word, 1982: 88–107.

Tichy, Noel M. *The Leadership Engine: Building Leaders at Every Level.* New York: Harper Business Essentials, 2002.

Tichy, Noel M., and M. A. Devanna. *The Transformational Leader.* New York: Wiley Publishing Inc., 1986.

Tilles, Seymour. "The Evaluation of Corporate Strategy." http://www.strategic- contro1.24xls.com/en157.

Tritle, Gerald. "The Wisdom of Business Mentorship." 2 *Business Reform* (2004): 12–15.

Tuckman, Bruce. "Forming, Storming, Norming, Performing Model." http://www.businessballs. com/tuckmanforming-stormingnormingperforming.htm.

Velsor, Ellen Van, Cynthia D. McCauley, and Marian N. Ruderman. *The Center for Creative Leadership Handbook of Leadership Development.* New York: John Wiley & Sons, 2010.

Welch, Jack & Suzy. *Winning: The Answers: Confronting 74 of the Toughest Questions in Business Today.* New York: Collins, 2006.

White, James Emery. "The High Road to Credibility." *Leadership* (Fall 1995): 53–56.

"Winston Churchill Biography," from *Nobel Lectures, Literature* 1901–1967. Amsterdam: Elsevier Publishing Company, 1969.

Womack, Sean. "Back to School." 1 *The Life @ Work Journal* October 1998:13–16.

Wong, Kenman. "Finding True North." 2 *The Life @ Work Journal* October 1999: 44–52.

Wooden, John, and Steve Jamison. *Wooden On Leadership.* New York: McGraw Hill, 2005.

Worley, Christopher G., and Yvonne H Vick. "Leading and Managing Change: Leading change Management Involves Some Simple, but too Often Forgotten Rules." 8 *Graziadio Business Report:* 2005.

Worman, Dave. "20 Ways to Motivate Your Employees without Raising Their Pay." http:// www.biztrain.com/motivation/stories/20ways.htm.

Yukl, Gary. *Leadership in Organizations* 7ᵗʰ ed. Upper Saddle River, New Jersey: Prentice Hall, 2010.

# ABOUT THE AUTHORS

## PHILLIP V. LEWIS

Phillip V. Lewis is a high-impact consultant, educator, author, and speaker.

Lewis's academic leadership experience includes twenty years as a dean in three locations: College of Professional Studies, which includes the Schools of Business, Education, and Engineering, at Oklahoma Christian University (Oklahoma City); School of Business and Management, Azusa Pacific University (Los Angeles County); and College of Business Administration, Abilene Christian University (Abilene, Texas). He previously was the Chair of the Department of Management Sciences at ACU. He also has taught at Oklahoma State University and Northern Arizona University. He has taught Strategic Management and Change; Ethics,

Decision Making, and Communication; Introduction to Business; Principles of Management; Organizational Behavior; Organizational Communication; Team and Group Leadership; and Leaders, Managers, and Entrepreneurs.

His business leadership experience includes working in retail clothing sales, management, and banking. He has served as president of Creative Management Associates (Abilene, TX), Leadership Resources (Claremont, CA), and the American Citizenship Center (Oklahoma City, OK). He has been the executive director of Enterprise Square, USA (Oklahoma City), and the vice president of Leadership Development Institute (Stillwater, OK). He also worked for the First National Bank (Westminster, CO) and S&Q Clothiers (Abilene, TX).

Lewis's writing experience includes authoring fourteen books, monographs, and training manuals. His book *Transformational Leadership: A New Model for Total Church Involvement* (BandH, Broadman & Holman Publishers), was a finalist for the Gold Medallion Christian Book of the Year Award presented by the Evangelical Christian Publishers Association. It was adopted by the Salvation Army, the Graduate School of Biblical Studies at Abilene Christian University, and other groups. His textbook *Organizational Communication: The Essence of Effective Management* (Wiley Publishing Co.) went through three editions. It was adopted by the US Chamber of Commerce and numerous colleges and universities. Lewis also has written over one hundred articles and papers for various publications and professional organizations and given an inordinate number of speeches to various groups. He has also written four children's books, and one of his hobbies is writing poetry.

His consulting experience includes conducting numerous workshops and seminars for business, industry, education, religious groups, and government in the areas of ethics, leadership, organizational communication, and strategic visioning. A sampling includes the following:

Author Table:

| | |
|---|---|
| Performance Dashboard Inc. | E-Z Serve Oil Co. |
| Salvation Army, California district | O. Smith West Texas Oil and Gas Society |
| Salvation Army, Western and Eastern territories | United Way Fund |
| | Burrough's Corporation |
| Pacific Shore Partners | First National Bank and Trust Co. |
| Beijing Lan Yuan Business Consultant Systems | Garden Way Manufacturing Co. Inc. |
| | Ernst and Young |
| ASP International Group | McGraw-Hill Book Co. |
| Glenkirk Presbyterian Church | Dana F. Cole and Co. |
| Bentley Mills | Oklahoma Hospital Personnel Association |
| Salta Pipe Co. | Stillwater National Bank and Trust Co. |
| Washington Gas Light Co. | Phillips-VanHuesen Corp. |
| International Manpower Development Gro | American Airlines |
| Leadership Development Institute | Reading and Bates Offshore Drilling Co. |
| National Republican Organization, The Co Group | Atkins and Merrill Inc. |
| | Frontier Federal Savings and Loan |
| Tinker Air Force Base | Stillwater Church of Christ |
| Ralston Purina Corp. | Daniel International Corp. |
| 70001 Ltd. | Swan Hose Division, Amerace Corp. |
| Educational Resource Associates | Resource Sciences Corp. |
| Oklahoma Department of Tourism and Recreation | Mid-American Savings and Loan |
| | Federal National Bank |

In addition, Lewis has received many honors during his career. He was named Oklahoma State University's "Teacher of the Year" by the Oklahoma Education Association. He was named an "Ambassador of Goodwill" for the State of Oklahoma by the governor's office. He received a "Distinguished Paper" award from the Southwestern Federation of Administrative Disciplines. He was named a "Fellow" of the Association for Business Communication, served a three-year term as editor of *The Journal of Business Communication,* and received ABC's Francis W. Weeks Award of Merit.

He received an Award for Scholarship from the College of Business Administration, Abilene Christian University. He received the outstanding service and dedication award as an Economic Development Partner by the Edmond (OK) Economic Development Authority. He received the Keith Weber Award for Respect from Leadership Edmond XVII. He received the Faculty Leadership Award, Oklahoma Christian University. He was named Professional of the Year by Strathmore's Who's Who Worldwide.

Lewis has served as president of the Association for Business Communication and was on its board of directors. He served as president of Southwest Association for Business Communication and was a member of the board of directors of Southwestern Federation of Administrative Disciplines. He also is a member of the Midwest Business Deans Association, Southwestern Business Deans Association, and the Christian Business Faculty Association. He is a past secretary of the board of directors for the Association for Collegiate Business Schools and Programs and is an active member, chairing accreditation visits each year. He was recently elected President of ACBSP, Region 6.

Dr. Lewis received a B.S. from Abilene Christian University, a M.A. from the University of Denver, and an Ed.D. from the University of Houston.

He is married to Dr. Marilyn Hermann Lewis, and they have two grown sons, Brook and Blair. He enjoys travel; speaking, teaching, and conducting seminars; reading and writing; and musicals and plays. You may contact him at phil.lewis@oc.edu.

## DR. MARILYN HERMANN LEWIS

Dr. Marilyn Hermann Lewis is an educator, editor, and speaker.

Her academic experience includes having been Associate Professor in the College of Arts and Sciences at Oklahoma Christian University. Prior to joining OCU, she served as an associate professor of education, coordinator of field experience and director of the APLE program in the School of Education and Applied Behavioral Studies at Azusa Pacific University, Azusa, California; assistant professor in the College of Business Administration, Abilene Christian University; director of development for the College of Liberal and Fine Arts at ACU; and instructor in the Department of Speech Communication, Oklahoma State University. She also has worked as a business consultant for a number of organizations.

She has authored several articles in professional magazines and is a frequent speaker to businesses, education institutions, and religious groups. She has conducted numerous workshops on topics as varied as nonverbal communication, hospitality, the in-law function, sales techniques, humor in the workplace, leadership skills for women, and conflict resolution.

Dr. Lewis has received several honors during her career. She has been named to Who's Who of American Women, received the Bronze Leadership Award from the National Junior Achievement (Abilene, TX); served as a judge for the Texas Women's Award; and coordinated City of Abilene's third place award in the State of Texas Keep America Beautiful Campaign.

She has served as a board member of LASS—Ladies Actively Serving Seniors (Southern California), Delta Kappa Gamma (Azusa Pacific University), American Marketing Association Club sponsor (Abilene Christian University), featured woman's speaker and writer—ACU Lectureship, Junior Achievement board member (Abilene); co-educational director for University Church of Christ (Abilene, Texas, and Stillwater, Oklahoma); educational consultant for Region 14 Educational Service Center (Texas); co-president, Stillwater (Oklahoma) PTA; vice president of the American Society for Training and Development (Oklahoma State University); vice president of the Graduate Student Council (OSU); extension consultant in communication skills at Oklahoma State University; and a member of the Oklahoma Christian Women's Association.

Dr. Lewis received a B.S. in elementary education from Abilene Christian University, a M.A. in education from Northern Colorado University, and an Ed.D. in organizational communication and higher education from Oklahoma State University.

She is married to Dr. Phil Lewis. They have two grown sons and three grandchildren. They are members of the Memorial Road Church of Christ in Oklahoma City. She enjoys travel, Bible study, swimming, reading, musicals and plays, baking, ethnic jewelry, and entertaining.

You may contact her at marilyn.lewis@oc.edu.

# INDEX